130561

# A Layman's Guide
## to
# Christian Terms

# A Layman's Guide to Christian Terms

by
Ellen C. Shannon

SOUTH BRUNSWICK AND NEW YORK:
A. S. Barnes and Company
LONDON: Thomas Yoseloff Ltd

A. S. Barnes and Co., Inc.
Cranbury, New Jersey 08512

Thomas Yoseloff Ltd
108 New Bond Street
London W1Y OQX, England

SBN
498 06429 8
Printed in the United States of America

*To the family and friends who made
it possible, this book is most
gratefully dedicated.*

# PREFACE

In preparing *A Layman's Guide to Christian Terms,* I have kept in mind the people who are growing more interested now than they have ever been before in examining and understanding the Christian religion. In the past, many of us, myself not entirely excepted, have repeated the formulas and used the vocabulary of Christianity without giving much thought, really, to the exact meaning of what we were saying. Now, the revitalized interest in theology and religion has made this attitude impractical, if not downright impossible, to maintain. For instance, it has become harder and harder to pick up a popular magazine without at least one article on some aspect of the subject of ecumenism, faith, or heresy.

I have, therefore, tried to cover a broad spectrum of words, terms, phrases, and names used in Christian churches, worship, faith, and history. Because much contemporary discussion is fairly technical, some technical terms, especially those likely to be heard or read by laymen, have also been included. In general, though, most technical theological terms have been omitted.

For the purpose of clarity, definitions often point up the differences in understanding between Catholic and Protestant or between popular and exact usages of terms. Pronunciation has been marked for many foreign words and phrases, and, I believe, for all those which the reader might want to use orally.

It is my hope that *A Layman's Guide to Christian Terms* will prove as helpful to the user as its preparation has proved pleasant to the author.

Ellen C. Shannon

Clatsop College
Astoria, Oregon

# PRONUNCIATION KEY

| | | | | | | | |
|---|---|---|---|---|---|---|---|
| a | fat | e | ten | i | is | o | lot |
| ā | āpe | ē | ēven | ī | bīte | ō | gō |
| â | bare | ê | here | | | ô | horn |
| ä | car | ẽ | ovẽr | | | | |

ə The schwa, as in *Webster's New World Dictionary of the American Language,* "has been used to represent the reduced, weakened, and dulled vowel of neutral coloration heard in the unstressed syllables of *ago, agent, sanity, comply,* and *focus.*" That is, in words where the schwa replaces *a,* it is pronounced like the *a* in *ago*; where it replaces *e,* it is pronounced like the *e* in *agent,* and so on.

| | | | | | | | |
|---|---|---|---|---|---|---|---|
| o͞o | to͞ol | oi | oil | u | up | g | get |
| oo | look | ou | out | ū | ūse | j | joy |
| | | | | ũ | fũr | y | yet |

| | |
|---|---|
| ch | chin |
| sh | she |
| th | thin |
| zh | leisure |

# A Layman's Guide
## to
# Christian Terms

# *A*

**ABBA.** The familiar word for "Father" in Aramaic, the language spoken by Jesus, according to Mark 14:36.

**ABBESS, ABBOT.** The governing official, often elected for life, of an abbey of nuns or of monks. In authority over all the abbey, the abbess or abbot is owed obedience by those in the abbey, and, in turn, bears full and ultimate responsibility, both physical and spiritual, for the residents.

**ABBEY.** A monastery, i.e., the permanent residence including cloisters, cells, and refectory of at least twelve monks or nuns, and governed by an abbot or an abbess.

**ABEL, ST.** The Old Testament son of Adam and Eve. His feast day is July 30.

**ABELARD, PETER** (1079-1142). A French scholastic credited with the founding of the University of Paris, Peter Abelard is famed for his application of logic to the truths of faith, and, with his wife, Heloise, for one of the most moving of all love stories and the letters in which it found expression.

**ABLUTIONS.** The washing of the thumbs and index fingers of the celebrant after a Communion service.

**ABSOLUTE, THE.** The title often used to refer to God, or the Deity. "Absolute" implies that which exists in its own nature and independently of all else.

ABSOLUTION. The forgiveness, pardon, or remission of sin or the penalty of sin. In the Catholic Church, absolution after confession and penance is given by a priest exercising the authority vested in him by God through Jesus Christ. The penitent must be sincere, and the confession, remorse, and intent to improve must be genuine for the absolution to be valid. If absolution is granted on the basis of an insincere or intentionally incomplete confession, the penitent is said to merit God's displeasure and the confession is deemed sacrilege.

Absolution, or Holy Absolution, is one of the seven Sacraments of the Catholic and Anglican churches, and is sometimes referred to as the Sacrament of Penance. It is given "on account of the merits and mediation of Our Lord Jesus Christ. It is conditioned upon our faith, love and repentence." As baptism remits original and ante-baptismal sin, so penance and absolution remit later sin.

In the Catholic Church, absolution after confession and penance is given to an individual in a private confessional. The private confessional, while available in many Anglican churches, is not so frequently used, and in general the practice of other Protestant churches is followed in which confession is made aloud by the congregation in unison or in silence, and the minister reassures or reminds the worshipers of God's pardon through Jesus Christ.

ABSOLUTION, CONDITIONAL. ". . . Absolution may and must be given conditionally if, were it given absolutely, the sacrament would be exposed to the danger of nullity, or if, were it denied, the penitent would be in danger of suffering grave spiritual loss." (*Catholic Dictionary*, p. 4)

ABSOLVE. To grant absolution.

ABSTINENCE. Generally, abstinence must be distinguished from fasting, the more total "giving up." Abstinence refers only to the practice of most Catholics, Anglicans, and perhaps others of refraining from eating meat on Fridays, Ash Wednesday, and other religious days, while fasting is a far more complete avoidance of food and liquids.

ABUSES. Those corrupt medieval practices within the Catholic Church which were corrected in the sixteenth-century reform movement. Among the abuses were the sale of indulgences and relics and various corrupt practices of the clergy in their private lives.

ABYSS. A once-popular term for Hell; also frequently used to refer to "the pit" of sin into which man might "fall," thus insuring his eventual descent into the final abyss.

ACACIANS. Followers of Acacius, a bishop of Caesarea in Palestine in the fourth century, who believed a semi-Arian heretical doctrine that can be simply stated as: "the Son is *like* the Father." Also *Homoeans*.

ACCIDIE (Gr. "don't-careishness"). Spiritual sloth; a capital sin, a "regret for the gift of faith because of the troublesome obligations involved." (*Catholic Dictionary,* p. 5)

ACCOMMODATION. Among interpreters of Scripture, this term refers to the fairly common practice among Christians of adjusting a word or a writing to mean something the original author did not perhaps have in mind. For example, the reference to the "suffering servant" and "Lord" in Isaiah 53 and elsewhere is taken to refer to Jesus. It is also sometimes said that Jesus "accommodated" his teachings to his audience, although he knew they were not strictly true.

ACCUMULATION OF PROBABILITIES. A frequently condemned basis for faith, this is the view that in the long run there is a greater chance that the Scriptures are true than that they are false; it is an amassing of "probablies," and is not accepted theologically as a sound basis for certainty.

ACOLYTE. Generally, a layman or boy who lights the altar candles and generally assists the priest in the service of the Mass in the Catholic or Anglican Church, although the practice has been extended to some Protestant denominations as well.

ACT. One of the steps in sinning.

ACT OF WORSHIP. A church service or, more freely interpreted, any devout act or act done devoutly for the greater glory of God. The Catholic Church restricts the term usually to refer to the Mass and Divine Office.

ACTS OF THE APOSTLES. A canonical book of the New Testament, directly following the four Gospels, and describing the progress of the new church. It was written in approximately A.D. 64 by St. Luke and is in part an eye-witness account.

ACTS OF FAITH. Any acts which bear witness to the performer's complete faith in God and Jesus. They may be external and related to others, as charity and forgiveness, or internal and related only to oneself, as silent or solitary prayer or repentance.

ACTS OF PAUL, THE. An apocryphal New Testament writing of the second century; the Acts of Paul differs from accepted teaching in making virginity almost a prerequisite for salvation and in partially opening the ministry to women. It is conventional, however, in referring to prayers for the dead and to the sign of the cross.

ACTIVE LIFE. Theologically, and particularly in Catholic theology, the active life is the opposite of the contemplative life; more generally it is understood to refer to a life dedicated to actively helping others, both spiritually and physically, and not only to a bodily active existence.

ACTIVE ORDERS. The religious orders and congregations whose work is active charity, perhaps teaching, perhaps preaching, or any of a variety of others. In the Catholic Church, the Jesuits among men and the Ursulines among women are examples of such orders.

ACTUAL GRACE. A gift of grace which affects the mind and will and which may come from the reading of Scripture, the hearing of a sermon, the seeing of something beautiful, or in any of a variety of ways. It enlightens the mind and helps the will achieve that of which, in its natural state without such a gift, it would be incapable.

ACTUAL SIN. A sin of commission or omission that is the outcome of a free act of the will.

ADAM, ST. The first man, usually called the first father, whose feast day in the Catholic Church calendar is December 19.

ADAMITES. Religious sects, varieties of which began early in the second century and which were active as late as the nineteenth century, which met naked for worship. Usually sincere and ascetic principles deteriorated into sensual and promiscuous practices.

ADESTE FIDELES (Lat.: Come, ye faithful; ä-des'-tā fē-dä'-les). An anonymous Latin hymn of the seventeenth or eighteenth century, best known by its English title, "O Come All Ye Faithful," with lyrics composed by Frederick Oakeley in 1841. It is heard most during the Christmas season.

ADJURATION. A prayer or a command to do or to refrain from doing something, offered in the name of God particularly during baptismal services.

ADMONITION. A warning not to do something sinful or criminal, or to stop doing something already begun. If the admonition of the church is not heeded, the religious body or person offering it can censure the offender at whom it was directed.

ADOLPH, ST. A thirteenth-century bishop in Westphalia, whose feast day is February 11.

ADONAI (Heb. "my lords," the pl. form of majesty). The name of God given to Moses in the burning bush was JHVH. However, out of pious reluctance to pronounce this name, the Hebrews, some centuries before Jesus, substituted their word "Adonai." Later, other Jews, to clarify texts, wrote the vowels from Adonai—A, O, A, I—under the consonants JHVH. Instead of clarifying the reading for still later Christians, however, this caused confusion and the misreading of the "whole" word as "Jahovahi," that is, Jehovah.

ADOPTION. The result of receiving grace and thus becoming adopted children of God and co-heirs with Jesus. "You have received the spirit of adoption of sons whereby we cry, Abba, Father." (Romans 8:15)

ADOPTIONISM. An eighth-century Spanish heresy which said Jesus was the son of man and the adopted son of God, i.e., a double sonship, which connected it with the Nestorian heresy that regarded Jesus as essentially human and raised at some time during his life to sonship with God. The second person of the Trinity was held to be "only-begotten," but out of a desire to stress the humanity of Jesus, theologians of this persuasion taught that the Son of Man was only adopted and that only the Son of Man could be said to have suffered and died.

ADORATION. Most correctly, acts of worship directed only to God and not, ideally, used to refer to reverence of anything less than God for which the term "veneration" should be used, as for saints and relics in the Catholic Church.

ADVENT. The preparatory season before Christmas which looks forward to the coming, the advent, of Christ. It begins on the Sunday nearest November 30 (St. Andrew's Day), and is the first day of the Catholic Church year; Advent extends through December 24. Purple is the color associated with Advent, a practice now rather widely adopted by Protestant churches, as is that of celebrating the season itself.

ADVENTISTS, SEVEN DAY. A Protestant sect founded in the early part of the nineteenth century by a variety of churchmen in England and now having over a million members throughout the world. Adventists accept the Bible literally; they believe in salvation through faith alone and hold that obedience to the Ten Commandments is evidence of, but not necessary for, that salvation. The name is derived from two beliefs: that Saturday, the seventh day, is the Sabbath and should be so observed; and that the second coming, or second advent, of Jesus is imminent though the exact date is unknown. The church opposes smoking and drinking and other practices that they hold violate the body as the "temple" of the soul. They support a strong missionary and educational effort, believing that part of their duty is to prepare as many as possible for the expected end of the world—or, as is sometimes said, the end of the age as we know it.

ADVOCATE, THE DEVIL'S. The nickname given the Promoter of the Faith, a position in the Catholic Church's process of beatification and canonization. It is the job of the Devil's Advocate to question and examine the virtue and miracles of the candidates for beatification and canonization with the greatest care in order to eliminate the possibility of error due to too much enthusiasm on the part of those who support the candidate, or from any other source. In other words, he must pick apart the reasons why some think a man or woman should be so honored in order to discover any indication whatsoever why the person should not.

AFFUSION. A method of baptism by the pouring on of water. It is often called "infusion," and should be compared to "aspersion."

"AFTER-CHRISTIAN". "An inhabitant of Christendom and a descendant of Christian ancestors who, implicitly or explicitly, repudiates Christianity as a revealed religion." The term is especially applicable in England and the United States, "where much contemporary educated public opinion regards religion in a merely humanitarian and pragmatic way." (*Catholic Dictionary* p. 11) Modern times are more often referred to as "post-Christian."

AGAPE (Gr. brotherly love). In the first and second century, an agape was a "love feast" which often included prayer, supper, and singing, and might extend from Saturday night into Sunday morning, perhaps terminating in the Eucharist. The Lord's Supper, however, soon disappeared as a part of this celebration, and the agape deteriorated into a scandalous practice against which action had to be taken by the church. By the eighth century the agape had been abandoned entirely, although it survives today in certain small Protestant sects as a pleasant form of church get-together. See *Love-feast.*

AGAPE (ä′gə-pē) and EROS. These Greek words are used in the New Testament to describe, or to stand for, God's love for man and for the love that unites man with man in brotherhood. The former, "agape," is evidenced in the incarnation of Jesus and is often contrasted with "eros," which refers to an always existent, always unfulfilled desire of the lower for the higher, or as the inclination of the higher (perfect) to the lower (imperfect). Eros is man's feeling of incompleteness and incorporates many elements of physical desire which can be realized fully only in the agape, while the agape itself has a certain element of Eros within itself.

AGAPETAE (Lat., fr. Gr.: beloved). In the first century of the

Christian era, Christian girls who took the vow of chastity but remained in the world instead of entering a closed community were called "agapetae." Unhappily, their practice of living as housekeepers in the homes of laymen who had taken the same vow often led to scandal, and by the fourth century the practice had to be forbidden.

The term is also sometimes used to refer to a group of Gnostics who held that "to the pure, all things are lawful."

AGATHA, ST. (third century). The story of St. Agatha is lost in legend, but it is an old legend, and, although almost entirely unsubstantiated by fact, has won this virgin martyr a place of honor in the Catholic Church. Briefly, having lived a life entirely devoted to God, the young virgin Agatha underwent cruel tortures at the command of a Sicilian magistrate which ended in a violent earthquake and the girl's death, though not her corruption. She was probably a victim of the persecution of Christians ordered by Decius; her feast day is February 5.

AGE OF FAITH. A name often used to refer to the Middle Ages, reaching a climax (religiously) in the thirteenth century. The period was distinguished by the consolidation of Christianity in Europe, the Crusades, the erection of fine churches, and the unquestioned acceptance of the teachings of the Catholic Church regarding God and itself. Religion was a set thing, not open to question, but man was as uncontrollable as ever, and tyranny, violence, immorality, and wickedness were widespread.

AGE OF REASON. The age at which a child is considered capable of making the decision of, or knowing the difference between, right and wrong; that is, the age at which he becomes morally responsible. For mentally normal youngsters, the age is usually seven years.

AGNES, ST. (third century). A virgin martyr whose feast day is celebrated January 21.

AGNOSTICISM (Gr.: not knowing). In general usage, "agnosticism" is the philosophical or religious condition of those who do not know whether there is or is not a God, and who refrain from making a positive statement either one way or the other. The "a" (*without*) and "gnostic" (from *know* or *to know*) combine to form a word that is best translated as "without knowledge," and the distinction is thus made clear between the agnostic, the person without knowledge, and the "atheist," the person "without a deity."

AGNUS DEI (Lat. Lamb of God; än'yo͞os-dā'ē). A title often given Jesus, as for example in John 1: 29, 36, where John the Baptist refers to Jesus as "The Lamb of God which taketh away the sins of the world." The lamb had long been a sacrificial animal in Hebrew worship, and Jesus' crucifixion at the time of the Passover, when such a lamb was traditionally slain, was of particular significance. The figure or picture of a lamb holding a cross or a flag is used to depict this concept.

The "Agnus Dei" is also the name given a small disk of wax stamped with a lamb and blessed by the pope. Also in the Catholic Church, it is the name used for a prayer in the Mass which begins with the words "Agnus Dei," and for the music to accompany it.

In the Anglican Church the name refers to an anthem beginning with the words, "O Lamb of God."

AGRAPHA OF JESUS (Gr.: "without writing"). Words supposedly spoken by Jesus but not found in the four Gospels. There are over seventy of these sayings, but their genuineness is seriously in question and is almost impossible to verify, the only authority for it being, as a rule, the antiquity of a writing.

AISLE. Because this term is derived from the Latin "ala," or "wing," the walk or passageway on one or both sides of the nave of a church is the only such area which can properly be called an aisle. In practice, however, the term is used to refer to any such passageway through the nave of the church, whether through the middle, often called "central aisle," or along one side. It may also be applied to any walk between pews or chairs left open to allow access. The confusion arose, perhaps, through associating "aisle" with the French word "allée" or "alley."

ALB. The long white linen garment with tight-fitting sleeves and belt that is part of the vestment of a priest of the Catholic Church. It may be embroidered, but as its symbolic significance is purity of heart, the decoration is not supposed to detract from its essentially simple character.

ALBAN, ST. (third century). An English saint who became a victim of persecution in that country. His home, Verulanium, is now called St. Albans. His feast day is June 22.

ALBERT THE GREAT, ST. (1193 or 1206–1280). Also called Albertus Magnus, St. Albert was one of the later Doctors of the Church. He was born a count in Swabia, an area in southwest Germany, and became a Dominican and teacher of theology. He was a highly influential thinker, an instructor of St. Thomas Aquinas, and one of those who contributed most to the reconciling of Aristotelian philosophy and Christianity. He was not only a scholastic philosopher but also a scholar in the natural sciences. The "Universal Doctor" was canonized by Pope Pius XI in 1931. His feast day is November 15.

ALBIGENSIANISM. A heresy of the Middle Ages, approximately the twelfth and thirteenth centuries, whose adherents believed that all matter was evil and all spirit was good. The physical Jesus was considered not truly physical but only physical in appearance. Albigensians rejected sacraments, and, as they looked upon the creation of children as clothing a spiritual entity, the soul, in evil matter, they particularly rejected the sacrament of marriage. Suicide was encouraged, as releasing the spiritual from the material. By the Catholic Church, Albigensianism was considered a dualistic heresy, separating the spiritual and the physical in Jesus, and a part of the Cathari movement. By some, Albigensians are considered not heretics but actually non-Christians.

The group flourished in France and, through enthusiasm and strong preachers, gained some powerful support. However, the spiritual force of the Catholic Church and the political force of the French king combined to overthrow their stronghold in the south of France and win Toulouse, center of their activity, for the throne in 1229, spelling the end of the group as a power of any consequence.

ALEXANDER, ST. (third century). Bishop of Jerusalem, St. Alexander was noted for his kindliness, for the library he founded, and for his friendship with such men as Origen. His feast day is March 18.

ALEXANDRIA, PATRIARCHATE OF. One of the original five great patriarchates of the Catholic Church, said to have been founded by St. Mark, and numbering among its famous bishops such men as St. Athanasius and St. Cyril. At present the three bishops of Alexandria have separate jurisdiction over a branch of the Orthodox Eastern Church, a dissident Coptic Church, and a church of Catholics of the Coptic Rites.

ALEXANDRINE LITURGY. Also called the Liturgy of St. Mark, it was the form used in the patriarchate of Alexandria during its great days of power before the Council of Chalcedon (451). Long out of use now, its place has been taken by Byzantine liturgy, primarily, in the Orthodox Eastern Church.

ALEXIS, ST. (fifth century). More legend than history, the story of St. Alexis has been popular since the tenth century or earlier. He was, the tale goes, the son of a Roman senator who was related to the emperor. Fleeing home on the eve of his marriage, he begged for his living for seventeen years on the church steps in the town of Edessa. Eventually returning to Rome, he hid his identity and entered his father's house, for his parents were both still living and his fiancée had remained faithful, and here, again, he stayed as a beggar for another seventeen years. A celestial voice revealed to Pope Innocent I that a "man of God" should be sought in the old senator's house, and when officials went there, they found Alexis, dead, with a parchment still held in his hand that revealed the whole story of his identity and his life. His feast day is July 17.

ALIENATION. A term used synonymously to express the feeling that results from sinning or lack of faith, a sense of being cut off from God, from other men, and even from oneself. It is used most by theologians influenced by existentialism.

ALITURGICAL DAYS. Days on which celebration of the Mass is not permitted in the Catholic Church. The only true aliturgical day is Good Friday in the Roman Catholic Church, while in the Orthodox Eastern Church wider limitations exist during Lent. Holy Saturday may be considered aliturgical, since the only Mass permitted is at night and is actually a part of Easter Day.

ALLELUIA (Heb.: Praise God, fr. HALLELU, praise, + YAH,

Yahweh, God). An expression of praise and of joy, widely used throughout the Psalms and in most Christian church services, especially during the Easter celebration. Also *Hallelujah.*

ALL HALLOWS. All Saints' Day. All Hallows may also be called Allhallows, Allhallowmas, or, in referring to the season or time itself, Allhallowtide, all the terms derived from the word "all" and the Anglo-Saxon word for saint, "halga."

ALL SAINTS' DAY. The day in the Catholic Church calendar set aside for commemoration of all saints, known and unknown, canonized or uncanonized. It is celebrated on November 1 in Western churches, on other days in other rites, and is a feast day of great importance. The association of witches, ghosts, spirits, etc. with All Saints' Eve (Hallowe'en) is of Celtic origin, and very ancient. The celebration of All Saints' itself began in Rome in the early ninth century.

ALL SOULS' DAY. Also called "The Commemoration of the Faithful Departed," All Souls' is celebrated on November 2. This day of prayer was instituted by St. Odilo at Cluny in France early in the eleventh century, and its observation quickly spread throughout Europe.

ALMIGHTY, THE. A title frequently used to refer to God.

ALMS GIVING. While generally understood in the context of financial help, alms giving may actually refer to any physical act of mercy done for the relief of another's need. Although it is up to the personal conscience of each giver to decide what/or how much to give, there is usually the understanding that one is bound to give only from what is extra and thus unnecessary to the needs of one's own family and maintenance of its way of life.

According to Attwater's *A Catholic Dictionary,* alms are not only for the deserving poor, as gifts to the deserving are not charity but simple justice; organizational charities or state institutions do not relieve the individual of his responsibility; further, "a man who makes it a rule never to give alms to ordinary beggars certainly commits sin, and . . . the precept of the divine law forbids 'the rich to be so mean that some men are forced to beg by necessity'."

ALPHA AND OMEGA. A and Ω, the first and last letters of the Greek alphabet, used symbolically to signify the all-encompassing nature of God, or God and Son as eternal; the All, infinite being itself, as for example in Revelation 1:8.

ALTAR. By definition, that upon which sacrifice is offered. In many Christian churches, worship services are led by a minister at an altar, a construction usually of wood, approximately four feet high, set at the front of the nave and directly facing the congregation. Many denominations recognize as an altar any construction or object from which worship services are conducted, although "pulpit" is by far the more proper term.

In the Catholic Church, however, an altar is the essential requirement for the offering of the Mass, and such an altar must be properly placed and consecrated, and is not used as a pulpit or lectern. If the fixed altar has not been consecrated it must hold, or have set into it, a consecrated altar stone containing relics, as do all consecrated altars.

ALTAR BREAD. The bread used in the Communion service.

ALTAR CLOTHS. In any church, the cloths which cover the altar at the church service. In the Catholic Church, three white linen cloths which have been blessed by a bishop or other in his place cover the altar at Mass. Symbolically they represent the linen in which the dead body of Jesus was wrapped.

ALTAR BOY. The boy or man assisting the minister at a worship service.

ALTAR LIGHTS. The candles placed on or at the altar in a church.

ALTAR RAILS. The fencelike construction which stands between the altar of a church and the congregation.

ALTAR STONE. A single, unbroken piece of stone usually square or nearly square in shape and about one inch thick. Carved in its surface are five Greek crosses, one at each corner and one in the center, and relics are usually sealed in a niche cut in the stone itself. Such an altar stone must be consecrated by a bishop; it may be used as a portable altar for the saying of Mass by a bishop or other member of the clergy granted the right, in any decent place except at sea. Altar stones are frequently used with altars which have not been consecrated, in order that Mass may be said therefrom.

AMANA SOCIETY. The general name used to designate the inhabitants of seven small towns in central Iowa which were settled in 1855 by members of the Community of True Inspiration, a religious sect which originated in 1714 in Germany. Under their leader Christian Metz (1794–1867), members of the group fled to the United States in 1843 to escape persecution at home, and eventually moved West from their first settlement near Buffalo, New York. Over the years, they developed a very successful communal society. In 1932, the economic activity of the community, which centered mainly around wool and wood crafts, was separated from the religious activity, and the society became a co-operative corporation.

AMBO. A small platform in the middle of the church from which the Epistle and Gospel were presented in the early Christian era, but now almost totally replaced by the pulpit and lectern.

AMBROSE, ST. (330?–397). One of the Doctors of the Church, noted for his able administration of his diocese in northwest Italy, his popularity with his people, and his effectiveness in dealing with the various emperors of the time. Most important, perhaps, was the influence of his teaching and personality on St. Augustine of Hippo, for it was under his tutelage that the latter rejected Manicheism and returned to his earlier Christian faith. For the Church, he secured, among other things, the outlawing of heresy and the support and protection of the state. He was a writer of religious treatises, and his name is associated with a type of plain song still known as Ambrosian chant. His feast day is December 7.

AMEN (Heb.: certainly; so be it). The word said at the conclusion of a prayer or as an expression of approval, agreement, or assent. It was used in the synagogue before it entered Christian worship in apostolic times, and is pronounced either a-men or ah-men.

AMICE. A rectangular white linen vestment worn under the alb and covering the neck and shoulders of the priest or other celebrant at Mass. In earlier times, a portion of the amice could be lifted over the head and symbolically it still represents the "helmet of salvation" as well as "discipline of the tongue."

AMISH. A sect of the original Mennonite Protestants, a Reformation movement that originated in Switzerland in 1525. Named after its founder, Jacob Ammann (1693), the Amish began emigration from Switzerland and Germany in the eighteenth century and settled primarily in Pennsylvania. In general, the Amish are more strict in their rules and practices than the Mennonites, the original break itself having been over a matter of rule enforcement.

The Bible is the rule of faith for the Amish, both physically and spiritually, and such things as electricity, gasoline engines and the like which are not mentioned in the Bible are rejected, so far as ownership is concerned, by conservative members. Beards after marriage and buttonless jackets and vests distinguish the appearance of the men, as long, plain dresses, white indoor caps and dark outdoor bonnets do the women. Good farms well managed, group cooperation and closeness, sobriety and earnestness of mien and behavior, and refusal to bear arms are identifying characteristics of the "Plain People." However, the most outstanding hallmark can best be identified as an overall resistance to the modern, or "gay," ways of outsiders.

The Amish folk are rarely joined by such outsiders, not even through marriage, and the increase in their numbers, from around 10,000 in 1900 to 50,000 today is accounted for almost solely by the large families they produce.

AMOS. A prophetical book of the Old Testament, named after its author, whose writings date from the eighth century B.C. and are the earliest extant prophecies.

AMULET. Any good-luck charm, usually a very small object inscribed with the charm, worn on a necklace as protection against evil. As superstitious objects, they are rejected by Christianity, although they are tolerated by some faiths if God is the origin of the hoped-for good luck, in which case they are considered not "magic" but "religious."

ANABAPTISTS (Gr.: re-baptizers). A group of sixteenth-century

Protestants who rebaptized by immersion those who wanted to become church members and who had previously been baptized as infants. The group held that only adults can choose to be baptized and that immersion is the only valid form. They upheld the separation of church and state, a belief for which they were persecuted, and remained disunited and generally opposed. Originally called Swiss Brethren, they were renamed Mennonites after their leader, Menno Simons, and as such today maintain several communities in Pennsylvania and the Midwest.

ANANIAS, ST. (first century). The man met by St. Paul on the road to Damascus, and instrumental in the conversion of the former persecutor of the first Christians. The story is recounted in Acts 9: 11–17 and 22: 12–16. Beyond this, little is known of Ananias, though he is thought to have been bishop of Damascus and a martyr by stoning. His feast day is January 25.

ANAPHORA. "A liturgical term for the canon of a Eucharistic Liturgy, especially in the Eastern rites." (*Catholic Dictionary,* p. 21) More generally, an "anaphora" is the repetition of a word, or perhaps of a phrase, at the beginning of successive sentences or clauses.

ANASTASIA, ST. Although there are a number of saints named Anastasia, two particularly stand out. The earlier, a woman of the first century, apparently became a martyr during the reign of Nero for burying the bodies of Sts. Peter and Paul. Her feast day is April 15. The later, St. Anastasia or Athanasia, lived in the fourth century on the island of Aegina where she directed a large convent during the latter part of her life. Her feast day is August 14.

ANATHEMA (Gr.: to set up; later, thing devoted to evil). A thing or person so wicked as to have received the condemnation of an organized religious body; thus, cursed or cast out because of extreme evil. In the Old Testament the usage is much broader, for at that time the word might be used to designate anything set up as an object of execration or consecration, and only at a later date did it come to refer exclusively to a curse or to something cursed or execrated.

ANCHOR. An early symbol of Christian hope often used to represent the cross, as an anchor approximates the shape of a cross.

ANCHORITE. A hermit, or one who confines himself to a single area, such as a room or house, for religious reasons.

ANCIENT CHURCH. The early Christian Church, a term usually designating the Church during the first three or four centuries of its history.

ANCIENT FATHERS. Great thinkers and writers of early Christianity who lived between approximately the second and the eighth centuries. These men gave definition and precision to Christian beliefs and shaped much of the dogma of the Church. They are distinct both from the Apostolic Fathers, who were earlier, and from the later Fathers of the Church.

Various lists exist, but a frequently used one names eight Ancient Fathers, all men of the fourth and fifth centuries. The four Greek Fathers are given as Sts. Athanasius, Basil, Gregory Nazianzen, and John Chrysostom, and the four Latin Fathers as Sts. Ambrose, Augustine, Gregory the Great (or sometimes Leo I), and Jerome. They are also referred to as the Ancient Doctors, and as the Fathers, or Doctors, of the Church.

ANCIENT OF DAYS. A frequently used name for God, derived from Daniel 7: 9, 13, and 22.

ANCYRA VIRGINS, MARTYRDOM OF THE. Seven women of the early fourth century, who were martyred by drowning near Ancyra (now Ankara) in Turkey. Refusing to become apostates, they were subjected to torture and humiliation, and were drowned during a pagan ceremony of bathing statues of Diana and Minerva in a lake near Ancyra. The written account of their deaths is perhaps not entirely reliable but cannot be entirely rejected, either. Their feast day is May 18.

ANDREW, ST. (first century). Apostle of Christ and the brother of Simon Peter, a fisherman of Capharnaum. He is especially mentioned during the choosing of the Apostles (Matt. 4:17–20). St. Andrew is believed to have carried the Gospel teachings into the area around the Black Sea and is said to have been crucified on an X-shaped cross in Achaia. The patron saint of fishermen and fishmongers, he is also invoked by women who desire to have children. His feast day is November 30, and the start of the Advent Season is the first Sunday thereafter.

ANGEL (fr. Gr. "messenger"). A supernatural or heavenly being used by God as a messenger. Angels are defined in Catholic theology as persons with acute intelligence and power but pure spirit, that is, not associated in any way with matter, as is the human soul. Angels as the "heavenly host" or "sons of God" figured prominently in the Old Testament and were carried over into the New Testament as well. Actually, human beings who die and go to heaven are not classifiable as angels, although popularly the term is applied to the image of white-robed, winged figures playing harps.

ANGELA MERICI, ST. (1474–1540). Of Italian birth, Angela Merici joined the third order of the Franciscans not long after her parents died and while she was still quite young. Distressed about the loss of family unity and the general laxity of the morality of the times, she was inspired to found an order "to restore family morality by the Christian education of future mothers" (*Lives of the Saints,* p. 240), and to that end founded the Ursulines in Brescia in 1535. For their patron saint, she chose St. Ursula, a fourth-century virgin martyr. This Company of St. Ursula was the first of the authorized women's teaching orders. St. Angela Merici's feast day is May 31.

ANGELIC HYMN, THE. The Gloria in Excelsis, or Greater Doxology, taken from the angels' song in Luke 2:14.

ANGEL OF THE SCHOOLS. See Aquinas, St. Thomas.

ANGELOLOGY. The part of theology dealing with the study of beliefs concerning the existence, role, and nature of angels.

ANGELUS, THE. A formal prayer in honor of the Incarnation, said in the Catholic Church at about 6 A.M., noon, and 6 P.M. The ringing of the angelus bell at each hour consists of three strokes, three pauses, and nine strokes.

ANGER. One of the seven deadly sins.

ANGLICAN. Used to refer to a person, practice, belief, etc., belonging to or characteristic of the Anglican Church, that is, the Church of England or the Episcopal Church in America.

ANGLICANISM. That faith which originated with King Henry

VIII's withdrawal of England's allegiance to the pope, an action confirmed by the Act of Supremacy of 1534. Essentially, the Anglican Church embraces the Church of England, the Episcopal Church of America, the Scottish Episcopal Church, and the Church of Ireland. Its worship is liturgical; that is, it follows a specific formulation and makes use of the Apostles', Nicene, and Athanasian Creeds. Doctrine is set forth in a catechism, the Book of Common Prayer, and the Thirty-nine Articles. The archbishop of Canterbury is the head of the Church, followed by the archbishop of York.

Many Anglicans consider the church to be in the line of the Apostolic Succession, and a branch of the Catholic Church. Ministers are usually called "priest," and may be referred to as "Father," as in the Catholic Church. Some Anglican churches have worship services which closely resemble the Catholic Mass, even perhaps to the point of using Latin for a portion of the service. However, in contrast to these "high churches" are those often called "low church," which may resemble in worship services and evangelical nature the least ritualistic of Protestant denominations. The latter omit, or drastically reduce, the use of genuflection, kneeling, making the sign of the cross, incense, and symbolism which characterize "high church" services.

ANGLO-CATHOLIC. The name given to a group or to an individual within the Church of England or any other Protestant Episcopal denomination following Catholic faith and practice very closely. Such persons or groups are often called, loosely, "high-church."

ANIMA CHRISTI (Lat.: Soul of Christ). A prayer to Christ in his passion, and also a hymn, "Soul of My Saviour," that is taken from the prayer.

ANNE, ST. By tradition, and according to the apocryphal gospels, the mother of Mary and grandmother of Jesus. The Scriptures do not mention her name, but other sources tell her story. Childless for many years, she and her husband, Joachim, lived saintly lives and were eventually blessed with the girl Mary. Eastern churches have been especially devoted to St. Anne, and in the West she has been popular since approximately the time of the Crusades. Her feast day is July 26.

ANNIHILATIONISM. The theological view that the souls of the damned are not punished eternally in Hell, but are destroyed, (annihilated) instead. It was condemned by the Catholic Church in the sixteenth century, but has attracted some notice since, for it defines a middle way between a view that seems to deny the redemptive love of God (eternal damnation) and a view that denies the power of man to reject God's love in saying that eventually all beings enjoy complete salvation (universalism).

ANNULMENT OF MARRIAGE. In the Catholic Church, the act of declaring void a sacramental marriage which has not been consummated. The term is often confused with Declaration of Nullity, a concept with much broader applicability.

ANNUNCIATION, THE. The angel Gabriel's announcement (annunciation) to Mary of God's decision that she, though virgin, is to bear a boy who will rule as the begotten Son of God. The story is fully recounted in Luke 1: 27–38. Annunciation Day, or Lady Day, is celebrated March 25.

ANOINTED, THE. A term used to refer to Jesus Christ, for the word "Christ" literally means "the anointed," and is derived from the Greek *chrein,* to anoint. *Chrism,* an anointing oil or unguent was applied to make sacred, or consecrated, a thing or a person, and the "Messiah" of the Old Testament would be "the Anointed," or consecrated one. The term was originally applied descriptively to Jesus, as "Jesus the Christ," or the Anointed, and then came to be used as part of the proper name.

ANOINTING. The application of a small amount of oil to a person or thing, to consecrate or bless it. It is of ancient usage in the Christian religion, and is still employed in the Catholic Church at baptism, confirmation, conferring of holy orders, and in the sacrament called Extreme Unction for the Sick.

ANSELM, ST. (1034–1109). Born in Italy and renowned as abbot and later archbishop of Bec, in Normandy, St. Anselm became archbishop of Canterbury, England, in 1093 and remained there until his death. He supported papal claims to the right to appoint bishops, and put forward the so-called ontological proof of the existence of God, i.e., that the mere fact that the human brain can imagine, or conceive of, the idea of an infinite Being means that such a Being must exist. His teachings, writings, and influence in the Church, especially in negotiating conflicts between the papacy and the English, earned for him a title as one of the later Doctors of the Church. His feast day is April 23.

ANTE-BAPTISMAL SIN. That sin incurred by a human being prior to baptism, but not including original sin, with which each is born.

ANTHEM. A song sung by the choir or congregation of a church, and often composed of Scripture verses set to music. The name is derived from the word "antiphon," and an anthem was originally a religious song sung antiphonally.

ANTHONY OF PADUA, ST. (1195–1231). A Portuguese Franciscan, and both a teacher and a preacher, St. Anthony has been called the most popular worker of miracles in the Catholic Church. His powers are particularly invoked to help find lost articles. Canonized only a year after his death, St. Anthony was declared a later Doctor of the Church in 1946. His feast day is June 13.

ANTHONY OF THE DESERT, ST. (250–356). A great ascetic who lived most of his life in the seclusion of the Egyptian desert. In spite of his desire for solitude, St. Anthony was visited by many admirers. He founded two monasteries and was, in fact, the great spirit behind the rise of monasticism in both the East and the West. His life was exemplary, and he died happily and at a great age in a solitary mountain cave. His feast day is January 17.

ANTHROPOMORPHISM. The attribution of human characteristics, physical, emotional, or intellectual, to God. Such references have long been made, and are intended to be taken figuratively and not literally, according to the vast majority of theologians.

ANTICHRIST. According to 1 John 2:18, the great enemy of Christ who will spread universal evil before the end of the world, but who will meet ultimate defeat at the time of the second coming of Christ. In some theologies, the coming of the antichrist is held to be one of the signs of, or one of the events which must occur prior to, the second coming.

The antichrist is often identified as the Beast of Revelation, and sometimes, though erroneously, as Satan. Among some Christians,

the term is used loosely to designate anyone who does not believe as they do, or who opposes or does not believe in Christianity.

ANTICLERICALISM. Opposition to, or negative attitude toward, the
church or clergy or religious beliefs in general. Specifically, it is
opposition to influence of churches or clergy in public affairs.

ANTINOMIANISM. A heresy, almost as old as the Christian religion
itself, which holds that Christians are not bound by moral law.
Some Protestant groups after the sixteenth century Reformation
carried the doctrine of justification by faith to this extreme, saying,
in effect, that so long as one believed, any behavior was allowable.

ANTIPHON. A psalm or a hymn sung or chanted in alternating
parts, often with one side or part of a choir responding to the
other or singing alternate verses. In the Catholic Church, a verse
of Scripture sung before or after certain songs or prayers is
called the "antiphon."

ANTIPHONAL CHANTS. Any chant sung antiphonally, but specifically, in the Catholic Church, the three chants sung at High
Mass, the introit, offertory, and Communion chants, which are
sung by the choir while something is going on and not just for
their own sake.

ANTIPOPE. A pope established in opposition to the one chosen by
Church law. In the Catholic Church there have been twenty-five
such antipopes, ten of them in the twelfth century alone, the last
one in the fifteenth century. The "alter-popes" of the Great
Schism of the Church are called "Clementine popes," because
their historical position is too uncertain to condemn them as pre-
tenders.

APOCALYPSE. (Gr.: to disclose). The last book of the New Testament, written by St. John perhaps before the end of the first
century, and called Revelation in the Authorized Version. It foretells what is to happen through the use of symbolic visions, dreams,
and prophecies, and is, theologically, quite difficult to interpret.
Some faiths accept the visions and dreams as literal forecasts
of the future while others emphasize that they must be taken
figuratively. It can be said certainly, however, that the Apocalypse

deals with the last events on earth, the identity of heaven, and the cataclysmic nature of the world's end.

APOCALYPTIC WRITINGS. Those writings foretelling the last events which will occur on earth. Apocalyptic literature was produced for two centuries before, and three centuries after, the birth of Jesus. The visions of Daniel and Zacharias, Jesus' prophecy of the second coming, and especially Revelation are apocalyptic in nature.

APOCRYPHA (Gr.: hidden things). An appendix to the Authorized Version containing books and writings deemed instructive and useful, but not canonical, by the scholars who worked on that Protestant Bible. The standard was inclusion in the Masoretic text, and those books not found therein were placed in the Apocrypha. Included are:

| | |
|---|---|
| 1 and 2 Esdras | Daniel 3: 24–90 |
| Tobit | Daniel 13 and 14 |
| Judith | Prayer of Manasses |
| Esther 10: 4–16 | 1 and 2 Maccabees |
| Wisdom | |
| Ecclesiasticus | |
| Baruch | |

With the exception of the Prayer of Manasses and 1 and 2 Esdras, all the books in the Protestant Apocrypha are considered canonical by the Catholic Church.

APOLLINARIANISM. A fourth century heresy, named for Apollinaris, bishop of Alexandria, which held that Jesus had no human intellect and that his body and divinity were one substance, the "human appearing" part having actually been brought with him from Heaven, and that it was actually God-the-Son who died on the cross.

APOLOGETICS. The study of the explanation and defense of the Christian religion, and not to be confused with the popular use and meaning of the word "apology."

APOSTASY. The rejection of the faith of Christianity by a person baptized and raised a Christian and once possessed of the faith.

APOSTATE. A baptized Christian who rejects his faith.

A POSTERIORI. Used to designate an argument which is from effect to cause; from observation of what exists to a conclusion about it, thus, empirical. The existence of God, for example, might be argued *a posteriori,* through observation of the world, nature, effects, etc. Cf. with *a priori* and see St. Thomas Aquinas.

APOSTLE, THE. Generally used in reference to St. Paul, the "Apostle of the Gentiles."

APOSTLE OF ENGLAND. See St. Augustine of Canterbury.

APOSTLES, THE. Although the word, when not capitalized, may refer to any person sent on a mission or as a preacher, the term "the Apostles" is generally used to designate the twelve disciples chosen by Jesus and sent to preach the gospel:

| | |
|---|---|
| Andrew | Judas Iscariot |
| Bartholomew | (replaced by Matthias) |
| James the Younger | Matthew |
| James the Elder | Philip |
| John | Simon the Canaanite |
| Jude | Simon Peter |
| | Thomas |

Further, the first Christian missionary who succeeds in converting a country is called its "apostle." Thus, St. Augustine of England is called "The Apostle of England."

APOSTLES' CREED. A brief statement of basic Christian belief, the Apostles' Creed may be a development of a rule of faith used in Apostolic times. One form was used by Tertullian in the third century, and the complete modern form, which follows, was extant by 750:

I believe in God the Father Almighty, Maker of heaven and earth; And in Jesus Christ his only Son our Lord, Who was conceived by the Holy Ghost, Born of the Virgin Mary, Suffered under Pontius Pilate, Was crucified, dead, and buried; The third day he rose again from the dead; He ascended into heaven, And sitteth on the right hand of God the Father Almighty; From thence he shall come to judge the quick and the dead.

I believe in the Holy Ghost; The holy Catholic Church; The Communion of Saints; The Forgiveness of sins; The Resurrection of the body, And the life everlasting.

APOSTOLIC CHURCHES. According to the more limited of two definitions of this term, Apostolic churches are those either founded or governed by one of the Apostles, or said to have been so. Among them are: Rome—St. Peter; Alexandria—St. Mark; Antioch—St. Peter; Jerusalem—St. James the Younger; Athens —St. Paul; Cyprus—St. Barnabas (not one of the original twelve Apostles, but probably closely associated with St. Paul).

According to a more general definition, "Apostolic church" may refer to any church which adheres to the doctrine of Apostolic succession.

APOSTOLIC FATHERS. Those writers who lived and wrote at or near the time of the Apostles and thus came closely under their influence. Very few such writings are extant, but among them are letters of advice to churches and individuals; the Didache; the "Letter of Clement"; a group of letters of St. Ignatius of Antioch; and the moral teachings of the Shepherd of Hermas. They are interesting in that they throw light on the practices and problems of the very early church.

APOSTOLICITY. One of the four characteristics which identify the Catholic Church alone, according to Catholic theologians. "Apostolicity" consists of the fact that the Church teaches the same doctrine as the Apostles taught, that the line of Apostolic Succession is indisputable, and that the Church is the same organization, or society, as that which the Apostles founded.

APOSTOLIC SEE, THE. The episcopal see of Rome, founded by St. Peter, and the ultimate seat of authority in the Roman Catholic Church. "See" is from the Latin, "seat," of authority, and thus an "apostolic see" is, more generally, a seat of authority founded by one of the apostles.

APOSTOLIC SUCCESSION. The religious doctrine that the authority and the mission given by Jesus to the Apostles have descended in a direct and unbroken line of bishops to the bishops of today. The Catholic Church holds that descent is necessary through St. Peter and Rome. The Orthodox Eastern Church and other Eastern churches, as well as the Anglican Church, adhere to the doctrine, although their claims are either not fully accepted or are almost totally rejected by the Catholic Church.

APOTHEOSIS. The deification of a living human being, as, for example, some Roman emperors were believed to become divine when they became emperors.

A PRIORI. Used to designate an argument which is from cause to effect, from a general observation to particular illustrative proofs; such an argument is based on theory rather than on experiment or observation. Cf. *a posteriori* and *see* St. Anselm.

APSE. Semicircular end portion of early Christian churches, the apse held the bishop's throne. It was usually at the east end of the church and usually had a high, domed roof.

ARAMAIC. The Semitic language spoken in Babylon and Syria and, after the Babylonian captivity, by the Jews in a form called "Palestinian Aramaic." Thus, Aramaic, rather than Hebrew, was the language spoken by Jesus.

ARCHANGEL. A chief angel, one of the highest rank. Michael, Gabriel, and Raphael are the traditional biblical archangels, and four more, Uriel, Raguel, Sariel, and Jeramial are named in the book of Enoch in the pseudepigrapha (Catholic apocrypha).

ARCHBISHOP. The highest ranking bishop, or chief bishop, who has authority over an archbishopric or archdiocese just as a bishop has jurisdiction over the smaller division called a bishopric or diocese, and a priest over the still more localized parish. There are twenty-seven archbishoprics in the continental United States.

AREOPAGITE, THE. See Dionysius the Areopagite.

ARIANISM. A heresy originating in the third century with Arias, a priest in Alexandria, who held that Christ the Son was inferior to God the Father, and, as the Word, was a creature more perfect than other creatures but not divine. It was combated by St. Athanasius and condemned at the Council of Nicaea in 325, but had widespread circulation, especially in Europe, and a considerable effect on the early church.

ARK OF THE COVENANT. A gold-overlaid wooden chest, sacred to the early Hebrews as it represented God, the Ark could not be touched under threat of death, and it had to be carried into battle on poles put through rings on its sides. David took it to Jerusalem and Solomon placed it in the most holy part of the Temple. It is thought by some to have contained the stone tablets engraved with the Ten Commandments, but the belief cannot be verified as the Ark has long since disappeared. The term now refers to the place in a synagogue where the scrolls of the Torah are kept.

ARMENIAN CHURCH. A highly divergent branch of the Catholic Church, founded in the third century, and, since the sixth century, isolated from the parent church and highly national in character. Theologically, an identifying belief is monophysism, that the humanity of Jesus was absorbed in his divinity; various attempts at reconciliation have failed, primarily because of Armenian adherence to this doctrine, branded a heresy by the Catholic Church. Armenian orders and sacraments are valid, however; at present the church has a membership of some two or three million.

ARMINIANISM. The rejection of the doctrine of predestination, election and grace, as taught by Calvinism, led by Jacob Arminius (1560–1609). Baptists and Methodists were divided at one time into Calvinistic and Arminian branches, but the teachings of Wesley himself were Arminian in nature, as he emphasized the need for a personal thinking-through of the relationship of God and man and rejected the idea that God elects some men to be damned.

ARTICLES OF FAITH. Generally, whatever a particular church defines or lays down for belief by its members. In some churches, and especially in the Catholic Church, failure to accept one such article of faith implies rejection of all of them and the total loss of theological faith, for each article is equal to every other article in importance.

ASCENSION. The bodily ascent of Jesus into heaven.

ASCENSION DAY. The fortieth day after Easter, which always falls on Thursday, when the bodily ascent of Jesus into heaven is celebrated (Acts of the Apostles 1: 9). Ascension Day is also sometimes called Holy Thursday, and in the Catholic Church is a Holy Day of Obligation. The three days preceding Ascension Day are Rogation Days when special prayers and supplications are offered. On Ascension Day, the paschal, or Easter, candle is snuffed out, symbolizing Jesus' departure from earth and the Apostles.

ASCETICISM. The religious belief that self-denial and self-discipline may help lead one to a higher spiritual state. Such measures may be either physical or mental, rigorous or mild, but they should not, according to religious teaching, be practiced for their own sake. Most Christian churches recommend self-discipline or self-denial to an extent, and emphasize that Jesus demonstrated these in his chastity, poverty, obedience, and humility. However, "asceticism" as a way of life is more recognized by the Catholic Church than by the Protestant denominations, and it is primarily from Catholicism that most true ascetics have come.

ASEITY. In theology, the characteristic of being self-derived, independent of derivation, and thus applicable to God only.

ASHES. Christian symbol of penitence and death, hence the origin of the custom of marking the forehead with a cross of ashes on Ash Wednesday, the first day of the penitential Lenten season.

ASH WEDNESDAY. The first day of Lent, deriving its name from the ancient custom described above.

ASPERGES, THE. "The ceremony of sprinkling the people with holy water before the principal Mass on Sundays . . . the rite is at least as old as the ninth century and refers to the purified state . . ." needed to participate at Mass. (*Catholic Dictionary*, p. 36)

ASPERSION. Baptism by sprinkling the head with water.

ASSENT. An act of the intellect in judging and agreeing, as contrasted to *consent*, an act of the will.

ASS, FEAST OF THE. A pseudo-liturgical celebration which occurred primarily in thirteenth century France, and which became an occasion for revelry and merry-making, so much so, in fact, that it had to be officially suppressed by the Church. It derived its name from Balaam's ass, and from the ass which bore Mary and Jesus into Egypt, and was celebrated on the day after the octave of Epiphany, January 14.

ASSUMPTION, THE. The ascent into heaven of the soul and body of the Virgin Mary at her death. Although held from early time, this belief was not made a dogma by the Catholic Church until 1950. It is celebrated on August 15.

ATHANASIAN CREED. The most exact and lengthiest statement of the beliefs of the Catholic Church, and, to a fair degree, of most Christian churches. It is particularly explicit regarding the Trinity, incarnation, redemption, resurrection, ascension, and the nature of the Holy Ghost. The Creed is a statement of the doctrines held by St. Athanasius, one of the Greek Fathers of the Church, and was once attributed to him. It is now considered an anonymous work of the fourth, or, more probably, the sixth century, that was designed to embody the teachings of St. Athanasius. It was written in Latin, whereas the briefer Apostles' and Nicene Creeds were written in Greek. It is sometimes called *Quicunque vult.*

THE ATHANASIAN CREED. Whosoever will be saved: before all things it is necessary that he hold the Catholic Faith, which Faith except every one do keep whole and undefiled, without doubt he shall perish everlastingly. And the Catholic Faith is this:
    That we worship One God in Trinity, and Trinity in Unity; Neither confounding the Persons: nor dividing the Substance. For there is One Person of the Father, another of the Son: and another of the Holy Ghost. But the Godhead of the Father, of the Son and of the Holy Ghost is all one: the Glory equal, the Majesty co-eternal. Such as the Father is, such is the Son; and such is the Holy Ghost. The Father uncreate, the Son uncreate: and the Holy Ghost uncreate. The Father incomprehensible: the Son incomprehensible: and the Holy Ghost incomprehensible. The Father eternal, the Son eternal: and the Holy Ghost eternal. And yet there are not three eternals: but one eternal. As also there are not three incomprehensibles nor three uncreated: but one uncreated and one incomprehensible. So likewise the Father is Almighty: the Son Almighty: and the Holy Ghost Almighty. And yet there are not three Almighties: but one Almighty. So the Father is God, the Son is God: and the Holy Ghost is God. And yet there are not

three Gods: but one God. So likewise the Father is Lord, the Son Lord: and the Holy Ghost Lord. And yet not three Lords: but one Lord. For like as we are compelled by the Christian verity: to acknowledge every Person by Himself to be God and Lord: so are we forbidden by the Catholic Religion to say there be three Gods, or three Lords. The Father is made of none: neither created nor begotten. The Son is of the Father alone: not made nor created but begotten. The Holy Ghost is of the Father and of the Son: neither made, nor created, nor begotten, but proceeding. So there is one Father, not three Fathers; one Son, not three Sons; one Holy Ghost, not three Holy Ghosts. And in this Trinity none is afore, or after other: none is greater, or less than another; but the whole three Persons are co-eternal together: and co-equal. So that in all things, as is aforesaid: the Unity in Trinity, and the Trinity in Unity, is to be worshipped. He therefore that will be saved: must thus think of the Trinity.

Furthermore, it is necessary to everlasting salvation: that he also believe rightly the Incarnation of our Lord Jesus Christ. For the right Faith is, that we believe and confess: that our Lord Jesus Christ, the Son of God, is God and Man; God, of the Substance of the Father, begotten before the worlds, and Man, of the Substance of His Mother, born in the world; Perfect God, and Perfect Man: of a reasonable soul and human flesh subsisting. Equal to the Father, as touching His Godhead: and inferior to the Father, as touching His Manhood. Who although He be God and Man: yet He is not two but one Christ; One: not by conversion of the Godhead into flesh: but by taking of the Manhood, into God; One altogether; not by confusion of Substance: but by unity of Person. For as the reasonable soul and flesh is one man: so God and Man is one Christ; Who suffered for our salvation; descended into hell; rose again the third day from the dead. He ascended into Heaven, He sitteth on the Right hand of the Father, God Almighty: from whence He shall come to judge the quick and the dead. At Whose coming all men shall rise again with their bodies: and shall give account of their own works. And they that have done good shall go into life everlasting: and they that have done evil into everlasting fire.

This is the Catholic Faith: which except a man believe faithfully he cannot be saved.

Glory be to the Father, and to the Son, and to the Holy Ghost. As it was in the beginning, is now, and ever shall be, world without end. Amen.

ATHANASIUS, ST. (295–373). An early Alexandrian patriarch and Doctor of the Church who was most forceful in fighting the wide-spread Arian heresy of the times, i.e., that the Son of God was begotten by God as the first creature, and was neither equal with God nor eternal. The opposing camps of Arians and Athanasians were fairly evenly balanced at least for a while, and to such an extent that Athanasius, upholding what was to become orthodox belief, was exiled five times. However, St. Athanasius' beliefs triumphed at the First Council of Nicaea, the first of the ecumenical councils, convened by Constantine in 325 to debate and decide about the divinity of Jesus. At this council the concept of the "consubstantial" nature of the Father and Son, that they are of the same substance and essential nature, and that, hence, the Son is divine, was adopted as official. The Athanasian Creed, although not written by Athanasius and generally accepted as a considerably later work, sets forth quite explicitly the beliefs held by him. His feast day is May 2.

ATHEISM (Gr.: without God). The belief that denies the existence of a deity; although in context the term usually designates one who denies the existence of the Judeo-Christian God or any other type of deity, it may be limited to apply only to one who denies the existence of the Judeo-Christian God, while admitting the existence of a divine principle that is more or less unidentifiable.

ATHEIST. One who denies that there is a God, although qualified as above. The atheist has more in common with the theist, insofar as certainty is concerned, than either has with the agnostic.

ATONEMENT, THE. The act of reconciliation of man and God accomplished through the suffering and death of Jesus, who thus made up, that is, atoned, for man's sins.

ATTRIBUTES OF GOD. The defining characteristics of God. Traditionally, there have been two methods for determining the nature of God, the simpler of the two being the Way of Negation. By this method, theologians define what God is by stating what he is not: "God is not complex, therefore absolutely simple; God is not finite, therefore infinite; not in time, therefore eternal; not subject to change, therefore immutable; not spatially limited, therefore omnipresent; not caused, therefore possesses aseity." (*Theological Terms,* p. 35)

The more complex, the Way of Analogy, has been much used by Catholic theologians and much attacked by their Protestant counterparts. St. Thomas Aquinas, particularly, developed the Way of Analogy, which says, essentially, that the nature of the Creator is analogous to the nature of the creature, since man is said to be created in the image of God. Among the difficulties encountered in this method is that of *how* analogous, or *how* similar, God is to man, a question proponents may answer by saying: not the same, but near enough to allow a meaningful comparison from which significant conclusions can be drawn. In general, God is said to be omniscient, omnipotent, and omnipresent, i.e., all-knowing, all-powerful, and everywherepresent; existent in eternity, not in time; self-actualized, that is, not made or created by any other being; and pure actuality, a fully realized Being containing no element of incompleteness or potentiality.

ATTRITION. Held by Catholic theologians generally to be imperfect contrition in so much as contrition is sorrow that comes from love of God and from having offended God by sinning, while attrition is sorrow that comes from fear of Hell or loss of Heaven through sinning. The belief that attrition is insufficient for penance and absolution has recently been somewhat modified.

AUDIENCE, PAPAL. Any meeting accorded by the pope to an individual of whatever rank or status.

AUGSBURG CONFESSION. Written in 1530 by Melanchthon, the Augsburg Confession was endorsed by Martin Luther and is still the official statement of the beliefs of the Lutheran Church. Melanchthon was a humanist, tending toward conciliatory feelings, and until he saw the Confession, Luther is said to have feared he might compose too mild a statement of faith. However, he did not. The Confession was moderate but firm, and set the Lutheran group very clearly over against the Catholic. In *Here*

*I Stand,* Roland Bainton has written, "One might take the date June 25, 1530, the day when the Augsburg Confession was publicly read, as the death day of the Holy Roman Empire." The Augsburg Confession stands with the Thirty-nine Articles and the Westminster Confession as the identifying creed of a major Protestant denomination.

AUGUSTINE, RULE OF ST. Although St. Augustine of Hippo did not draw up a full set of rules as St. Benedict did, his teaching about monastic life was set down in various letters, and these teachings, considered together, have formed the basis for the constitutions of the Canons Regular as well as for those of the Dominicans, Knights Hospitallers, and other orders. Specifically, St. Augustine set down the precepts of prayer in common and no ownership of individual property, and he emphasized unity and charity in living the common life of the monastery.

AUGUSTINE OF CANTERBURY, ST. (d. 605). The first archbishop of Canterbury, England, where he and a number of other Roman Benedictine monks were sent by Pope Gregory I during the time of King Aethelbert of Kent in the late sixth century. He gained the favor of the king, whose wife was a Christian, and who later was converted himself, and he was allowed to preach and teach freely. Known as the Apostle of England, for he was the first truly successful missionary to that country, St. Augustine introduced the rites of the Roman Catholic Church to England, and these later replaced the Celtic forms which were followed in the north of the country. The exact date of his death is not known, but his feast day is kept on May 28, or, in England, on May 26.

AUGUSTINE OF HIPPO, ST. (354–430). St. Augustine, one of the Latin Fathers of the Church, was born at Tagaste, in Numidia, North Africa. He was raised in the Christian faith by his mother, Monica, but as a young man in school he became an apostate and turned to Manichaeism. This religion, ascetic and dualistic, originated in Persia; its spirtualization of the struggle between good (light) and evil (dark) seemed to the young man a better answer than Christianity to the riddle of the world. As a Manichaean he became a teacher of rhetoric in Milan, but while in that city he came under the influence of St. Ambrose, then its bishop, and returned to his former Christian faith. Back in Ta-gaste, he became a religious hermit, but later he was made bishop of Hippo Regius, now Bone, in North Africa.

While a Manichaean, St. Augustine lived a life he later depicted as self-seeking and immoral. He did not marry, though a match was arranged for him, but he was apparently faithful to the concubine he took instead. He deeply loved a son, Adeodatus, or Gift of God, whom she bore him; the boy died shortly after he and his father had received baptism into the Christian faith. After his conversion, or re-conversion, St. Augustine followed an ascetic life, during which, with a few friends, he founded in 388 the oldest Western monastic order, the Augustinians.

A master of theology, St. Augustine was not only a highly educated and literate man, but one willing to use his learning actively in argument against the various heresies of his day, among them Pelagianism, Donatism, and the Manichaeism of his earlier belief. In his fight against Pelagius, he defined and defended the Church's position on grace and salvation through God and belief in Christ as against the more open position of Pelagius who held that any good man, pagan or Christian, could be saved. This was the earliest spelling out in detail of the orthodox position on faith and good works.

Probably no churchman had a greater influence than St. Augustine on the Church of the Middle Ages, and, indeed, his thinking has been important not only to Catholicism but also to all Christian theology. Among laymen, he is best known for his *Confessions,* a moving exposition of his own search for faith, and for *The City of God,* an examination of the ideal in comparison to the actual, or the "City of Man," in a Christian society. His feast day is August 28.

AUGUSTINIAN CANONS AND AUGUSTINIAN FRIARS. See Canons Regular of St. Augustine and Hermits of St. Augustine.

AUGUSTINISM. A formulation by St. Augustine of Hippo stressing the "universal necessity of divine grace in every act that tends to salvation, the reality of the guilt of original sin, the divine election and predestination, but at the same time the complete liberty of the human will, and the reconciliation of these apparently conflicting doctrines." (*Catholic Dictionary,* p. 39)

AUREOLE. The gilt, representing a luminous cloud, or light, surrounding the whole figure of Jesus, Máry, or Joseph in religious pictures; it symbolizes the glory of God. It is not to be confused with "nimbus" or "halo."

AURICULAR CONFESSION. Private, as opposed to a public or general confession, the term literally means "to the ear." In practice, the confession may be written rather than spoken. It is the standard type of confession in the Catholic Church.

AUSTIN CANONS AND AUSTIN FRIARS. Short forms of Augustinian Canons and Augustinian Friars.

AUTHENICATION OF RELICS. In the Catholic Church, relics such as the bones of saints are venerated. While only those which have been properly approved as genuine, and this is a careful process, may be given public honor in churches, such authentication is not to be understood as a guarantee of genuineness. It merely insures that the object is not clearly spurious and that the authenticator does not know of any good reason why the object should not be venerated.

AUTHORIZED VERSION. The King James version of the Bible published in England in 1611 during the reign of James I. Regarded as the greatest of English translations, it is the standard Protestant Bible. It is often abbreviated A.V.

AUTO-DA-FÉ (Span. act of faith). A body of the Spanish Inquisition which heard the public recantation of errors of faith (this recanting being the "act of faith") made by the accused individual. This body set penance and reconciled the sinner to the Church. Anyone who refused to recant was handed over to civil authorities, however, and was frequently executed by a public burning, so "auto-da-fé" often refers to the public burning of a heretic.

A.V. Initials standing for Authorized Version

AVE BELL, THE. The bell rung for the Angelus.

AVE MARIA (Lat.: Hail, Mary; ä′vä-märē′-ä). In the Catholic Church, the most frequently used prayer to the Virgin Mary: "Hail Mary, full of grace. The Lord is with Thee. Blessed art thou amongst women, and blessed is the fruit of thy womb, Jesus.

Holy Mary, Mother of God, pray for us sinners now and at the hour of our death."

The origin is to be found in Luke 1: 28. The prayer has often been set to music, notably by Schubert and Gounod; the arrangement by the former is the more highly popularized, or commercialized, and the lyrics, in English, are not the Ave Maria prayer of the Catholic Church.

AVIGNON POPES. The seven legitimate popes who, from 1305 to 1370, governed the Catholic Church from Avignon, France, instead of from Rome, during the so-called "Babylonian captivity."

AZYME (Gr.: unleavened). The unleavened bread used at the Eucharist in the Catholic Church.

# B

BABINGTON CONSPIRACY, THE. The 1586 plot to assassinate Queen Elizabeth and place Mary Queen of Scots, a Catholic, on the English throne. Mary was apparently involved in the plot, but it took its name from Francis Babington, one of the conspirators. It failed, but Elizabeth, frightened, allowed the execution of her cousin Mary to proceed.

"BABYLONIAN (-LONISH) CAPTIVITY." The exile of seven popes from Rome to Avignon, France, during the fourteenth century (1309–1378). The name refers back to the captivity of the Jews in Babylon in the sixth century before Christ.

BALDACCHINO (bal'də-kē'-nō). A canopy to cover an altar; the name is derived from Baghdad, the place of origin. Also *baldachin*.

BAMBINO. An image of the baby Jesus, often in a crib.

BAPTISM. The sacrament by which original sin is removed and the subject is spiritually regenerated and received into a church. For a baptism to be valid in many, but not by any means all churches, it is only necessary for the person baptizing to have that sincere intent, to apply ordinary water to the head of the subject, and to say at that time "I baptize thee (or 'this person is baptized') in the name of the Father and of the Son and of the Holy Ghost."

Various churches have various ways of baptizing. The Baptist Church, for example, practices immersion of adults, the Catholic Church infusion (flowing water on the head), and many churches aspersion (sprinkling water on the head). Anointing with oil may also be customary.

Baptism is one of the two sacraments, the other being the Holy Communion or Eucharist, accepted by almost all Christians as being instituted by Jesus and the Scriptures, and as necessary parts of worship. Martin Luther was primarily responsible for casting doubt on the authenticity of the remaining five: Confirmation, Penance, Marriage, Holy Orders, and Extreme Unction.

BAPTISTS. A Protestant denomination founded by English separatist John Smyth in Amsterdam about 1608. A London group originated in 1611, and Roger Williams organized the first American branch in Providence, Rhode Island, in 1639. Essentially, Baptists believe that baptism is for adults, not children, since children cannot be believers in the true sense, and that it must be by immersion. Many branches of the Baptist Church have tended toward conservative Christianity and a literal or nearly literal acceptance of the Bible. They are congregational in form with nongoverning general associations such as the American Baptist Convention and the Southern Baptist Convention. Branches are numerous, and the total membership is over 25,-000,000 in the United States alone.

BAPTISTERY. That portion of the church, or a chapel, or even a separate building, containing the font for baptismal water and before which the sacrament of baptism is performed.

BARNABAS, ST. (first century). An early Christian, an apostle, and a friend of St. Paul. He came from Cyprus to Jerusalem and was influential in the first Christian community there and in the missionary work he pursued later. According to tradition, he died a martyr in Salamis in about A.D. 60. His feast day is June 11.

BARTHOLOMEW, ST. (first century). Very little is known of this Christian aside from the fact that he is given as an apostle in the Synoptic Gospels and that his name is linked with that of Philip, from which some conclude that they were close friends. Others have conjectured that he was also known as "Nathanael," also mentioned in conjunction with Philip. His feast day is August 24.

BASIL, ST. (330–379). One of the early Greek Doctors of the Church, St. Basil was a brilliantly educated man, an expert in philosophy, doctrine, politics, and oratory, as well as a productive and fine writer. An ascetic for a period of some five years, he became "the monastic legislator of the East, as later St. Benedict was of the West." (*Lives of the Saints,* p. 261.) In resisting Arianism, quite popular in his time not only with certain branches of the Church but also with the Emperor Valens, he helped establish doctrinal unity within the Church. His writings are numerous and include homilies, discourses, treatises, and several hundred letters. An adult convert to Christianity, St. Basil became one of the shapers of the Church, and is one of the three ecumenical doctors of the Greek Church, the others being St. Gregory of Nazianzus and St. John Chrysostom. His sister, whose influence led to his conversion, was St. Macrina, and his younger brother was St. Gregory of Nyssa; his maternal grandfather died a martyr; his friend, and the man he succeeded as bishop of Caesarea, was the remarkable Eusebius. Basilian monks, the monks of the Eastern Church, still maintain notable monasteries under his rule at Mt. Athos and Mt. Sinai. His feast day is June 14.

BASILICA. The name frequently given various ancient churches in Rome and elsewhere built in the fourth century and later. Their form followed that of large Roman halls. A portico and colonnaded atrium were characteristic, and the church proper was divided into a nave with side aisles and an apse with the altar at the front and the bishop's throne against the back wall. The shape was rectangular. In more modern times, "basilica" has become a title of honor with certain rights attached to the clergy of the church so designated. Among newer basilicas is the Grotto at Lourdes.

BEADS. In the Catholic Church, the Rosary. This arrangement of beads on a cord or chain is a device to help the memory when repetition of numbers of prayers is important. Beads for thus counting prayers are also used by Hindus, Buddhists, and Mohammedans. See *Rosary* and *bede.*

BEATIFICATION. The lengthy process carried on by high authorities in the Catholic Church whereby the sanctity of a deceased person is evaluated and he or she is officially deemed worthy of veneration on a general, national, or local level. Many years are usually required to subject the life, teachings, writings, and alleged miracles of the candidate to the critical scrutiny of many judges, and to the final decision of the Pope. Beatification usually, but not necessarily, leads to canonization.

BEATIFIC VISION, THE. The vision, or seeing, of God face to face by souls in Heaven. Such an immediate knowledge of God is said to be the greatest joy of the saved.

BEATITUDES, THE. The eight blessings pronounced by Jesus at the beginning of the Sermon on the Mount found in Matthew 5:3–10.

BECKET, ST. THOMAS (1117–1170). Born of a wealthy English family of Norman origin, Thomas Becket was first chancellor (prime minister) under Henry II, King of England and a portion of France, and later archbishop of Canterbury. After ordination as a priest in 1162, Becket exchanged his worldly life of pomp and display for one of austerity and devotion to his role as chief of the Church in England. He upheld papal rights and Church authority against the king, especially in matters of the law where he defended indefatigably the right of the Church to try clerics of any degree in ecclesiastical courts, rather than submit them to Henry II's secular courts. He was forced once to flee for his life to France, but returned as determined as ever to defend Church prerogatives. Although he and the king had once been close friends, Henry was thoroughly exasperated with the man whom he believed he had elevated, and, according to tradition, exclaimed, "Cursed be they that eat my bread unless they deliver me from this insolent priest!" Certain courtiers took him literally and slew Thomas Becket with swords in his cathedral. His death as a martyr was followed by miracles, some authenticated, many occasioned by the hysteria of believers at the murder of the head of the English church. His feast day is December 29.

BEDE. An Old English word for "prayer."

BEDE THE VENERABLE, ST. (673–735). The Venerable Bede is honored by the Catholic Church for his influence and instruction within the monastery where he spent most of his life, and by historians for his invaluable *Ecclesiastical History of the English People.* He was a devout man, a scholar, and a copious writer; although many of his works have been lost over the centuries, the

*Ecclesiastical History,* written in Latin, is considered excellent for its style, accuracy, and inclusiveness. The title is a little misleading, for it is not solely a church history. Rather, it covers the history of England from its origins to about 731, and he used for it, according to his epilogue, "old documents, ancient traditions, and what I have been able to see with my own eyes." It is a short book by modern standards, and is divided into chronologically arranged chapters. Within it also is recorded Bede's account of the gift of song to Caedmon, the first English poet known by name. St. Bede's feast day is May 27.

BEELZEBUB. Satan or any devil, although in the Hebrew the term meant "god of insects"; in Milton's *Paradise Lost* Beelzebub is identified as Satan's chief lieutenant.

BEING. This most important and difficult concept of both philosophy and theology has probably been debated more than any other. Although laymen identify "being" as "existence," and speak of God as the Supreme Being, any delving into the underlying meaning or meanings of the word will reveal at once the problems confronting professional thinkers. *Being* has been said to be the fulfillment of all possibilities with the resultant elimination of potential. A question arises: If God, then, is supremely realized, hence changeless and unchangeable, how can his knowing, loving, and being affected by man's problems be fitted into the definition? This was, and is, a problem faced but unresolved by theologians.

Identification of God with Being has been accepted and rejected over the years, and indeed "The rejection of the science of Being (ontology) as a vehicle for theology has particularly characterized liberal Protestantism as well as neo-Reformed thought . . ." (*Theological Terms,* p. 41). The question is far from settled. In the meantime, laymen can do worse than consider *being* as existence, recognizing humankind as finite beings, i.e., possessed of both existence and potential since their essence is not their existingness alone, and God as an infinite Being or existence, whose very nature is to *be.*

BEL AND THE DRAGON. The story in Daniel 14, a chapter found in the Apocrypha of the *Authorized Version,* recounts Daniel's clever outwitting of the priests of the pagan god Bel and his slaying of a dragon or beast worshipped as a god, for which he was thrown into the lions' den and protected by God.

BELIAL. In the Old Testament, wickedness as an actively evil force was termed *Belial;* in the New Testament, Belial is identified as Satan, and in Milton's *Paradise Lost* as one of the fallen angels.

BELIEF. The assent of the mind to doctrines or truths as expounded by a religious group or arrived at independently through thought.

BELL. The ringing of church bells to call worshipers to divine service has been a common practice since the eighth century. Otherwise, individual Protestant churches use bells at their own discretion. In some, they are tolled for the dead; they may be rung most frequently during the joyous Christmas season; they are often entirely silenced on Good Friday (unless one is tolled to mark the end of the Three Hours) to be rung again Easter morning.

In the Catholic Church, the hand bell rung during Mass directs the congregation's attention to the most solemn parts of the service, such as the Sanctus and the elevation of the Host, although the use is not omitted at private Masses when no congregation is present.

BELL, BOOK AND CANDLE. A term designating the now disused ceremony of public and solemn declaration of excommunication. In the past, a bishop read the sentence of excommunication from a particular book, priests holding candles threw them to the ground to symbolize the extinguishing of grace and joy, and the bell was rung to add solemnity to the occasion.

BENEDICITE, THE. The Song of the Three Children, Ananias, Azarias, and Mishael, in the fiery furnace. (More common names, given in Daniel 1:7 are Shadrach, Meshach, and Abednego.) The Song begins "All ye works of the Lord, bless [or 'praise ye'] the Lord," and is found in the Daniel, of the Aprocrypha of the *Authorized Version* since it is believed to have been added by an author of about 160 B.C.

BENEDICT, ST. (d. c.547). St. Benedict was born and educated in Italy and became a monk at Subiaco. Around him in his hermit's cave gathered many disciples, and eventually he founded twelve monasteries for them, placing about twelve monks in each. Later, he went to Monte Cassino, long a shrine for Venus, Jupiter, and Apollo, and after destroying all signs of the pagan gods, built an abbey there and founded an order and a rule that made him not only the Father of the Benedictines but also, in a very true sense, the Father of Western Monasticism. His rule was based on silence and prayer, work, contrition, and respect for the human being. At one time, some forty thousand monasteries followed this Rule of St. Benedict. His feast day is March 21.

BENEDICT, THE RULE OF ST. The standard rule for most monasteries in the West, the Rule of St. Benedict was written in the first part of the sixth century for the ordering of Benedict's own monastery at Monte Cassino. It covers government and organization of monasteries, the nature of daily community life and enclosure, the services to be held, and appointments and recruitment. The three vows of poverty, chastity and obedience, as well as of stability and conversion of manners (family life under monastic conditions), are defined, and a moderate degree of austerity is prescribed. All in all, the rule was reasonable, practicable, and filled with a wisdom especially remarkable for the times.

BENEDICTINE ORDER. A religious order in the Catholic Church founded in 529 and based on the Rule of St. Benedict, which stressed manual work and daily celebration of the Divine Office in choir. The various houses do not constitute a single religious order but exercise varying degrees of independence. In many cases, manual work has been replaced by teaching, ordinary parochial labors, or missionary efforts. The habit is usually black, and the vows taken are poverty, chastity, obedience, stability, and conversion of manners, i.e., common life in the monastery.

Benedictine nuns are an enclosed, contemplative order, though some schools are conducted.

BENEDICTION. A blessing, or a request for divine blessing, usually said by the minister at the conclusion of a church service.

BENEFIT OF CLERGY. Commonly, though incorrectly, this term is used with the negative "without" to designate an illicit or temporary union between a man and a woman. It denotes, actually, an obsolete English custom which once made it possible for a monk or a nun charged with any felony short of treason or arson to be tried in an ecclesiastical instead of a civil court. In post-Reformation times, it referred to the English custom of giving the well-educated guilty person a much lighter sentence for a felony in a civil court than would be given an illiterate individual. It was a practice that was much abused, but was not entirely abandoned until the nineteenth century.

BENJAMIN, ST. (d. c.422). This fifth-century Persian martyr stood up to the king in refusing to worship the sun and fire or to cease teaching the Christian faith in his country. As a consequence, he suffered death by torture and the stake, rejecting constant orders and requests to apostasize. His feast day is March 31.

BERNADETTE, ST. (1844-1879). Bernadette Soubirous was one of those rarities, an apparently authentic modern-day visionary and saint. Her story is fairly well known, having been told by Franz Werfel in *Song of Bernadette,* from which a popular film was made. This young French peasant girl of Lourdes was visited several times by an apparition of the Virgin Mary, the Immaculate Conception, between the months of February and July of 1858. Thereafter, Bernadette was educated at a house of the sisters of Nevers in Lourdes and later became a nun of the order. She was always humble and frequently ill, though she carried out her duties as well as her health allowed; she was often subjected to a certain amount of scorn and persecution, even by her superiors, but she never denied her visions of Mary or attempted to gain prestige through them. She was canonized in 1933; her feast day is April 16.

BERNARD OF CLAIRVAUX, ST. (1090-1153). One of the later Doctors of the Church, St. Bernard was probably the most powerful churchman of his day by virtue of his brilliance, strong character, and holiness. He founded a Cistercian monastery at Clairvaux in France, his native land, and worked from it the rest of his life, although he received bids to higher church offices. He was a remarkably fine writer and speaker, whereby he was able to launch the Second Crusade and to achieve the condemnation of Abelard, whom he believed to be in error and a threat to dogma of the Church. He was a great reformer, and his influence reached from the clergy through the Benedictines (though he was not able to get them to remove art works from their churches) to Rome. He was also notable for his kindness and his protection of the weak, as in his defense of the Rhineland Jews against oppression. His feast day is August 20.

BIBIANA (VIVIAN), ST. (d. 363). This Roman girl, daughter of a former prefect of the city, was a victim of the conditions which obtained during the rule of Julian the Apostate. Although Christians were not precisely persecuted during Julian's rule, as they were, for example, under Diocletian, they were thoroughly and officially rejected, and could often be tortured and killed without fear of punishment. Thus Bibiana's father was sent into slavery, her mother was beheaded, and she herself was beaten to death for refusing to give up her virtue. Her feast day is December 2.

BIBLE, THE. Primarily thought of as the sacred book of the Christion religion, and always so intended when the word is capitalized, *bible* means, literally, a collection of writings, and is a Greek term derived from the Egyption for "papyrus bark." The Christian Bible contains Old and New Testaments, and, in the Catholic *Douay Bible* much of the material relegated to the Apocrypha of the *Authorized Version*. The Old Testament is referred to as the Hebrew Bible, and the Koran may correctly be called the Moslem Bible. In the *A.V.* the Old Testament consists of thirty-nine books, the New Testament of twenty-seven, and the Apocrypha of twelve, counting additions to Esther and Daniel as books.

BIBLICAL CRITICISM. Primarily a product of the enlightened historical and scientific research of the eighteenth and nineteenth centuries, biblical criticism essentially questions the text of the Bible on all points and thus must be said to reject it as unerringly and literally true, the revealed Word of God. It questions the authenticity of texts, the truth of reported events, the authorship of most books; it examines literary style in relationship to the times, the intentions of the writer, and the beliefs of those for whom the writing was intended; it casts light on the history of biblical times, the social and intellectual environment, and the traditions of ancient societies.

Biblical criticism may be somewhat artificially subdivided into lower criticism, having to do with the authenticity of texts; higher criticism, having to do with most other questions; literary criticism; and historical criticism. The truth is that most areas overlap, and that to attempt to criticize from one viewpoint only is often to risk distortion and misinterpretation. It is impossible to ask, for example, what the most important ideas are in a certain piece of writing without being aware of the history of the people for whom they had their importance, their traditions and social milieu, and their ideas of what constituted an effective presentation of a belief or admonition.

Inevitably, biblical criticism found its own critics. Fundamentalists and Catholic theologians particularly attacked the so-called "higher criticism," although the Catholic Church has modified considerably the 1902 stand of its Biblical Commission which was taken to guarantee that Catholic scholars did not come up with historical ideas that went against dogma. Liberal Protestants have, as a rule, formed the vanguard in biblical criticism.

Many traditional beliefs about the Bible were shattered by the first wave of critics: Moses was not the author of the first five books of the Old Testament; The Book of Isaiah was not a single book, but two, or perhaps more; the Gospel According to St. John bore faint resemblance to the Gospels of Matthew, Mark, and Luke, and of those three, Matthew and Luke took a good portion of their material from the work of Mark; a history of Jesus' ministry simply cannot be reconstructed. And so on. At stake was the authority of the entire Bible.

That authority now is seen by most biblical critics and by many Protestant theologians to rest on the witness the Bible bears either to the "mighty works of God" or to God's goodness, both culminating in Jesus; the Word of God remains for them the Word of God, but is accepted as having been communicated through humans in a framework of history.

BIBLICISM. The point of view which accepts the Bible, word for word, as literally true, and which refuses to accept any truth as Christian which cannot be found there. Also *bibliolatry*.

BIDDING-PRAYER. The present custom in many churches of reading at some point during the worship service the names of those people most needing prayers, or the names of the recently deceased. It probably originated from the older bidding prayers which mentioned as specifically as possible those for whom special prayers should be said, from the highest church and state authorities through pregnant women to individuals in need of some special help. The custom in the Catholic Church was called "bidding the beads," or actually "praying the prayers," the name taken from the Old English "bede" meaning prayer.

BILOCATION. The capacity of being in two places at the same time, an argument sometimes used to explain how Jesus' body could be present at many places at the same time. Some few saints, also, are believed by some to have possessed this remarkable capability, as certain events in their lives are difficult to explain without resorting to it.

BINDING AND LOOSING. That power conferred by Jesus on his apostles and through them on bishops and priests, according to Matthew 16:18–19. It is also called the "power of the keys."

BINITARIANISM. In contrast to Trinitarianism, or a belief in the Trinity, Binitarianism holds that there are only two persons, God the Father and God the Son, and no God the Holy Ghost. The term is sometimes used to refer to a church or theology which slights the Holy Ghost, also, through failure to mention or teach the concept.

BIRETTA. The square cap with three ridges on its top and a tassel; it is worn by the Catholic clergy, except monks and friars, when entering and leaving the church for services and at certain times during the service itself. The color is usually black, but cardinals wear red birettas and bishops wear purple ones.

BISHOP. A clergyman of high rank who has authority over a diocese, or bishopric. The term "episcopal" refers to churches governed by bishops, such as the Protestant Episcopal Church, the Anglican, the Methodist, and the Catholic.

BLACK. The liturgical color for mourning. Most churches use black draperies of some sort on Good Friday and in association with funerals.

BLACK FAST. In the Catholic Church, a fast day on which only one meal was allowed, and that one in the evening, when milk, eggs, meat, butter and cheese were forbidden. The practice has virtually disappeared.

BLACK FRIARS. The Dominicans; the name came to be used because for outdoor wear Dominicans have a black cloak and hood.

BLACK MADONNA. Any statue or picture of the Virgin Mary which for any reason, such as age, material used, or environment, has turned black, or dark. The statue of Notre Dame du Pillier in Chartres Cathedral is, however, most often the one referred to by the term, as it is the most famous.

BLACK MASS. (1) A requiem Mass, when black vestments are worn. (2) A blasphemous rite performed by those who reject and mock Christianity, and, it is said, by those who worship the Devil. The Black Mass, in this sense, may be a parody of the Catholic Church service.

BLACK MONKS. The Benedictines, who wear an all black habit.

"BLACK POPE," THE. The nickname once given the superior generals of the Jesuits, who wear black cassocks, whereas the pope's is white, and who are, or were, erroneously believed to wield great power in the Catholic Church.

BLAISE, ST. (d. c.316). A native of Armenia, St. Blaise was a famous physician, as well as a hermit, and a church authority. He is particularly invoked by those having ailments of the throat and is deemed also a protector of animals, for he had great skill in handling even wild beasts. Tradition tells that he was beheaded after successfully walking on the waters of a lake into which he had been thrown and then inviting the pagans who abused him to show their gods' power by doing the same; they drowned, to a man. His feast day is February 3.

BLASPHEMY. Speech, writing, or even thought which shows intentional or unintentional contempt for, or dishonor toward, God. Common expressions, such as "God damn," and similar uses of the name of God or Jesus are usually unintentionally blasphemous, but are condemned nevertheless by Christian churches.

BLASPHEMY OF THE SPIRIT. Malicious attribution to the Devil of works that are manifestly of God. This has also been referred to as the Sin against the Holy Ghost, which is alternately defined (by St. Augustine) as final impenitence. Blasphemy of the Spirit and final impenitence have the same result, actually, since an inability to repent and thus be forgiven, and a pride and perversity that make repentance impossible, both lead to eternal damnation. (Matthew 12: 31–32 and Mark 3:29)

BLESS. Derived from an Anglo-Saxon word for blood, and early denoting a making holy, or consecrating, by sprinkling with blood; *bless* has, today, a variety of meanings. It may still denote a making holy, or a consecrating of a person, place, or thing; it may mean to ask divine favor upon, as in "Bless this house. . ."; it may signify a feeling of gratitude, or a desire to wish well to something or somebody.

BLESS ONESELF, TO. To make the sign of the cross on oneself, essentially from forehead to breast and from left shoulder to right, done with the right hand. This practice obtains in the Anglican and Catholic Churches and the gesture is commonly made at mention of the Father, Son, and Holy Ghost, or of any member of the Trinity. In the prayer book or missal, the points are marked by a small cross.

BLESSED. In the Catholic Church, the title for anyone who has been beatified but not canonized. In more general usage, *blessed* designates a person, object, or event which is for some reason felt to have received a special gift of God's grace, and thus to be to some extent holy.

BLESSED SACRAMENT. The Sacrament of the Eucharist; the supreme sacrament.

BLESSING. In most Christian churches, the rite by which the minister dedicates a person or group of people, a building, or an object to a holy purpose. In homes, the blessing at meals dedicates the food to the nourishment of the body as the house of the soul.

BLOOD, BAPTISM OF. Suffering martyrdom for the Christian faith or for some Christian virtue. It is a supreme act of love, and is accepted by the Catholic Church as being one of the two substitutes for baptism by water, the other being baptism of desire, although the martyr must have felt *attrition* for his sins.

BLUE. This color, although used by many churches, and particularly the Catholic Church, in connection with the Virgin Mary, is not considered a liturgical color.

BODY OF CHRIST. A synonym for the word "Church," when that term is used to define not a particular denomination but rather all those who "have accepted the preaching of the Gospel of Jesus Christ, participated in the symbolic rite of death and resurrection (Baptism), received the gift of the Holy Spirit (the new life), and gathered together for common worship and the celebration of the Eucharist." (*Theological Terms,* p. 51) Some Christian denominations, of course, may take a narrower view of the expression than that above, although those whom they exclude from the Body of Christ would doubtless take exception to the exclusion, and thus negate, or at least neutralize, their exclusion.

BOGOMILI, THE. Adherents of a heretical sect which existed in southeastern Europe and especially in Bulgaria from the tenth to the fifteenth century, and which took its name from the Priest Bogomil. Partial dualism (God was given a supreme position) was a portion of their faith shared with Paulicians and Messalians, but they also had a very well developed mythology.

BONAVENTURE, ST. (1121–1274). Born John Fidanza near Viterbo, Italy, St. Bonaventure joined the order of friars minor (Franciscans) when he was twenty years old and became a writer, teacher, reformer, and eventually a cardinal and a bishop. He is called the "Seraphic Doctor," and is rated along with St. Thomas Aquinas as philosopher and theologian. He was instrumental in bringing about the reunion of Eastern and Western Churches in 1274, and died only eight days afterwards. His feast day is July 14.

BONIFACE, ST. (680?–755). Born in Wessex, England, St. Boniface entered an abbey when he was only seven years old, obtained his education there, and formed his ambition to convert barbarian Frisia and Saxony in Germany, those areas from which Angles, Saxons, and Jutes had come to England. To that end, he went to

Rome, where his English name, Winfrid, was abandoned for Boniface. He was sent not to barbarian Germany but to that portion known as Roman Germany—Thuringia, the Rhineland, and Bavaria—which had once been Christianized, but which had returned to pagan worship. He worked there for almost thirty years, and was highly successful, establishing monasteries, training missionaries, and creating a strong episcopal organization. However, at the age of seventy-five he undertook to realize his lifelong dream, and with a group of priests and monks journeyed down the Rhine toward Frisia. Very shortly thereafter, his group was set upon by the pagans of the area and was slain. For his conversion of most of Germany, however, he is known as the Apostle of Germany. His feast day is June 5.

BOOK OF COMMON PRAYER. The book setting forth prayers, hymns, scriptures, etc., for the worship service of the Anglican Church. The first Book was made up from both breviary and missal and appeared in 1549, with revisions added by Thomas Cranmer in 1552. After being suppressed by both Catholics and Puritans, it was established as official and compulsory by the Act of Uniformity during the reign of Charles II. In the United States, the Protestant Episcopal Church uses a revised version, though one very similar to the Anglican Book, the first having been adopted in 1789.

BOOK OF HOURS. An illustrated prayer book of the Middle Ages.

BOOK OF LIFE. A name given to the divine predestination to supernatural life, as "His name is recorded in the Book of Life." The Book of Life is said to contain the names of those predestined to everlasting glory.

BOWING. In Catholic and Anglican churches, bowing is a sign of respect and reverance, and in some cases replaces the genuflection. The bow may be merely an inclination of the head, a medium bow of the top portion of the body, or a profound bow from the waist. Ministers and assistants at worship services bow frequently, but in general a bow is made toward the cross on a high altar, and any altar where Mass is being said unless the Blessed Sacrament is reserved there.

BOY-BISHOP. The boy elected on December 6 to act as "bishop" on the eve of Holy Innocents Day (December 28) in medieval England. The boy, dressed in cope and miter and carrying a staff, led a procession of boys to the Innocents' altar, as well as performing other "duties." The ceremony was a time for feasting and merry-making.

BRANCH THEORY. The theory that the true Catholic Church, or Church of Christ, is composed of three branches, the Catholic, Eastern Orthodox, and Anglican. In general, the theory is held more by Anglicans than by the others.

BRAZEN SERPENT. The brass serpent made by Moses while he and his people were traveling in the wilderness. Anyone bitten by a poisonous snake could look at it and be saved from death. It is also a type of Christ, represented as saving man from sin and death (John 3:14–16).

BREAD, ALTAR, COMMUNION, OR EUCHARISTIC. The bread especially prepared for the sacrament of Communion. It is often, but not always, unleavened.

BREAKING OF BREAD. This term may be used to designate anything from a simple joining together for worship and fellowship, or dining, to the specific preparation of the altar bread in the Catholic Church. Symbolically it represents unity in the fellowship of Christianity and is a reminder of Jesus' last supper with the apostles.

BORROMEO, ST. CHARLES (1538-1584). A nephew of Angelo de' Medici, who became Pope Pius IV in 1559, Charles Borromeo was a leader in the Catholic reform movement. In fact, he devoted his great fortune to helping the poor. He was able to accomplish reforms among clergy and educationalists, partly because of his place as a cardinal and bishop of Milan, and partly because of the example of devotion and humility which he set. His feast day is November 5.

BREECHES BIBLE. A nickname for the English language Geneva Bible of 1560, so called because Genesis 3:7 was translated "they sewed fig leaves together and made themselves breeches."

BRETHREN. An archaic word for brothers, now used to designate members of certain religious groups.

BREVIARY (Lat.: a compendium). The book which contains all the prayers, hymns, lessons, etc., necessary for a clergyman in the Catholic Church to recite the Divine Office. It is usually printed in four volumes, but a one-volume edition is also available.

BRIGID OF KILDARE, ST. (d. 525). One of the patron saints of Ireland where many parishes (and girls) bear her name, Brigid was born in Ulster and founded many convents in her native land. Her feast day is February 1.

BROAD CHURCH. In the Anglican Church, the large middle group of worshipers that is neither High Church nor Low Church.

BROTHER. In the Catholic Church, the term used to designate novices and postulants of religious orders, lay-brothers, members of religious congregations who are not priests, and various friars when addressed formally. In general, the term is used by Protestants as an expression of the brotherhood of man under the fatherhood of God, and was probably more commonly heard in past centuries, when the members of numerous churches addressed each other as "brother" and "sister" than it is today.

BROTHERHOOD OF MAN. This Christian belief is derived from Acts 17:26 "And hath made of one blood all nations of men . . . ." It is also consistent with the idea of God as father of all mankind.

BYZANTINE RITE. The rite of the Orthodox Eastern Church, first used only at Constantinople but now extending throughout the Eastern Church and embracing some hundred million Christians, second only to the Catholic Church. Chant, arrangement of the church, Communion practices (Communion is received in both kinds), the exclusion of statues, the lack of seats for the congregation, the forbidding of the use of musical instruments in churches, and different liturgies distinguish it from the Catholic Church rite. There are, also, some seven million Catholics of the Byzantine Rite.

# C

CAJETAN, ST. (1480–1547). An Italian churchman and scholar, Cajetan is often remembered primarily as the cardinal who strove to keep Martin Luther within the Catholic Church. He was a man of great integrity and plainly not unaware of ecclesiastical abuses of the time, for he founded an order of priests whose main aim was to set a good example for others to follow. They lived in great poverty and dedicated their lives to the care of the sick and to helping other afflicted people. St. Cajetan's feast day is August 7.

CALENDAR (KALENDAR), CHURCH (ECCLESIASTICAL). A chronological list of the feast days, saints' days, fasts, vigils, etc., of the Catholic year. Calendars may differ from diocese to diocese according to which saints are particularly venerated therein, but the main body is the same as that given in the General Calendar of the Roman Catholic Church.

CALVARY. The mount on which Jesus was crucified; the Aramaic name was Golgotha, "skull," or "place of a skull." In the Catholic Church, Calvary is represented by a cross or crucifix mounted on three steps, or by a crucifix with figures of Mary and St. John.

CALVIN, JOHN (1509–1564). The French Protestant reformer who actually determined the nature of puritanism as well as Presbyterianism. He held that the Bible was the sole source of God's law and set out to run the city of Geneva, Switzerland, according to religious law. Christian virtues that he stressed, and which had a far-reaching effect on the economy of Europe just then emerging from the Middle Ages, included thrift, industriousness, sobriety, and responsibility. He rejected papal authority, accepted justification by faith, and went much farther than Martin

Luther in developing the doctrine of predestination. According to this doctrine, salvation was for the elect alone, and, as a free gift of God, could not be had through good works. A man was "elected" before his birth, either to eternal grace or eternal damnation, and nothing which he did or did not do could alter the divine decree one iota. His *Institutes of the Christian Religion* sets forth Calvinistic faith in lengthy detail, a faith which came to be identified with narrowness of thought, intolerance of mind, and rigidity of spirit.

CALVINISM. The theological tenets of John Calvin, but which particularly refers to the doctrine of predestination. (See above.) Calvin's central principle was actually the dependence of everything on God, but in practice this developed into absolute predestination and the permanence of grace, as well as into the belief that the state should be absorbed by the church. Calvin also emphasized the sufficiency of the Bible as a law and way of life, but Calvinistic emphasis on the one God as a God of vengeance and arbitrary decision, picking one soul to be saved and another to be damned in spite of the also foreseen goodness and wickedness of each, has tended to obscure other teachings. Presbyterianism, the modern Calvinistic church, has modified his emphasis greatly.

CAMPANILE (Lat.: a bell; köm'pǝ-nē'lä). A bell tower or belfry. In Italy, the most common architectural form is Romanesque.

CAMPO SANTO (It.: Holy Field). A cemetery, but more specifically one with earth in it said to have been brought from Jerusalem.

CANDLE. Most Christian churches use candles during some ceremony or procession during the church year, perhaps at Christmas or Epiphany, often called the Festival of Lights. Symbolically, candles represent joy and the light Jesus brought, and show honor to God or to holy things. In the Catholic and Anglican churches they are used on the altar during the service of the Mass.

CANDLE, PASCHAL. That large candle which is lit in the Catholic Church as one of the most solemn of the Easter ceremonies.

CANDLE, VOTIVE. Those candles lit in front of the Blessed Sacrament, at shrines, and before images in the Catholic Church. The origin of the usage is unknown, but the candle, burning and consuming itself, may represent a form of sacrifice. "In the Middle Ages it was common for grateful persons to 'measure themselves' to a particular saint; i.e., a candle was set up the same height or weight as the person who had received or desired some favour." (*Catholic Dictionary,* p. 69) Its burning represented a vicarious sacrifice of the person who erected or purchased it. There is also the possibility that the light, smoke, and heat of the candle "carry" prayers upward.

CANDLEMAS DAY. February 2, the feast of the Purification of Our Lady, when blessing and distribution of candles precedes the main Mass in the Catholic Church. Such blessed candles may be lit during the year at times of trouble or temptation, or at childbirth or at the hour of death.

CANON. (1) An unchangeable object, or writing, by which changeable things are measured. (2) A list of recognized genuine works. (3) A person in the Catholic Church appointed by the bishop to be a member of a cathedral chapter, having among his rights and duties a voice in the chapter, a stall in the cathedral choir, residence in the cathedral city, and a voice in the government of the diocese. Other canons are members of collegiate chapters and have many of the same rights and duties except that they assist in the administration of the college rather than of the diocese.

CANON LAW. The laws, called in Latin *Corpus Juris Canonici* or "body of the canon law," that governed the Catholic Church before 1918. They were at that time replaced by the *Codex Juris Canonici,* or "code of the canon law," but the expression "canon law" is still widely used to refer to the body or code of laws under which the Church operates.

CANON OF THE MASS, THE. In the Catholic Church, the fundamental and set part of the Mass beginning with the prayer after the hymn that starts "Holy, Holy, Holy, Lord God of Hosts, Heaven and Earth are full of thy glory" (the Sanctus), and ending with the Great Amen before the Lord's Prayer. The canon of the Mass in its present form can be traced back to the seventh century.

CANONICAL HOURS. In the Catholic Church, the eight offices (services of prayers, psalms, lessons, etc. distinct from the Mass) which together make up the Divine Office, the services which all priests are required to recite daily. The Hours are Matins, Lauds, Prime, Terce, Sext, None, Vespers, and Compline. Prime, Terce, Sext, and None are named after the time when they are recited, the "prime hour" being the first hour of the active day, 6 A.M.; Terce the third hour, or 9 A.M.; Sext the sixth hour, or noon; and None the ninth hour or 3 P.M. Vespers is the evening service, held around 6 P.M., and Compline, the night prayer, is recited at approximately 9 P.M. For all practical purposes, Matins, which should technically be recited at Midnight, and Lauds, which should be said at 3 A.M., are combined as the night office, whether said late at night or quite early in the morning.

CANONICAL SCRIPTURES. Those books of the Old and New Testaments which are deemed to be inspired works. The Catholic Canon of Scriptures includes those Old Testament books placed in the Apocrypha of the Authorized Version, but Catholics and non-Catholics accept as canonical the same books of the New Testament. Thus for Protestants, the canonical Scriptures are all those found in the A.V. and for Catholics those found in the Douay Bible.

CANONIZATION. In the Catholic Church, "a public and official declaration of the heroic virtue of a person and the inclusion of his or her name in the canon (roll or registry) of the saints." (*Catholic Dictionary,* p. 72) The process of canonization, which must be preceded by beatification, is both lengthy and careful. Two miracles must have been wrought in the candidate's name after his beatification, and this, and other qualifications of life and work, are thoroughly examined before the elaborate and costly ceremony of canonization itself can be carried out. The Catholic Church emphasizes that just because a person has not been canonized does not mean he or she was not a saint, but since the twelfth century public veneration of the uncanonized without special permission has been unlawful.

CANONS REGULAR. Priests bound by the vows of religion, i.e., poverty, chastity, and obedience, and living in a religious community under a rule. They differ from monks in that monks have not necessarily taken holy orders (become priests), and also in that canons regular must be prepared to undertake active work in the world.

CANTICLE. A sacred song, the words of which are found in the Bible.

CANTICLE OF CANTICLES, THE. An alternate name for the book of the Old Testament called the Song of Solomon, or Song of Songs, literally, "the best song of all songs."

CANTOR. The choir master of a cathedral, collegiate, or monastery church, or, sometimes, the clergyman in charge of making the arrangements for worship service. The word is also sometimes used to refer to the leader of the choir who is dressed in a cope and sings at the lectern at solemn servics.

CAPITAL SINS. The chief and deadly sins, usually numbered at seven and consisting of pride, covetousness, lust, anger, gluttony, envy, and sloth.

CAPUCHINS (It.: a long hood; kap'yoo-shin). An independent branch of the Franciscans begun in 1525 to restore to that order a more literal observance of the Rule of St. Francis. Plainness and poverty are emphasized; sandals, a simple habit of coarse brown cloth belted with a cord, and a long, pointed hood are worn. Capuchins are bearded.

The Capuchins' churches are plain, their life is strict, and their Divine Office is recited without chant, the night office at midnight. Missionary work is emphasized, and lay brothers must beg.

CARDINAL. In the Catholic Church, one of the counsellors and assistants of the pope in the government of the Church through the Sacred College of Cardinals. The "sign of the Cardinal" is the red hat. Cardinals are nominated freely by the pope but must be at least priest prior to nomination. A cardinal has numerous privileges, but among his many obligations is to reside in Rome, unless he is the bishop of a foreign see, in order to be available to function as an active member of the College. As cardinals are nominated by the pope, so do the cardinals, in turn, nominate a new pope when the papal see becomes vacant.

CARDINAL VIRTUES. The four great moral virtues of prudence, justice, fortitude, and temperance which were propounded by

Plato and other Greek philosophers and adopted by Christianity. Together with the three theological virtues, faith, hope, and charity, they match in number the seven deadly sins.

CARMELITE ORDER. Also called White Friars from the color of the mantle they wear over a brown tunic, the Carmelites trace their origin to early hermits who lived on Mt. Carmel in Palestine, though their history really begins in 1155 with the founding by St. Berthold of a hermitage on that mountain. The sixteenth century reforms of St. Teresa and St. John of the Cross gave rise to two independent branches of the order; for the reformed branch, Discalced or Barefoot Carmelites, rules regarding abstinence, night office, fasting, silence, and the like are very strict. Carmelites engage in ministerial work, preaching, and missionary endeavor. Their chant is distinct to them alone, and their rite, though resembling the Dominican, is based on the ancient one used by the Latin church in Palestine during the twelfth and thirteenth centuries. Nuns of the order are required to live in poverty and strict enclosure, and observances of silence, abstinence, and manual work are rigorous, especially for those which follow the primitive or non-mitigated rule as set up by St. Teresa.

CARNIVAL (Lat.: *carnem levare,* to remove flesh-meat). The three or more days just before Lent, during which feasting, dancing, and revelry are prevalent in most Catholic countries and in such cities as New Orleans, historically a Catholic city. Carnival there and elsewhere is known also as Mardi Gras, and in England as Shrovetide. The custom originated during the years when a strict observance of Lenten restrictions was required, and was a last gay time before the sombre season.

CAROL. A hymn adapted for popular singing and associated with a religious festival, especially Christmas. True carols have the simplicity of folk songs; almost all the popular Christmas melodies are hymns and not carols, though they are called by the latter name. "To carol" invariably means to sing joyously, as it has since the Middle Ages.

CARTHUSIAN ORDER. A very strict religious order originated in France in 1084 by St. Bruno. The members' lives are devoted to prayer, a hermit-like existence, and self-discipline. They wear hair shirts, observe perpetual abstinence, and interrupt nightly rest for a long night office. Members' heads are closely shaven except for a narrow rim of hair. Neither the monks nor the nuns of the order are numerous, but the strict rules have always been maintained, and the order has never needed reforming.

CASSOCK. The outer garment of Catholic clerics, long and close-fitting and fastened down the front with many small buttons. The usual color is black, but the pope's is white; the cardinals' is red, and bishops' and other prelates' is purple for special use. It is the ordinary dress of the clergy.

CATACOMBS. The underground passages and chambers in which the early Christians in Rome buried their dead. As cemeteries of the Jewish type, and at first associated with family vaults of upper-class converts, the catacombs enjoyed legal immunity from disturbance. Their safety and the fact that they held the bodies of martyrs accounted for their being used as places of worship. Over two dozen catacombs have been discovered in Rome and are entrusted to the care of the Holy See.

CATECHISM, THE. Now a term denoting a method of religious instruction still used by several Christian denominations, the "question and answer" method was once almost universally used to instruct about church doctrine. A catechism is a summary of religious beliefs, the question put by the examiner, the answer, containing the church's teaching, memorized and recited by the candidate for confirmation or baptism or both.

CATECHUMEN. (kat'-ə-kū'-mən). Any person receiving instruction in the doctrines of Christianity and of a particular church which he intends to join. The term is usually not applied to children.

CATHARISM (Gr.: pure). The general name given the dualistic heresy which taught that all material things were created by Evil, all spiritual things by Good, i.e., God. Chief among the sects were the Albigensians in the West and the Bogomili in the East. Although called a heresy, Catharism was more accurately a new, or different, religion, and, by emphasizing the evil of procreation (which believers saw as clothing a spirit in flesh), was a rather dangerous one. It was prevalent in Europe, however, for almost four hundred years, 1000-1400.

CATHEDRA (Gr.: a chair, kə-thē'-drə). The chair, throne, or other seat of a Catholic bishop in his cathedral church, and thus considered the seat of authority.

CATHEDRAL. Also called the cathedral church, this edifice is the main church of a diocese, and is the one in which the bishop has his chair, or "cathedra." It may not be the largest or the most beautiful church in the diocese, but it is usually the most venerable, by virtue of its age or historical associations. The cathedral is referred to as the mother church of a diocese and its clergy enjoy preference.

CATHEDRAL SCHOOL. A school established in association with a cathedral for the education of boys. In ancient times, and also during the Middle Ages, cathedral schools were frequently the only schools available, and the level of instruction offered was excellent.

CATHERINE OF ALEXANDRIA, ST. A virgin martyr, probably of the fourth century, St. Catherine's "mystical marriage" with Jesus was the subject of many art works, especially during the Renaissance, but the famous Catherine wheel has probably been more frequently depicted on a popular level.

According to the medieval legend, Catherine was a beautiful and brilliant princess who was converted to Christianity and baptized in order to have a bridegroom as handsome and wise as herself. As the tale goes, this bridegroom was the infant Jesus, presented by his mother, who also gave Catherine a golden ring thus signifying that she was the mystical bride of Christ. Maximus, emperor of the Roman Empire at the time, ordered all his subjects to thank the pagan gods for certain great victories he had achieved, but Catherine refused to do so. In fact, she argued so wisely with the men who confronted her that she converted both wise men and soldiers, whom the furious emperor put to death at once. Being particularly enraged at Catherine herself, he had built for her torture and death the instrument which was to become known as the Catherine wheel. Two legends tell the rest of the story. One says that her mutilated flesh was removed from the barbs and saws of the four-wheeled device and carried to Mt. Sinai by angels; the other that the wheel broke at her touch and she had to be beheaded.

Philosophers and scholars venerate St. Catherine for her learned mind, while grinders, millers, wheelwrights, etc., took her as their patron saint because of the machine by which she (perhaps) died. Her feast day is November 25.

CATHOLIC. By definition, this Greek word means "universal," and is so intended when written with a small letter "c." It was applied to the original Christian church in this sense, and occurs in the Apostles' Creed with this meaning.

CATHOLIC CHURCH, THE ROMAN. The Christian church with headquarters at Rome, recognizing the bishop of Rome, i.e., the pope, as its earthly authority. It was, until the sixteenth century, the only Christian church in the West, although the Orthodox Eastern Church had become in 1054 the recognized Christian church in the East. Since severing itself from the parent church at that time it has been considered in a state of schism.

The *Catholic Dictionary* defines the Catholic Church as "the One, Holy, Catholic, and Apostolic Roman Church which is the one Church of Christ . . ." and a Catholic as "any person who, having been baptized, does not adhere to a non-Catholic religion or perform any act with the intention or effect of excluding himself from the Church." (p. 81.) Membership for the Roman Catholic Church in the United States is approximately 46,000,000.

CATHOLIC EPISTLES. Also called General Epistles, to distinguish them from the epistolary books of the New Testament usually ascribed to St. Paul. There are seven: James, 1 and 2 Peter, 1, 2, and 3 John, and Jude.

CATHOLICISM. A liturgical religion; the main Catholic worship service is called the Mass, which has an established form, recently modified for the use of vernacular languages and greater contact between the celebrant and the congregation. The use of ritual, symbolic colors, incense, candles, handbells, and the like distinguish the experience of a Catholic worship service from the experience of a Protestant one, but in recent years many Protestant churches have re-adopted at least some of the Catholic forms for use, and this with the modernization of Catholic ritual has reduced considerably the difference between the two forms.

As summarized by the *Catholic Dictionary,* "The principal articles of faith of Catholicism are: the unity of God in three divine Persons (the Holy Trinity); the fall of Adam and the resulting original sin of all mankind; that sanctifying grace was given to man at the beginning, lost by Adam, restored by Jesus Christ; the incarnation, passion, death and resurrection of Jesus Christ in whom are united two natures, human and divine; the one, holy, catholic and apostolic Church established by him; the immaculate conception, divine maternity and perpetual virginity of his mother, Mary; the real presence by transubstantiation of the body, blood, soul and divinity of Christ in the Eucharist; his institution of seven sacraments for our salvation; the absolute need of grace for salvation; purgatory, the resurrection of the body and everlasting life in Heaven or Hell; the primacy of jurisdiction and the infallibility of the pope of Rome; the Mass a true and proper sacrifice; the lawfulness of the veneration of saints and their images; the authority of Tradition and Scripture; the necessity for salvation of membership of the Church, at least invisibly; the obligation of the moral law." (p. 82.)

CAUSA SUI (Lat.: cause of itself, kôz'ə sōō'-ē). Used as a technical synonym for God considered as the Being whose nature is to exist, "that which does not depend for its existence on something else . . ." (*Theological Terms,* p. 48)

CECILIA, ST. Although St. Cecilia has been one of the more popular saints, and is the patron saint of musicians, even the period in which she lived is not known with any exactness. That it was early, probably within the first four centuries of the Christian era, is fairly certain, for she was one of the martyrs buried in the catacombs. Her beheaded body is still said to be in a coffin at Trastevere.

According to the legend, St. Cecilia was a young patrician of Rome, married, against her will, to Valerian of Trastevere. Both the young bridegroom and his brother became devout Christians, and, during a time of persecution, gave a decent burial to martyrs whom authorities refused to have interred. They were themselves beheaded, and St. Cecilia buried their bodies in her villa, the act which was at least partly the cause of her own death by beheading. Her feast day is November 22.

CELEBRANT. In Catholic and Anglican churches, the priest who says or sings the Mass.

CELESTIAL HIERARCHY, THE. According to general teaching of churchmen, especially of past centuries, there are nine choirs, or ranks, of angelic creatures each having distinct powers and authority. The nine are derived from a variety of references throughout the Bible. The choirs, from lowest to highest, are: angels, archangels, virtues, powers, principalities, dominations, thrones, cherubim, and seraphim.

CELESTINE ORDER. Extinct since the eighteenth century, the Celestines were members of a Benedictine congregation which was founded in Italy in the thirteenth century, and which later spread to Germany and France. Members led a strict, hermit-like existence.

CELL. The separate room, or a small dwelling, of a monk, hermit, friar, or nun. Although furnishings are simple, the accommodation is not uncomfortably small or bare, but rather is provided with necessities such as bed, table, chair, etc. The exception may be found in the cells of hermits, who may choose to live with no amenities whatsoever.

CENACLE, THE (Lat.: a dining room). The upper room in which Jesus and his apostles had the last supper; in which Jesus was seen after the Resurrection; and in which the apostles were gathered for the Pentecostal meal when the descent of the Holy Spirit occurred.

CENOBITE, COENOBITE (Lat.: convent; from Gr. forms for "common life," sen'-ə-bīt). A member of a religious order who lives in the community of a monastery or convent as distinguished from an anchorite or hermit who lives alone.

CENSER. A thurible, i.e., the vessel in which incense is burned during the Mass.

CERULARIUS, SCHISM OF. The break between the Roman Catholic Church and the Orthodox Eastern Church occasioned at least in part by the patriarch of Constantinople, Cerularius, whose ecclesiastical policies led to his excommunication in 1054 from the then still united Catholic Church. In fact, it only exacerbated the separatist tendencies already present within the Eastern branch, but it is from that year that its independent existence is dated.

CHAD, ST. (d. 672). An early English bishop, a man of apparently humble bearing and dedication to his task of helping and praying for his people, St. Chad was briefly bishop of York, but spent much of his mature life as bishop of Lichfield. He was revered for his custom of living with the poor and as the poor, and never heeded the suggestion of Archbishop Theodore of Canterbury that he should make his long journeys, at least, on horseback. His feast day is March 2.

CHALCEDON, COUNCIL OF. In 451, the fourth and one of the most important of all ecumenical councils was held in Chalcedon, a Greek city in Asia Minor. Its most significant work was doctrinal, for it stated the official position of the Church on the dual nature, human and divine, distinct but inseparably united, of Jesus. This declaration particularly reversed the heresy of Eutyches (Monophysitism) as set forth in the illegal Robber Synod in 449, and was a vital element in the construction of an orthodox and universal faith.

CHALICE. The stemmed cup or other vessel used to hold the Communion wine. In the Catholic Church, such a cup must be gilded at least on the inside, must be consecrated, and must not be touched by anyone except clerics or authorized laymen.

CHALLONER'S BIBLE. A revision of the Rheims-Douay Bible, and a close approximation of the *Authorized Version,* made between 1749 and 1752 by Bishop Richard Challoner, an Englishman and a Catholic. It is a vastly improved and modified version of the Douay Bible, clearing up the ambiguities of that often obscure rendering of the Vulgate into English. Nevertheless, the Catholic Bible is still usually called the Douay, and not the Challoner, Bible.

CHANCEL. The part of a church which is around the altar and between the altar and the nave; the chancel takes its name from the railings (Latin, *cancelli*) with which it was originally enclosed, though these have been replaced in most modern churches by the communion rail. The use of the chancel is usually reserved to clergy and choir.

CHANTRY. Small chapels added on to, or formed inside of, a larger church, or even built separately, in which a special chantry priest says Mass for the founder who might have his tomb therein.

CHAPEL. A separate room in, or a small addition to, a building or a larger church, containing an altar and often pews or seats for a small number of worshipers. Chapels may be dedicated to a special purpose, or they may be set aside for the use of a particular family or group. The name is derived from the sanctuary which held the enshrined cloak (cope or cape) of St. Martin of Tours (316-397).

CHAPEL-OF-EASE. A little church especially for the convenience of worshipers who live in an isolated part of a parish and hence find it difficult to get to the parish church for services.

CHAPLAIN. A member of the clergy who exercises his ministry attached to an institution such as a hospital, orphanage, or prison, or in a branch of the armed services.

CHAPLET. A general name for devotions said with beads, e.g., the rosary.

CHAPTER. A group of canons under the leadership of a dean, often those associated with a cathedral or collegiate church. A chapter house is the room or building in which their meetings are held.

CHAPTER OF FAULTS. The meeting together of members of a monastery for the purpose of self-accusation of flaws and weaknesses, and for the discussion of matters pertaining to the life of the community.

CHARISMATA (Gr.: divine gifts, kâr'-iz-mä'-tä). Gifts or graces given by God to someone for the good of others, as, for example, a gift of prophecy, rather than for the good of the individual recipient. Such are described in Romans 12:6-8.

CHARITY. One of the three theological or supernatural virtues, the others being faith and hope. See also CARDINAL VIRTUES.

CHARLEMAGNE, ST. (742-814) The achievements of Charles I
of France, called Charles the Great, included the Christianizing
of parts of Europe; having the Pope crown him emperor, thereby
creating the idea, at least, of a Holy Roman Empire; founding
a palace school led by Alcuin that was to become the heart of
the Carolingian Renaissance; and bringing to his reign concepts
of justice for the poor and well-being for all that were little
short of revolutionary for that day. He was so renowned and
so well loved that it was not long after his death that marvelous
legends began to grow around his character and exploits, and it
was not much longer until he was venerated as a saint. He was
never officially canonized, but canonization by an anti-pope in
1165 was never declared invalid, and his feast day is still marked
on January 28.

CHASUBLE. The distinctive outer vestment worn by the celebrant
of the Mass. Essentially, it consists of two rectangles of silk ornamented with a cross, reaching often to the ground. Symbolically,
it has several meanings, among them being the all-encompassing
charity and the Yoke of Christ.

CHERUBIM. The second rank, or choir, in the celestial hierarchy
which kept the gates of paradise after the Fall, according to
Genesis 3:24.

CHILDREN'S CRUSADE. An almost incredible event of the early
thirteenth century during which 50,000 or more children, mostly
between the ages of ten and sixteen, attempted to reach and
capture Jerusalem from the Infidels. Three groups set out from
France and Germany, one under the direction of a French shepherd boy named Stephen, and one led by a German boy, Klaus
(or, according to some accounts, Nicholas). All the efforts of
parents, king, and priests to deter them failed. It was not a rabble,
by any means, for many of those who joined were from wealthy
and landed families, and the inspiration for the hopeless venture
was idealistic, perhaps a youthful response to the miserable failure of the Fourth Crusade.

Perhaps as much as half of the group perished in crossing the
Alps, of cold, hunger, disease, and the attacks of wild animals.
Many more were kidnapped later and sold as slaves by Barbary
pirates and Moors. Papal authority persuaded some to turn back

from Italy, but only a remnant ever reached their homes again. So far as is known, not a single one of the youngsters ever got to Jerusalem.

CHOIR. The men or women or mixed group that sings anthems, hymns, responses, etc., during a church worship service, or elsewhere. In many churches, the choir has a gallery in which members sit, and special robes, frequently black or deep blue, which are worn. The part of the church for choir members may be called the "quire" to distinguish it, as far as spelling is concerned, from the singers themselves. The area may also be called the choir loft.

CHOIR MONK. A member of a religious order for men who has the responsibility of saying the Divine Office daily in choir with other members, and thus differs from the lay brother. The vast majority of choir monks is required to take holy orders. Several orders of nuns also have divisions of choir sisters and lay sisters.

CHOIRS OF ANGELS. The nine choirs, or ranks, that form the celestial hierarchy.

CHOSEN PEOPLE. The Jews, so designated in the Old Testament (Genesis 17) as having been chosen by God from among all people as those with whom he would establish a covenant.

CHRISM. In the Catholic Church, olive oil with which a little balsam (balm) is mixed and which has been consecrated by a bishop on Maundy Thursday. The union of oil and balm represents the union of the divine and human natures in Jesus, and its use represents the fullness and diffusion of grace. It is used in the sacrament of baptism and in the consecrations of churches, altars, etc.

CHRIST (Gr.: the Anointed one). In the Old Testament, the Hebrew term *Mashiah,* or Messiah, is used to refer to the Anointed one, i.e., the one consecrated to the sacred purpose of delivering the Jews. The Greek word for the Hebrew "anointed" is "Christos," and, in the New Testament Greek, Jesus, recognized by followers as the expected Messiah, is called Jesus the Christ. The title was later incorporated in the name, to form Jesus Christ.

CHRISTEN. A frequently used synonym for baptism, "to make Christian." Sometimes the baptismal formula may be given "I christen thee," instead of "I baptize thee," and the ceremony is called christening.

CHRISTENDOM. A general term to refer to all Christians considered collectively, or to all those areas of the world whose inhabitants are predominantly Christians rather than Moslems, Buddhists, or other. It would include North and South America, Europe, Australia, and Russia, for example.

CHRISTIAN. One who accepts Jesus as the Christ and professes belief in the religion based on his teachings. The term may be used descriptively to refer to a person showing generosity, piety, humility, tolerance, or any of the "Christian" virtues defined by Jesus.

CHRISTIAN BROTHERS. A congregation of laymen bound by the religious vows of poverty, chastity, and obedience, founded by St. John Baptist de la Salle in 1684 for the education of the poor.

CHRISTIAN NAME. The one or more names which precede the family name and which may be given at the christening or baptismal service.

CHRISTMAS. Literally, Christ's Mass, the common name for December 25 which is celebrated as the birthday of Jesus. It early became an occasion for festivity, and was abolished as a holiday by the Puritan government of England in 1644; it was reinstated after the restoration of the monarchy.

CHRISTMASTIDE. The time between December 25 and either January 1 or January 6 (Epiphany).

CHRISTOCENTRIC. A theology or, sometimes, a person or a church, which makes the person and the work of Jesus the basis for all theological and moral conclusions.

CHRISTOLOGY. The study of all things pertaining to Jesus, his nature, role, person, teaching, words, history.

CHRISTOPHER, ST. Although St. Christopher is one of the most popular of all saints, being invoked particularly in modern times by those who travel by car, nothing factual whatsoever is known of his life. The more interesting legend by far is the Latin one, although the Greek, which identifies him as a converted barbarian who died a martyr in about 251, may be closer to the truth.

The Latin tale tells that he was a giant eighteen feet tall who understandably wanted to serve only the strongest king on earth. He entered the service of the ruler having that reputation, but soon observed that the man crossed himself every time a minstrel sang the word "devil" in a particular song. Upon having his suspicions confirmed, that the devil was stronger than the king, Christopher left and entered the devil's service. But Satan, he saw, trembled when he passed a cross, and admitted that he was afraid of Jesus Christ, whereupon Christopher left him to serve Jesus. A hermit instructed him, and while learning his prayers, Christopher was set the charitable task of helping travelers across a very dangerous river without requiring pay for the assistance. One night he was called to carry a child across—and the child was the Infant Jesus.

St. Christopher was especially venerated during the Middle Ages, and may still be invoked against sudden death, storms, toothache, and impenitence at death. His feast day is July 25.

CHRYSOSTOM, ST. JOHN (345?-407) [Gr.: goldenmouthed, kris'-os-təm]. The great Greek Doctor of the Church, St. John Chrysostom was known for his attempted reforms, his excellent and definitive homilies in accomplished Greek style, and his oratory. He was born in Antioch in Syria, and became a priest and, in 397, a bishop of Constantinople. Prior to his public positions, he had lived ascetically as a hermit, and he was always a strict moralist. Because the morality of the times was in general quite lax, he found many opposed to his stand that monasteries, court, and people all needed reforming, and he was exiled toward the end of his life for his unpopular demands. Nevertheless, he exerted a tremendous influence during the formative years of Christianity. His feast day is January 27.

CHURCH. For the Greek word *ekklesia* used in the Bible to designate the group who followed Jesus' teachings, translators chose to substitute the word "church," actually from a Late Greek word *kyriakon,* house of the Lord. It may designate a building or place of Christian worship, the membership of a particular denomination, or all Christians, considered together.

CHURCH, NATIONAL. By common definition, a church which is self-governing within a nation but which enjoys recognition as the official church or religion of that nation. An example is the Anglican Church or the Church of England, and Anglicanism is referred to as the "state religion." The monarch is invariably a member of the Church of England, and religious portions of official ceremonies employ Anglican ritual and are carried out by a prelate of the Church of England. The existence of a state religion does not mean that other denominations do not enjoy freedom, although that was the case some centuries ago. By contrast, however, the application of the idea of separation of church and state, as in the United States, particularly prohibits the official association of any church or religion with national, state, or local government.

CHURCH EXPECTANT. According to Catholic theology, those souls of the saved in purgatory where they are purified before entering heaven.

CHURCH MILITANT. As this term is used by some Protestants it refers to all Christians on earth; according to Catholic theology it refers to all living members of the Catholic Church, considered the Church of Christ, or the visible church on earth.

CHURCH OF ENGLAND. The established church, or state church, of England. See ANGLICANISM.

CHURCH OF ROME. The Roman Catholic Church headed by the bishop of Rome, i.e., the Pope. Called in this book simply the Catholic Church, it may also be termed the Western Church or the Roman Church.

CHURCH SUFFERING. An alternative term for the Church Expectant.

CHURCH TRIUMPHANT. All the souls in heaven.

CHURCHING OF WOMEN. In the Catholic and some Anglican churches, the thanksgiving and blessing of the mother after childbirth. The idea that a woman may not attend worship services after a baby's birth until she has been "churched" persists in spite of its being untrue.

CHURCHWARDEN. Especially in the Anglican Church, a layman who has been appointed to help administer church property.

CIBORIUM (Gr.: a cup, si-bôr'-ē-əm). A metal container like a lidded chalice in which the bread is kept for distribution during the Communion service. Also, a canopy of some material used for covering an altar.

CILICE, CILICIUM (Gr.: goat's hair garment; sil'-is, sil-i'-sē-um). The hair shirt worn under the clothing by members of certain religious orders, or by others, as a form of self-mortification.

CIRCUMCISION, FEAST OF THE. Celebrated January 1, when, according to tradition, the baby Jesus underwent the required Jewish ritual of circumcision, bestowal of name, and assignment of godparents. In the Catholic Church it is one of the Holy Days of Obligation.

CISTERCIAN ORDER. A religious order founded in 1098 at Citeaux (Lat.: Cistertium), France, for the purpose of observing more strictly the Rule of St. Benedict. The order, also known as the White Monks from the color of the habit, expanded rapidly under St. Bernard of Clairvaux but declined slowly after about 1400. Cistercians of the More Strict Observance, as distinct from those of the Common Observance, are frequently but incorrectly called Trappists, probably because that name was applied to monks of a monastery at La Trappe, France, where a reform movement began around 1660. The La Trappe Cistercians were absorbed into the Cistercians of the More Strict Observance in the late nineteenth century, and, technically, "Trappists" per se no longer exist. The work of such Cistercians is farming, primarily; their life is strictly regulated; they observe perpetual silence, except in necessity, and abstinence from meat, fish, and eggs; they rise for the night office at 2 A.M. Cistercians of the Common Observance, on the other hand, have a modified rule. The habit is white for choir monks, and brown for lay brothers. Nuns of both observances are strictly enclosed and contemplative.

CLARE, ST. (1193?-1253). Born in Assisi of a noble family, Clare, while not yet twenty years old, ran away with her cousin to join St. Francis in his work. He cut the girls' hair, gave them garments of brown wool characteristic of the Franciscans, and helped them establish a new order for women, to be called the Order of the Poor Ladies, or the Poor Clares. From this origin in 1212, the order grew rapidly, appealing to women who wanted to put into practice the teachings of St. Francis which stressed penance, prayer, poverty, the need for spiritual joy and the necessity of helping others. The order survived on alms alone, often in considerable need. St. Clare's mother and sisters eventually joined the order, also, but its founder was always particularly devoted to St. Francis, who, in turn, watched over her until his death. St. Clare's feast day is August 12.

CLEMENT OF ROME, ST. (d. c. 100). St. Clement was probably, though not by any means certainly, the third bishop of Rome after St. Peter. His tone in the *Epistle to the Corinthians* is authoritarian, suggesting that the position he held already carried a special degree of power. This and other writings once attributed to him are now included in the pseudepigrapha. His origin and death are both obscured, but according to certain traditions, he was either a converted Jew or a freed slave, and died a martyr.

CLEMENTINE POPES. Those popes, self-styled Clement VII and Benedict XIII, who held court at Avignon during the fourteenth century Schism of the West. They are neither true popes nor antipopes, but are "called popes in their obedience."

CLERGY. Persons of a church qualified according to the established procedures of the church to administer the sacraments, exercise jurisdiction, and minister to members, although not all members of the clergy may be invested with the same authority.

CLERIC. Any member of the clergy.

CLOISTER. A covered passageway, often open on the inner side, which surrounds a quadrangle around which a monastery, convent, portion of a church, or similar building is set. Cloisters were once used as work rooms, but are now mostly hallways to allow convenient access to the buildings they join. The enclosed life of monks or nuns may be called "cloistered."

CLOUD, ST. (d. 560). Son of King Clodomir of Orleans, Cloud, or Clodoald, renounced a secular life for the existence of a hermit and churchman. In Provence, St. Cloud was highly venerated, and later in Paris he became a priest. Jealous uncles who had murdered his brothers were relieved to see that their remaining nephew was completely disinterested in worldly matters, and gave him a piece of land on the Seine not far from Paris. There he built a church and lived out his life, and it is there that the town called St. Cloud now stands. His feast day is September 7.

CLUNIACS. Members of the now extinct Congregation of Cluny, founded on the Rule of St. Benedict in 912 at Cluny, France. It became a great feudal institution, minimizing the family life of Benedictines and stressing, instead, the primary importance of the recitation of the Divine Office as the work of monks. Hence church services were both numerous and elaborate. The group flourished for about 250 years and then declined rapidly, but its influence lingered on in the Benedictine Order.

CODE OF CANON LAW. The law of the Roman Catholic Church that was put into force in 1918, replacing the Body of Canon Law. It contains 2,414 canons.

CODEX, THE. The Code of Canon Law. Also, a volume in manuscript form of one or more of the books of the Bible (or, sometimes, a classical work), such as were written mostly in Greek between the fourth and the eighth centuries.

COENOBITE. See CENOBITE.

COLLATION. The light meal taken on fasting days in addition to the full meal, or, sometimes, any light meal. This usage was derived from a monastery custom of reading orally some religious writing during a meal, the writing itself being the "collation." The term may also refer to the appointment of a clergyman to a benefice.

COLLECT. A short prayer particularly suitable to the time of the church service during which it is used. In the Catholic Church, it is said or sung before the Epistle.

COLLEGE OF CARDINALS. The cardinals of the Catholic Church considered as a group. There are seventy cardinals in all, a figure established in the sixteenth century, and almost half are Italian. The chief duty of the College is the administration of the Holy See whenever it is vacant, and the election of popes. It also acts as something of a privy council.

COLOSSIANS, EPISTLE TO THE. A book of the New Testament that is a letter of St. Paul to Christians in Colossae and Laodicea. It emphasizes the union of Christians in the mystical body of Christ.

COMFORTABLE WORDS. Various words of comfort and reassurance spoken by Jesus to those who believed in Him.

COMFORTER, THE. The Holy Spirit, John 14:16.

COMMON PRAYER, THE BOOK OF. See BOOK OF COMMON PRAYER.

COMMANDMENTS, THE TEN. Those commandments received by Moses from God on Mt. Sinai, Exodus 20:1-17.

COMMUNION. In Protestant churches, the reception by church members of the sacramental bread and wine (or a nonalcoholic substitute) in the celebration of the Eucharist or Communion service. Christ is considered present, body and blood, in the sacramental elements, although more symbolically or spiritually than physically. It is often said that the bread and wine "represent," or are "reminders of" Christ's body and blood that were sacrificed for mankind, although consubstantiation is an element of Lutheran faith. Remembrance of the Last Supper is usually stressed, the fellowship as well as the sacrament.

In the Catholic Church, communicants receive the consecrated bread, or Host, after the celebrant has received the wine, or Precious Blood, a form called Communion Under One Kind in contrast to the Protestant Communion Under Both Kinds. For Catholics, it is of faith that the whole substance of both bread and wine are converted by transubstantiation into the body and blood of Christ, and that Christ is received whole under either kind by itself. The change from Communion Under Both Kinds to the present-day form was not made final until the fifteenth century, and reasons given for the alteration vary. The possibility of spilling the consecrated wine, or of similar desecrations occurring was greater when the laity received both bread and wine; the time required increased as the number of communicants grew; the anxiety attendant upon communicants required to sip from the same cup no doubt mounted during the fourteenth century when the plague swept through Europe. Whatever the cause, the ruling was made official at the Council of Constance in 1415.

COMMUNION OF SAINTS. This term, occurring in the Apostles' Creed, may be interpreted in two ways. It may refer to the communion that Christians on earth share in such things as the Communion or other "holy things" (a possible reading of the Latin *sanctorum* of the original); or it may refer to the communion that exists among all Christians both living and dead. As the Apostles' Creed is translated into English "communion of saints," it has, of course, the second meaning.

COMMUNION SERVICE. That religious service in a Protestant church which has as its primary action the reception of the sacramental bread and wine and the recitation of appropriate prayers, hymns, etc. It may also designate a regular worship service into which at some point the Communion service is inserted.

COMMUNION SUNDAY. In Protestant churches, that Sunday on which a Communion service is inserted into the morning worship service. In some churches, one Sunday a month is so designated, in others, Communion Sundays are quarterly.

COMMUNION UNDER BOTH KINDS. See COMMUNION.

COMMUNION UNDER ONE KIND. See COMMUNION.

COMPLINE. The night prayer of the Catholic Church, which may be said right after vespers or around 9 P.M. It is the eighth and last of the canonical hours and has sleep and waking, life and death, sin and grace as its subject matter.

CONCILIAR THEORY. This idea, that an ecumenical council is superior in authority to the Pope, was quite popular once among Catholics and was only condemned finally at the Vatican Council of 1870.

CONDITIONAL IMMORTALITY. That view, condemned by the Catholic Church in the early sixteenth century, which held that a soul is not necessarily immortal, but rather that its immortality may be rewarded after the body's death if the character of its earthly life merited it.

CONFESSIO, THE. Originally the tomb of a martyr, now the crypt beneath the high altar that holds a martyr's relics, and specifically that which holds St. Peter's.

CONFESSION. The admitting of sins, with the accompanying repentance, penance, and absolution in the Catholic Church. In some Protestant churches, the congregation makes a general confession, while others use no form of confession but stress that each Christian must make his own private confession of his sins to God. See also CREED.

CONFESSION OF AUGSBURG. See AUGSBURG CONFESSION.

CONFESSIONAL. That area provided in a Catholic Church and in some Anglican churches for the priest to hear the confession of penitents. The priest is seated behind a grating which prevents, or is intended to prevent, any identification of the penitent, who kneels facing the grating. The confessional is private and enclosed, and secrets of the confessional may not be revealed by the clergyman. Sometimes the confessional is called "the box."

CONFESSIONS OF FAITH. Also often called creeds, these are statements of doctrines and beliefs. The important early confessions are the Apostles', Athanasian, and Nicene Creeds. Important ones within the Protestant churches are the Augsburg Confession (Lutheran), the Confession of Dort (Calvinist), the Scottish and Westminster Confessions (Presbyterian), and the Thirty-Nine Articles (Anglican).

CONFIRMATION. In the Catholic and Anglican churches, one of the seven sacraments. As a baby customarily receives the sacrament of baptism, so may an older child (or a baptized adult) be "confirmed" in his faith through the sacrament of confirmation. The sacrament is ordinarily administered by a bishop and includes the laying on of hands, prayer, anointing, and signing the candidate with the sign of the cross. Many other Protestant churches besides the Anglican use some form of confirmation, often to recognize publicly the individual's membership in the church.

CONFITEOR (Lat.: I confess, kǝn-fit' i-ôr). A formal prayer containing a general confession of sins which is used at the beginning of Mass, before the Eucharist, when extreme unction is administered to the dying, and at other points where the confession of sins is necessary.

CONGREGATIONALISM. A modern and modified form of Calvinism, the Congregationalists have as a hallmark the complete, or nearly complete, autonomy of each congregation, being governed neither by presbyters nor bishops. They recognize the Gospels as their sole rule and basis of faith, and Jesus as the single religious authority.

The denomination developed in sixteenth- and seventeenth-century England among separatists who protested the state control of the Anglican Church and the formal, ritualistic worship of the church itself. The puritans are probably the best known early American Congregationalists, and the church, which they brought to America, flourished here. In 1931, the Congregational Church and the Christian Church merged in the United States and now have combined (1961) with the Evangelical and Reformed Church to form the United Church of Christ with a membership of more than two million.

CONSECRATION. The act of setting something or someone apart for a religious use, office, or work; a more solemn and specific act than blessing, which leaves the object or person in its original use and condition.

CONSISTORY. The assembly of a church council, as of cardinals, bishops, deacons, or presbyters, or the session held by such a group, or the place where it meets.

CONSTANCE, COUNCIL OF. The sixteenth ecumenical council of the Catholic Church held from 1414 to 1418, which condemned John Wycliff's views and had John Huss condemned and burned at the stake. The purpose of the council was to put down heresy, reform the Church, and end the Schism of the West. It succeeded in the latter by electing Pope Martin V, and achieved something against heretics. However, so far as reforms were concerned, the Church itself was still too divided a body to act effectively upon itself, and the few measures that were taken were insignificant.

CONSTANCE, ST. (d. c.354). A daughter, or perhaps a niece, of the Emperor Constantine, Constance was miraculously cured, legend says, of leprosy and thereafter was baptized. She was instrumental in turning her fiancé, General Gallicanus, to Christianity; after his conversion they decided not to marry, and he dedicated his life to good works and died a martyr. Constance converted his two daughters by a previous marriage to the faith, and they lived out their lives together. Her feast day is February 18.

CONSTANTINOPLE, COUNCIL OF. The first Council of Constantinople, the second ecumenical council of the Catholic Church, was convened in 381; it is probably the most significant in so far as the familiar history of Christianity is concerned, since it completed the Nicene Creed in a form almost identical with that used today. Its other accomplishments were against the heresies of Arianism and Apollinarianism, and in a ruling that made the patriarch of Constantinople second only to the pope.

CONSTANTINOPLE, PATRIARCHATE OF. One of the five great patriarchates of the early Christian church, the patriarchate of Constantinople has had mixed fortunes through the years. It was second only to Rome at one time, and wielded great power in the East, imposing its liturgy on other patriarchates of the area and leading them into schism with the Western Church during the earlier Middle Ages. Reunion, brief and unsatisfactory, was followed by a temporary extension of its jurisdiction, but a decline followed, and today the patriarchate has only about 100,000 members, mostly Greek residents of Turkey.

CONSUBSTANTIAL (Lat.: to be of the same substance). A term used to define the relationship between God the Father and God the Son and God the Holy Spirit, who are in traditional theology considered "three persons in one substance." The Son is "consubstantial" with the Father, the Father with the Holy Spirit, and so on, there being no difference in the "substance" of either.

CONSUBSTANTIATION. A doctrine put forward by Martin Luther to counter the Catholic doctrine of transubstantiation, *consubstantiation* says essentially that the substance of the consecrated bread and wine of the Eucharist remain bread and wine, but that Christ is bodily present "in" and "under" both during the church service. It may be that Luther himself never used the term, although it is identified with his teachings on the matter.

CONTEMPLATIVE ORDER. A religious order dedicated exclusively, or almost exclusively, to prayer and worship, so that work in the world is replaced entirely with contemplation and seclusion. Carthusian and Cistercian monks, and Carthusian, Carmelite, Poor Clare, and some Dominican nuns are included, while certain Benedictine monasteries and most Benedictine convents may be. The exact degree to which an order must be contemplative to be called a "contemplative order" is not precisely defined.

CONTINUITY THEORY. That theory which states that the Anglican Church, including the Protestant Episcopal, has an "unbroken organic continuity" with the Catholic Church, and is an integral part of that body. Anglican orders were condemned by Pope Leo XIII in 1896, and the Catholic Church has considered the question settled since that time.

CONTRITE HEART. See CONTRITION.

CONTRITION. Sorrow of heart, and the resolution not to sin again, because of the love for God and the regret at having offended him and caused him pain. The Catholic Church defines *contrition* most explicitly, distinguishing it, for example, from *attrition,* and Protestant bodies speak often of the "contrite heart." According to Catholic belief, valid or perfect contrition cannot be based on anything except reverence and love for God; it must include a hatred of sin as the greatest of evils, as it is an offense against the deity. Imperfect contrition may arise from other motives such as an awareness of the disgusting nature of the sin, fear of punishment, fear of Hell, and the like, and may be called *attrition.* The "contrite heart" is the true feeling of contrition by the person who has sinned.

CONTRITION, ACT OF. An action that demonstrates contrition (see preceding); often a formula of prayer or confession which expresses the sorrow of the penitent, a plea for pardon for having sinned against God and for grace not to sin again. An act of perfect contrition "blots out sin before the reception of the sacrament (though the obligation of confession remains)." (*Catholic Dictionary*, p. 121)

CONVENT. In general usage this term almost invariably refers to a house, or set of buildings, which are occupied by an order of nuns. Actually, it may be correctly applied to the house of any "conventual," i.e., religious order or community, whether of nuns, monks, or friars.

CONVENTUAL. A partial synonym for "religious" or "monastic," *conventual* refers to a religious life or a monastic order, or to things having to do with either, as the "conventual church" is the church of a monastery, and a "conventual mass" is the daily Mass heard by a community of nuns or monks.

CONVERSION. A change from one belief to another or from a lack of faith to faith.

CONVERSION OF ST. PAUL. It may well be that no one single event, after the life, death, and resurrection of Jesus and the descent of the Holy Spirit, has had more impact on Christianity than the conversion of St. Paul on the road to Damascus where he was going to persecute Christians. From that time when Jesus appeared to him, as in a vision, he became without doubt the most influential and indefatigable apostle of all times. His conversion is celebrated on January 25; the story is recounted in Acts 9:1–8.

CONVERT. Any adult or child, who has reached the age of reason and who leaves a previous faith or a state of no faith to accept the teachings and beliefs and to join the church of his choice. Thus the convert is distinguished from one who was baptized and raised in the particular church by being, instead, "changed over" or converted into a believer and church member.

COPE. A full-length mantle, held together in front by a clasp or flap, and part of the vestment of a priest or other cleric during processions and at most solemn offices with the exception of Mass.

COPTIC CHURCH. Since "Copt" means Egyptian, this term literally means "Egyptian Church," and in fact refers to the Egyptian Christian Church, Catholic in origin, whose orders and sacraments are still recognized as valid by the parent body, though differing in many ways from Catholic forms. The Coptic Church originated, according to tradition, from St. Mark's work in Alexandria; today's membership is approximately one million.

CORINTHIANS, EPISTLES TO THE. Two letters from St. Paul, making up two books of the New Testament. The first rebukes the Corinthians very generally, touching upon Christian doctrine, and the second is personal. They were addressed to the church in Corinth.

CORNELIUS, ST. (first century). The centurian whose story is recounted in Acts 10. His feast day is February 2.

CORONA. (Lat.: crown). Within the Catholic Church, and to a degree in other denominations, *corona* may refer to any one of three things: the five mysteries of the rosary; a circle of candles or other lights, e.g., a chandelier, in a church; or the usually narrow band of hair left around the head of a tonsured monk.

CORPUS CHRISTI (Lat.: the Body of Christ). Designated a festival in 1264, Corpus Christi falls on the Thursday after Trinity Sunday, which is the first Sunday after Pentecost, while Pentecost itself is the seventh Sunday after Easter. It celebrates the institution of the sacrament of the Eucharist, which could not be properly commemorated on its most appropriate day, the Thursday during Holy Week, when the Last Supper took place, because of other liturgical obligations even more appropriate to that most solemn of all Christian times. The festival of Corpus Christi was most important during the Middle Ages, and was then, and still is to a certain extent, the occasion for an obligatory procession, the Procession of the Blessed Sacrament.

COSMAS AND DAMIAN, STS. (d. c.300). The two Christian brothers from Arabia who practiced medicine in Syria and always followed the Gospel of Matthew 10:8: "Heal the sick, cleanse the lepers, raise the dead, cast out devils: freely ye have received, freely give." At the same time, they also converted many to the Christian faith, and it was this activity which lead eventually to their torture and martyrdom. Their feast day is September 27.

COSMIC DRAMA. The orderly and universal life story or life cycle from creation through aging and maturity to death and regeneration, repeated over and over again throughout the universe.

COTTA. A short surplice, one of the vestments which members of the clergy may wear.

COUNCIL, ECUMENICAL (Gr.: of or from the whole world, ek-yōo-men'-i-k'l). The meeting together of all officials of a church, such as the bishops, the presbyters, and the clergy, who have voting power within the body to discuss and act upon business of the church, either temporal or spiritual or both. See CHALCEDON, CONSTANCE, and NICAEA.

COUNTER REFORMATION. The sixteenth-century movement of reform within the Catholic Church, also sometimes called the Catholic Reformation. Such a reform was long overdue, a fact which had been apparent to conscientious churchmen for many years, and had been prevented in part at least by the schism within the church itself. The church was riddled with abuses which ranged from the immorality and secularism of the clergy to such practices as the selling of indulgences and pardons to the laity and the wholesale peddling of far-from-authenticated relics. Names outstanding in the reform movement are those of Pope Gregory XIII and Sts. Philip Neri, Charles Borromeo, Ignatius, Francis Xavier, and Teresa.

COVENANT. A voluntary agreement or compact between two or more parties to uphold their relationship and to keep faithfully to certain conditions of it. Perhaps the best known covenant is that between God and Israel, when God freely elected the Israelites as his chosen ones and gave them the Law as the outward sign of the covenant. The term is often used to designate a legal relationship established by self-interested parties for their mutual benefit, but such usage distorts the real meaning.

COVERDALE'S BIBLE. Important as the first complete English translation of the Bible to be printed, Miles Coverdale completed the work and had it printed in Europe, rather than in England, in 1535.

COVETOUSNESS. The second of the so-called Seven Deadly Sins, covetousness is a greedy craving for something, often for something that is the property of another.

COWL. By a common mistake, "cowl" is often understood only to mean "hood," though in fact it may also refer to the cloak or wide-sleeved coat of which the hood or cowl is a part. Such a garment is usually associated with monks, sometimes with nuns.

CRANMER'S BIBLE. Editions of the Great Bible that appeared during 1540 and 1541 in England carried a preface by Thomas Cranmer, Archbishop of Canterbury, and these are called Cranmer's Bible, thus distinguishing them from the earlier editions that appeared during 1539, called Cromwell's Bible.

CREATION, THE. The bringing into being of the world and universe by God as described in the Old Testament book of Genesis.

CREATIONISM. The doctrine of the Catholic Church which states that the soul is created by God out of nothing either at the moment of conception or when the foetus takes the human form. Other theologians may hold that the soul is created in a like fashion, but only at birth. This doctrine is contrary to those of Traducianism and Emanationism, each of which, in its own way, denies the "creation out of nothing" hypothesis.

CREDENCE. A small table beside the Communion table which holds the bread and wine before they are consecrated, and which may hold, as well, other small items necessary to the sacrament's administration.

CREDO (Lat.: I believe, krā′dō). Sometimes used as a synonym for "The Creed," and often called the "I Believe," the term may designate either the Apostles' or the Nicene Creed, as "Credo" is the first phrase in the Latin of both.

CREED. A summary, or the briefest possible statement of the doctrines and beliefs held by a faith. The Apostles', Nicene, and Athanasian Creeds are the earliest known to have been used in the Christian church. Of these, the Apostles' and the Nicene are statements of the basic beliefs (with some few elements excepted) of almost all Christians, while the Athanasian is more specifically a statement of Catholic belief concerning the Trinity and the Incarnation. The Augsburg Confession is the official creed of Lutheranism, the Thirty-nine Articles of Anglicanism, and the Westminster Confession of Calvinism with modifications for Presbyterianism and Congregationalism. As a rule, *creed* may be used synonymously with *confession* or *confession of faith*.

CRIB. The manger in which the baby Jesus was laid, or a representation of the manger or of the Nativity itself, including Mary, Joseph, the Baby, and perhaps angels, shepherds, wise men, and domestic animals. St. Francis of Assisi is credited with initiating in 1223 the custom of ceremoniously placing a figure of the baby Jesus in the crib during the midnight service on Christmas Eve. Since that time, churches and more recently individual homes have adopted the use of a "Crib," "Manger Scene," "Nativity Scene," or "Creche" as an appropriate part of Christmas services or decoration.

CRISPIN AND CRISPINIAN, STS. (d. 285). These Christian brothers were born into a noble Roman family and, together, went as missionaries to Gaul (France). In order not to be too conspicuous in their work, they became shoemakers, and were especially well thought of because they refused to accept pay from the poor for work that they willingly did for them. They were quite effective, too, in converting people to their faith—so effective, in fact, that they eventually suffered martyrdom for their efforts. After their deaths, stories about the two brothers spread widely throughout Europe; many churches were dedicated to them and they became the patron saints of shoemakers and dealers in leather. Their feast day is October 25.

CRITICISM, BIBLICAL. Often misunderstood by devout Christians as implying negative or destructive criticism of the Bible, biblical criticism is actually the attempt by scholars and scientists to ascertain the historicity of the Bible (historical criticism); the correct reading of the actual texts as originally written (textual criticism); and the sources upon which a biblical book has drawn as well as the time and circumstances of its writing (higher criticism). For a more detailed discussion, see BIBLICAL CRITICISM.

CROMWELL'S BIBLE. See CRANMER'S BIBLE; and GREAT BIBLE.

CROSIER, CROZIER (Lat.: a shepherd's staff, akin to English crutch; krō'-zher). The common name for the pastoral staff, an ornamented staff of metal or wood about six feet long, which is carried by, or in front of, a bishop or an abbot in processions. It symbolizes the bishop's office and jurisdiction and, by extension, the rod of correction and the shepherd's crook as well as the shepherd's responsibilities.

CROSS. In modern times, the most commonly used and most highly venerated symbol of Christianity, the cross, represents in whatever form it may appear the Cross upon which Jesus was crucified. Several forms are used by Christians around the world. The *patriarchal* is most frequently used in Heraldry; the *St. Andrew's* is so called because that saint according to tradition was crucified on one of that shape; the top bar of the *Russian* represents the title placed above the crucified Jesus and the bottom bar represents the footrest; the *Maltese* was the emblem used by the Knights of Malta during the Middle Ages.

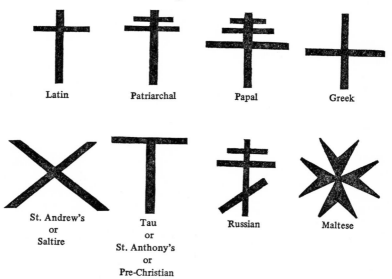

Latin      Patriarchal      Papal      Greek

St. Andrew's
or
Saltire

Tau
or
St. Anthony's
or
Pre-Christian

Russian      Maltese

CROSS, RELICS OF THE TRUE. According to tradition, the True Cross was found by the Empress Helena, mother of the Emperor Constantine the Great, sometime after her conversion to Christianity in 313. During a pilgrimage to Jerusalem, the Empress was instrumental in having excavations made to discover the site of the Holy Sepulcher, and sometime later the True Cross was also unearthed. At any rate, veneration of the main portion of the cross in Jerusalem was described by an eye-witness around 385. Many relics of the True Cross are said to be still in existence and to be of pine, thus discounting popular legends which identify various other trees as being the "tree of the Crucifixion."

CROWN OF THORNS. The circlet of thorns placed on Jesus' head before he was crucified, and thus one of the most significant symbols of the Christian church. The corona of tonsured monks represents this crown of thorns.

The true crown of thorns, or, more accurately, its reconstructed rush base is said to be preserved in Notre Dame at Paris, a spot it reached after many vicissitudes including loss of the thorns. Many of these were given away in golden reliquaries by St. Louis, and one such reliquary is now in the British Museum.

CRUCIFIX. A cross on which the figure of Jesus is represented, either in painting, carving, statuary, or other form. The use of the most frequently seen crucifix, one showing Jesus dressed in a loin cloth and suffering or dead, dates back only to the thirteenth century and only came into general use during the sixteenth century, at the time of the Counter Reformation. The older type of crucifix that shows Jesus reigning from the cross and clothed in robes and a crown dates from about the sixth century.

CRUCIFIXION, THE. The execution and death of Jesus on the Cross, the consummation of his actions as a man in the redemption of the human race.

CRUSADES. There were ten crusades launched by European Christians between the eleventh and the fourteenth centuries, of which the First through the Fourth, and perhaps the tragic Childrens' Crusade, are the best known. The name was derived from the emblem of a cross (Lat.: crux, crucis) worn by participants and from the fact that crosses were distributed to those attending the Council of Clermont (1095) when the idea of a "Crusade" was first presented. All the Crusades had as their main objective the recapturing of the Holy Land, and especially Jerusalem, from the Turks, i.e., those who followed the religion of Islam. All were failures in the final account. Worse yet, many of them degenerated into expeditions for looting, personal aggrandizement, and adventure.

The First Crusade got out of hand at once. It was begun officially in France, but a peasant mob led by Walter the Penniless and Peter the Hermit began it unofficially by pillaging its way across Europe and slaughtering many of the Jewish residents of the Rhineland. Once in Asia Minor, members were inevitably defeated by the Turks. The organized group was more successful, conquering Jerusalem in 1099. The Second Crusade (1147–1149), called for by St. Bernard of Clairvaux after Christian defeats in Asia Minor, ended in failure, but the Third Crusade (1189–1192), especially identified with its leader Richard I of England, succeeded at least in securing Christians free access to the Holy Sepulcher. The Fourth Crusade (1202–1204) degenerated from its inception into a plan to enrich Venice, which was accomplished in part by the sacking of the Christian city of Constantinople. The dismay and disillusionment with crusaders and crusading which followed this debacle is thought to have inspired the children of Europe to go on the ill-fated Childrens' Crusade (1204) which ended in death for thousands of French and German youngsters and which never even reached the Holy Land.

The Fifth Crusade (1217–1221) ended in failure, but the Sixth (1228–1229), a peaceful venture, secured the surrender of the Holy Places. The peace was not kept, and the Seventh Crusade (1248–1254) as well as the Eighth (1270), launched to regain lost privileges to access as well as territory, were both adversely affected by the death of Louis IX of France. The Ninth Crusade (1271–1272) led by Edward I of England never really got started, and by 1291 the last Christian stronghold in the area, Acre, fell. (For further details about the Childrens' Crusade, see entry under that heading.)

CRUTCHED FRIARS. A group of friars founded before the twelfth century and suppressed in the mid-seventeenth century who first carried a staff with a cross and who later wore a habit upon which a cross was sewn, from which the name is derived (Middle English *crouch,* a cross, derived from Anglo Saxon *cruc,* taken in turn from the Latin *crux,* cross).

CRYPT. An underground burial place, often beneath the floor of a church.

CURATE. A priest or clergyman who helps the rector of a parish, though strictly speaking "one with the cure of souls," the usage derived from the Latin *curatus,* one having a charge, and cognate with the French *curé,* or parish priest.

CURE OF SOULS. Literally, the care by the pastor or clergyman of the members of his congregation. This concept extends from the most highly placed member of a church to the minister or priest in each church district or parish and covers the carrying out of the religious worship service, preaching, caring for and comforting the poor and the sick, and watching over the spiritual and physical welfare of the children. A clergyman with such responsibilities is said to have "the cure of souls."

CURIA. Usually used to refer to the Curia Romana, the organized bodies, considered together, that assist the pope in the administration and government of the Catholic Church.

CUTHBERT, ST. (d. 687). Until the Reformation, St. Cuthbert was among the most popular saints in England. A native of that country, he was first a shepherd, then a monk, then prior of the abbey on the island of Lindisfarne off the eastern coast, then a hermit on a tiny island nearby. The latter style of life was his preference, and after serving somewhat reluctantly as abbot-bishop of Lindisfarne, he retired again to his island, where he died. He is the patron saint of sailors; his feast day is March 20.

CYPRIAN, ST. (200?–258). One of the great names in early Christianity, St. Cyprian was a teacher and lawyer before his conversion in about 245; he was for some fifteen years bishop of Carthage. He apparently led a productive as well as a holy life, for his writings and correspondence contain ideas on dogma, morals, and church discipline, and his support of the concept of the primacy of St. Peter is particularly important. He suffered martyrdom for refusing to recognize the pagan gods of Rome. His feast day is September 16.

CYRIL OF ALEXANDRIA, ST. (d. 444). One of the early Fathers of the Church, St. Cyril was an active opponent of nonbelievers and heretics, especially Nestorians, who held that Mary should not be called the Mother of God, since the baby Jesus was a human baby into which divinity later descended. St. Cyril, whose argument later became the orthodox faith, was that Christ was the "very Word taking birth in flesh," thus God being born, and that therefore Mary should be called the Mother of God. His feast day is February 9.

# D

DALMATIC. A garment with short, wide sleeves and open sides worn under the chasuble by deacons in the Catholic Church.

DAMN. To condemn to eternal punishment in Hell.

DAMNATION. The state of being condemned to eternal punishment in Hell.

DANIEL. A prophetic book of the Old Testament named after its chief character and supposed author who lived around 600 B.C. It contains the familiar stories of the three children in the fiery furnace, Daniel in the lion's den, and the handwriting on the wall at Belshazzar's feast. The book is also apocalyptic, containing in its second half several visions of the world's future. Stories of Susanna and the Elders and Bel and the Dragon are to be found now in the Apocrypha of the Authorized Version.

DANIEL, ST. (Heb.: God is my judge, or, God's judge). The Old Testament prophet, priest, government official, and author of the book of Daniel. His feast day is July 21.

DARK NIGHT OF THE SPIRIT. In general usage, a time of loss of faith and of desolation; a feeling of abandonment by, yet a yearning for, God. It usually precedes a time, often sudden in approach, of an exceptional renewal of faith that is greater and more confident than that which preceded the "dark night." In Catholic theology as expounded by St. John of the Cross it designates much the same experience, although it is more specifically defined.

DAVID, ST. (c. 1015 B.C.). The Old Testament shepherd boy who became Israel's great king, David also is credited with the composition of some of the psalms, although modern biblical scholars do not believe as many are his work as was once thought. His story is recounted in I and II Samuel and I Kings; his feast day is December 29.

DAY HOURS. All the hours of the Divine Office, or Canonical Hours, with the exception of Matins.

DEACON. In Catholic and Anglican churches, a clergyman whose rank is just below that of priest; in some Protestant churches, a layman appointed to assist the minister, usually in secular affairs.

DEACONESS. A woman appointed to help in the church or the district, for instance, in visitation of the sick and needy.

DEADLY SINS, THE SEVEN. A popular term for the capital sins: pride, covetousness, lust, anger, gluttony, envy, and sloth.

DEAN. The chief dignitary or presiding official of a chapter in a collegiate or cathedral church. The term is derived from the Latin *decanus,* the leader or head of ten, as monks or soldiers, which in turn was taken from the Latin *decem,* meaning ten.

DECADE. A term referring to one-fifth of the usual Rosary. Each decade consists of one large bead and ten smaller beads and the prayers used are the Lord's Prayer, the Hail Mary, and the Gloria Patri.

DECALOGUE (Gr.: *ten* and *word* or *speech,* dek'-ə-lôg). The Ten Commandments; Exodus 20:2–17.

DECLARATION OF NULLITY. That action which may be taken by the Catholic Church to declare the nullity of a marriage, i.e., that it is "invalid owing to a diriment impediment or lack of consent or defect of form." It is not to be confused with annulment, a term which is often incorrectly used when declaration of nullity is meant. Actually, no consummated sacramental marriage can be annulled, though it may be declared null. It was such a declaration which was sought by Henry VIII to free him from Catherine of Aragon.

DECREES, ETERNAL. The theological concept that God has, from all eternity, decreed what should and should not be, and that he executes his own decrees. This belief is basic to Calvinistic predestination, but critics fault it as a doctrine because it leads inevitably to denial of the free will of man and, perhaps more objectionably, to the conclusion that God is the source of evil.

DECRETALS. Papal letters that are sent in response to specific questions and that have "the force of law within the Pope's jurisdiction." (*Oxford Dictionary of the Christian Church.*)

DEFENDER OF THE FAITH. The title bestowed in 1521, by Pope Leo X, on King Henry VIII of England in gratitude for his written defense of the seven sacraments and papal supremacy in refutation of Martin Luther. By virtue of a 1543 act of parliament, after the English break with the Church in Rome, "Defender of the Faith" was kept as a title by British monarchs.

DEISM. A form of rationalism, developed in England in the eighteenth century, which admits the existence of God as the original creative force but which rejects or minimizes his action in the world since that time. The deist's God is remote, an observer of the order he has created, and is not one to tamper with that order, or Law of Nature, through any supernatural means. Understandably, then, the deist maintains that reason and not revelation is the source of religious knowledge.

DEITY. In general usage, God is called "the Deity." Theologically, a distinction is made between "God" and "Deity," the former signifying the divine essence in the possessor and standing for a divine, identifiable person, the latter representing an abstract concept, a divine essence apart from any possessor or person. Even in common usage, a similar distinction can be seen between God and Jesus, for it would be unusual to hear Jesus referred to as "the Deity," although reference is made to "the deity of Jesus."

DEITY, THE. An alternative term for God.

DEMON. A fallen angel, or an evil spirit; as "the Demon," Satan or the Devil himself.

DENIS (OR DIONYSIUS) THE AREOPAGITE, ST. (ar′ē-op′ə-jĭt). A first-century Athenian converted by St. Paul following that apostle's address to the assembled members of the philosophical court of judges (the Areopagus, the name derived from the hill, Greek *pagus,* of the god Ares, where the group met). St. Dionysius, or Denis, later became bishop of Athens and is thought to have suffered martyrdom for his faith. His namesake, a third-century martyr who was an evangelist near Paris, is sometimes confused with him. St. Denis the Areopagite's feast day is October 9.

DEO GRATIAS (Latin: Thanks be to god; dā'ō-grä'ti-äs). A frequently occurring formula of thanksgiving in the Catholic Church, "Thanks be to God," or "Thanks to God."

DEONTOLOGY. (Gr.: that which is binding or necessary, dē'ontol'-ə-jē). Ethics, or a science of moral duties. A system of ethics that is based on the "I ought," and which stresses what is right, and moral duty, and means to ends, is called deontological. On the other hand, a teleological system stresses what is good and is more concerned with consequences and end results. In regard to God's law, a deontological approach recognizes it as an expression of God's will, while the teleological sees it more as a plan that completes human life. (*Good* should be understood here to refer to virtuousness, moral soundness, and piousness, while *right* refers to what is just, lawful, proper, or required by duty.)

DEPRAVITY, TOTAL. The Protestant concept that, since the Fall, nothing in man remains unaffected by the sin. It does not mean, as the name seems to indicate, that man is all bad, but it does mean that all of man is *some* bad!

DE PROFUNDIS (Lat.: Out of the depths; dā'prō-fun'dis). The opening words in Latin, in English "Out of the depths," of Psalm 130, which is often used as a prayer for the dead.

DESCENT INTO HELL. This phrase, found in the Apostles' Creed as "he descended into Hell," is alternately interpreted from the Latin *descendit ad inferna* to mean "he descended into the place of departed spirits." This allows considerable leeway in interpretation, e.g., he descended into the fringes of Hell, or limbo, purgatory, or the place of all departed spirits, spiritual suffering, or the abode of the Devil. Catholic belief differs from Protestant, and Protestants differ among themselves; agreement is on the fact that Jesus, between the Crucifixion and the Resurrection, was in some form elsewhere than in the tomb.

DESIRE, BAPTISM OF. Catholicism recognizes two substitutes for baptism of water: baptism of blood (essentially, martyrdom for the faith) and baptism of desire. The latter consists of an act "of perfect contrition or pure love of God," which usually presupposes a desire for baptism of water. It is limited, for obvious reasons, to those who are capable of performing such an act, and consequently excludes babies, but a "heathen, believing, even though in a confused way, in a God whose will should be done and desiring to do that will whatever it may be, probably has Baptism of desire." (*Catholic Dictionary*, p. 144)

DETERMINISM. In its theological application, this term usually refers to the belief that God foreordains and has foreknowledge of all that is to happen for all eternity. It rests on the belief in the omnipotence and omniscience of God and figures prominently in the Calvinistic doctrines of predestination and "the elect."

DEUTERO-CANONICAL BOOKS (Gr.: *deutero*, second or subsequent, plus canonical; dōō'-tĕr-ō-kə-non'-i-k'l). The books included in the Apocrypha of the Authorized Version. They were accepted as canonical after the other books by Catholic scholars, and are not included in the Hebrew Bible.

DEUTERO-ISAIAH. Also called the Unknown Prophet or the Second Isaiah, this unidentified author is credited with writing the fortieth through the sixty-sixth chapter of the book of Isaiah in the Old Testament. The tone of Deutero-Isaiah is optimistic; he prophesies the coming of the Messiah of peace and gives significance of a deeper and more enduring nature to the suffering of the Jews, holding that their suffering is not caused by divine punishment but rather that it is so that all men may be redeemed. The date of Deutero-Isaiah is about 540 B.C., or some two hundred years later than the preceding thirty-nine chapters of Isaiah.

DEUTERONOMY. The fifth book of the Old Testament, and the last of the Pentateuch, Deuteronomy dates from approximately 350 B.C. in its present form, though it is a repetition of much of Leviticus which was composed during the Exile. It recounts some events of the wandering in the wilderness and includes the death of Moses.

DEVIL. Lucifer, Satan, the Devil, or any of the other "fallen angels" or evil spirits believed to be the inhabitants of Hell. Milton in *Paradise Lost* tells the story of Lucifer's sin of pride which led to his expulsion from Heaven. Belief in the Devil and devils has declined in modern times, but by those who do believe, such spirits are held to be immaterial beings, wide-roaming, and capable of "possessing" or afflicting humans (I Peter 5:8). The Devil is credited with seducing Eve in the Garden of Eden, and is often treated as the sole cause of man's many sins on earth, though theology recognizes that "the world, the flesh, and the Devil" are mutually and sometimes independently responsible for the temptation and the transgressions of mankind.

DEVIL'S ADVOCATE. A popular name for the Promoter of the Faith and by extension used to refer to anybody who has the task of examining evidence critically to discover both the pros and the cons of a question, or who has the job of arguing for the unpopular side, or who for the sake of being contrary upholds the side that is obviously wrong. In the Catholic Church, the Promoter of the Faith, examines carefully all the evidence about the life of one named for canonization, in order to discover what reasons there may be why canonization should not take place.

DEVOTION. A great love for God, and the will and desire to serve God and do his will, i.e., to devote oneself to God.

DEVOTIONAL. Prayer, scriptural reading, or other act of worship or a worship service showing "devotion" to God and Jesus.

DEVOTIONS. Prayers.

DIASPORA (Gr.: a scattering, dī-as′-pə-rə). The dispersion of the Jews after the Babylonian captivity; also, a term designating the Jewish Christians living outside Jerusalem.

DIDACHE, THE (from Gr., the teaching; did′-ə-kē). This anonymous work, also called "The Teaching of the Twelve Apostles," was prepared before the end of the second century, but was only rediscovered in 1875. Its historical value as a record of the practices and procedures of the very early Christian church is great. It covers such things as moral teachings, baptismal and Eucharistic procedures, and directions to leaders of the young faith.

DIEGO (DIDACUS), ST. A Spanish Franciscan friar born early in the fifteenth century, St. Diego was first a porter, then a lay brother in the monasteries where he served. While in Rome for a jubilee year celebration, he gained renown as a healer, even of the dying, during the epidemic that spread through the city. His reputation as a miracle-worker continued after his return to Spain, where he died in 1463. His feast day is November 13.

DIES IRAE (Lat.: Day of Wrath; dē'-ās-ē'-rā). The day of the Last Judgment, and a thirteenth-century hymn about this day that begins with the Latin words "Dies irae." It is now frequently used as a requiem or funeral hymn.

DISCIPLE (Lat.: a pupil). One of the early believers in or followers of Jesus, but especially used to refer to one of the twelve Apostles or to one of the seventy appointed according to Luke 10:1. The term may be used to designate anyone who follows Christian teachings rigorously or who leads an evangelical life, or, when capitalized, to a member of the church called the Disciples of Christ.

DISCIPLES OF CHRIST. A Protestant church established in the early nineteenth century by Thomas and Alexander Campbell and having an evangelical and conservative inclination. The Bible was accepted as the sole basis of faith. The other half of the movement called itself Christians, and was the less progressive of the two. In 1957 the name was changed to the International Convention of Christian Churches (Disciples of Christ) with a United States membership of about two million.

DISMAS, ST. (first century). The one of the two thieves crucified with Jesus who said to him, "Lord, remember me when thou comest into thy kingdom," and to whom Jesus replied, "Today shalt thou be with me in paradise." In the Authorized Version this story of "the good thief" is recounted in Luke 23:39-43; the name Dismas is found only in Apocryphal gospels. His feast day is March 25.

DISPENSATION. To relax, do away with, or dispense with a certain church law or penalty for a special case or occasion, is to grant a "dispensation."

DIVES. The name used for the rich man, otherwise nameless, described in Luke 16:19-31. The name is derived from the Latin word for wealthy, but is usually pronounced *Di'-vēs*.

DIVINE. Holy; sacred or sacrosanct; of God. In past times, and to a certain extent at present, a theologian or a minister might be called a "divine."

DIVINE OFFICE, THE. The daily worship of the Catholic Church outside the Mass. The offices of the Canonical Hours are the Divine Office and are found in the Breviary. Each service consists of psalms, appropriate antiphons, hymns, lessons, prayers, etc., to be recited daily by priests and certain other clerics, and said or sung by monks, friars, and most nuns in choir.

DIVINE SERVICE. The worship service of a church; the term is often reserved to the main Sunday worship service, although this is a matter of custom solely, and to speak of the "divine services" of a church may properly refer to all worship services considered together.

DIVINITY OF CHRIST. Christ as God, not as a messenger of God, a superman, or an especially good man, but truly God. While modern Christianity and Christians ordinarily take Christ's divinity for granted, this matter was the cause of many disputes and much bloodshed in the early years of the faith. For more detailed discussions see the entries under HERESY.

DOCETISM. A common heresy, dating from the earliest days of the church, which asserts that Jesus was pure God, entirely divine, and only appeared to have a human body and lead a human life. It is also called Illusionism. For comparison with other heresies, see GNOSTICISM, MANICHAEISM, and PAULICIANISM.

DOCTORS OF THE CHURCH. Great writers and thinkers on ecclesiastical matters, and usually shapers of religious dogma and doctrine. The early Greek doctors are: Basil the Great, Gregory Nazianzen, John Chrysostom and Athanasius; the early Latin doctors are: Ambrose, Augustine, Gregory the Great, and Jerome. Later doctors include, but are not limited to: Saints Thomas Aquinas, Anselm, Pope Leo the Great, the Venerable Bede, and John of the Cross. Doctors may also be called Fathers of the Church.

DOCTRINE. The body of belief taught by any denomination; "Christian doctrine" refers to the body of beliefs held by Christians in general about their faith.

DOGMA. A principle or tenet of faith in which members of the specific church are required to believe. By common application, "dogma" has arbitrary connotations, although in no church is such a tenet arbitrarily determined, but rather is held to be firmly based in revealed truth. *Dogma* is also used as a collective term to refer to the body of doctrines which a church formally and authoritatively affirms.

DOM. In the Catholic Church, the title for professed monks of certain religious orders. It may also be used, followed by a period, as an abbreviation for Dominican.

DOMINIC, ST. (1170-1221). Dominic Guzman, a Spaniard of Castile and a canon regular, was sent to southern France to attempt to convert the Albigensian heretics, more accurately the non-Christian Cathari. He was not as successful as he had hoped to be, but observation of the group he opposed opened his eyes to weaknesses of his own people. As a result, he gathered together priests who were devout and who followed the life of poverty and work that their vows entailed and formed a "preaching order" which grew into the Order of Preachers or Dominicans who led a life of commendable poverty, preaching, and teaching. St. Dominic urged study and thoughtful questioning as a prime concern of those who followed him, and the Dominicans today are prominent as teachers and educators. His feast day is August 4.

DOMINIC, THE RULE OF ST. St. Dominic left no rule in the formal sense, but the Rule of St. Augustine is generally followed, with additions from the Rule of St. Benedict and modifications to include the Dominican emphasis on teaching and preaching. He set up a body with fixed rules governed on elective principles and following the observations of poverty, silence, fasting, and common life.

DOMINICAN ORDER. A religious order of mendicant friars, more correctly called the Order of Preachers, founded by St. Dominic in 1216, and now devoted primarily to preaching and teaching.

There are nuns of the order, also. The white habit is covered by a black cloak, hence the name by which Dominicans are often known: Black Friars.

DOMINICAN RITE. The form of the Latin liturgy used by the Dominican order. Variations from the standard Catholic usage seem minor, but have interesting historical implications, e.g., they tend to give the rite a more "medieval" flavor, and in fact the form is similar to the medieval "Sarum use" determined by St. Osmund in 1099 for use in his diocese of Salisbury (Sarum), England. The variations include, but are not limited to: the offering together of the host and the chalice at Communion; the preparation by the celebrant of the chalice at the altar before Low Mass; and the order of certain prayers.

DOMINUS VOBISCUM (Lat.: The Lord be with you; dom'-ə-nəs vō-bis'-kəm). An ancient Christian greeting, now used in either Latin or the vernacular in the liturgy of the church, especially the Catholic and Anglican. The minister gives the salutation, and the response, "And with thy spirit," or *"Et cum spiritu tuo,"* is said by the choir or congregation.

DONATISM. The fourth-century heresy, or schism, taking its name from its leader, Donatus, of Casa Nigra in Africa. This heretical doctrine, which disturbed the church for about one hundred years, stated that sinners could not be church members and that sacraments administered by unworthy (sinful) ministers were invalid. Much violence arose out of this extreme moralistic position, and the Donatists seceded from the church and established their own groups. They were condemned by the Synod of Arles in 314, but were not really defeated until attacked by St. Augustine, approximately 450.

DOOMSDAY. The Day of Judgment, that day when "the quick and the dead" will be finally evaluated and sent to Heaven or Hell. The word is from the ancient "doom," or Old English "dom," sentence of law.

DOOR MONEY. A small contribution made voluntarily upon entering a church, and used for upkeep expenses.

DOROTHEA, ST. (1347-1394). Dorothea Swartz, one of the most famous of visionaries, is credited with many revelations, ecstasies, and miracles. After a hard life with a husband who was apparently insensitive at best and brutal at worst, albeit nominally devout, she spent some time in Rome, from where she returned to find her mate dead. She had always wanted to lead a religious life, and after a two-year probationary period she was allowed to do so on her own terms. At her request, a small room was built into the cathedral of Marienwerder. Here, in great austerity and suffering, she experienced visions and heavenly visitations before her pain-racked death about a year later. The patron of the Prussians, St. Dorothea's feast day is October 30.

DOUAY BIBLE. The English translation of the Bible made from the Latin Vulgate at the English college in Douay, France, and also at Rheims, and published in whole in 1609-1610. It is also sometimes called the Rheims-Douay Bible. It was for many years the standard Catholic Bible, but it was superseded in the eighteenth century by Challoner's Bible, a much clearer and more comprehensible text based in part on that of the Authorized Version. The Douay, or more properly the Challoner Bible, was replaced to a certain extent by a nineteenth-century revision, but the name Douay continues to be used.

DOUBLE MONASTERY. A now extinct type of monastery housing monks and nuns, though the groups came together only in church services. Usually all members were under the command of the abbess, but sometimes under that of the prior. This type of monastery was common throughout Europe in the Middle Ages and survived in Poland until the middle of the nineteenth century. In England, St. Hilda's monastery of Whitby, described by Bede in the *Ecclesiastical History,* is probably the most famous.

DOVE. The frequently used Christian symbol for the Holy Spirit, the church, peace, hope, and love.

DOXOLOGY (Gr.: glory; praise; doks-ol′-ə-jē). A formula of praise of the Father, Son, and Holy Spirit. Perhaps the best known among Protestants is the hymn beginning "Praise God from whom all blessings flow." A distinction is made between the "Greater Doxology," the *Gloria in Excelsis,* or Angelic Hymn, which begins "Glory to God in the highest," and the "Lesser Doxology," or *Gloria Patri,* which begins "Glory be to the Father and to the Son and to the Holy Ghost." The words "For thine is the kingdom, and the power, and the glory, forever," included at the close of the Lord's Prayer by Protestants and the Eastern Church as it is found in Matthew 6:13, is also a doxology.

DRY MASS. The informal name given the Catholic service, not truly a Mass, of prayers without offertory, Communion, or other essentials of the true Mass. It was once used when a Mass could not be said, and still survives in the private devotion of the Carthusian order. The blessing of the palms on Palm Sunday is the public service which most closely resembles it.

DUALISM. A religious and philosophical position which holds that the universe is the battleground of two equally powerful and co-eternal forces: good and evil, God and the Devil. Over the centuries, a variety of heresies have sprung up within the Christian faith which tend toward dualism, such as Albigensianism, though a strong case can be made for considering this not a Christian heresy but a non-Christian religion. Among dualistic religions, Zoroastrianism is outstanding, and among borderline Christian groups might be placed the Cathari. See also MANICHAEISM and GNOSTICISM.

DULIA (from the Gr., service; do͞o-li'-ə). In the Catholic Church, the homage due saints and angels as distinct from the adoration due God and Jesus and the special honor paid the Virgin Mary.

DUNSTAN, ST. (d. 988). A popular English saint; at least two churches in London still bear his name. He was a primate of Canterbury and was active in reforming monastic life in England. His feast day is May 19.

# E

EARTH, BLESSED. Ground which has been blessed or consecrated to a religious purpose, as, for example, a cemetery. Also, earth scattered on a lowered coffin.

EARTHLY PARADISE. The Garden of Eden.

EASTER. The Sunday on which is commemorated and celebrated the resurrection of Jesus. Easter falls on the first Sunday after the first full moon after, or on, March 21, and thus may be in either March or April. In date it corresponds roughly with the Jewish Passover, and is often called "Paschal Sunday," from that festival. The name "Easter," however, is derived from the pagan goddess of the dawn, Eastre, or East, and the celebration almost coincides with the ancient pagan spring festival.

EASTER CONTROVERSY. The dispute in the very early Church about the day on which Easter should be celebrated, and especially the debate between St. Augustine of Canterbury and Celtic Christians in the seventh century. Besides confusion caused by frequent mistakes in early calendars, the problem arose from the need to reconcile the Jewish lunar year with the Roman solar year, and different practices among different peoples. The Easter Controversy was resolved at the Synod of Whitby (664) when the Northumbrian King Oswy decided in favor of the Roman system for determining the date.

There is some feeling that a set date for Easter, rather than the movable date, would be allowable from a theological viewpoint, but since the day has always been determined at least partially by the date of the Jewish Passover, any change would be quite a radical departure from ancient custom antedating even Christianity. Nevertheless, considerable evidence points to April 9 of the year A.D. 30 as the most probable historical date.

EASTER EGG. The custom of coloring eggs at Easter may be derived from an ancient pagan custom, as eggs are a symbol of fertility and Easter heralds spring, the rebirth of the year, and a time of planting and growing. However, within the early Christian context, eggs and similar protein foods were usually forbidden during Lent, and were allowed again at Easter, so that one need not explore pagan folklore for a reasonable explanation of the connection of eggs and Easter. The practice of coloring the eggs brightly is an ancient one, also, and many places still observe the old custom of bringing painted eggs to church to be blessed on that day.

EASTERN CHURCH, THE. Catholics of the Eastern rites of the Catholic Church, for example, those of the Byzantine rite and Catholic Armenians, Ethiopians, etc., represent a return, mostly during the sixteenth and seventeenth centuries, from the dissident Eastern churches. They are considered fully Catholic, but keep their own liturgies. Compare with EASTERN CHURCHES.

EASTERN CHURCHES, THE. This general name embraces both the Orthodox Eastern Church and the Nestorian, Armenian Coptic, Ethiopic and Syrian Jacobite churches, all of which deny the supremacy of the pope, but have "valid" orders and sacraments as far as the Catholic Church is concerned. Thus it is possible for a priest of any of the Eastern Churches to administer absolution and communion almost interchangeably with a priest of the Catholic Church.

EBIONITE. An adjective that designates Christian groups or studies which do not accept wholly the doctrine of Jesus' divinity, or which tend to ignore or by-pass it. Original "Ebionites" were Jewish Christians of the first century who emphasized the importance of Hebraic law and consequently rejected the teachings of St. Paul regarding such matters. They also considered Jesus more as a great prophet than as the Son of God, and it is from this latter tenet of their faith that the term derives its present usage. The word comes from the Hebrew for "the poor," which may have described the condition of the members of the group.

ECCE HOMO (Lat.: Behold the man; ek'-ā hō'mō). An image, usually the head, of Jesus with the crown of thorns. The term is derived from Pilate's words when presenting Jesus to the people (John 19:5) before the crucifixion.

ECCLESIA (Gr.: assembly of the people; i-klē′-zi-ə). "The church," whether referring to the church building or to the members of the congregation.

ECCLESIASTES (Gr.: preacher; i-klē′-zi-as′-tēz). A book of the Old Testament, generally attributed to Solomon, though probably erroneously. It dates from about 150 B.C. and expresses profound pessimism and disappointment, although interpretation may find in it the message that, though earthly matters are stale and worthless, satisfaction is to be found in and with God. The Hebrew title was *Qohaleth,* the preacher; Ecclesiastes is a Greek rendering.

ECCLESIASTIC. A minister, priest, bishop, or other cleric who represents a church.

ECTASY. An act of contemplation and prayer so intense that the soul seems to leave the body. In some "ecstatics" bodily functions may be slowed, and the soul left freer to receive the spiritual illumination that the person seeks. Genuine ecstatics have been rare in the history of the Christian faith; true ecstatic states are brief and do not weaken the body, contrary to the claims of some who have held themselves to be ecstatics.

ECUMENICAL (Gr.: of or from the whole world; ek′-yōo-men′-i-k'l). The councils of the Christian Church until the split between East and West were those originally known as "ecumenical councils," for they represented the thought of the entire church. The Catholic Church recognizes as ecumenical any council called by the pope, but in general, non-Catholics do not, and hence look upon only seven as ecumenical while Catholics recognize twenty such, excluding the Second Vatican Council. In recent times, the word has been used by Protestant churches to designate their general church councils, and still more recently, the "ecumenical movement" has developed in the hope of unifying all Christian churches. The word is also sometimes spelled *oecumenical.*

EDMUND, ST. (1170?-1240). Edmund Rich of Abingdon near

Oxford, England, came from a good family that lived an intensely religious life. He was well educated, a university teacher in the sciences and then in theology, later a priest and archbishop of Canterbury. He preached the cause of the Sixth Crusade (1228), and, seeming to follow in the footsteps of the earlier Thomas Becket, another primate of Canterbury, struggled against his sovereign (Henry III) for the preservation of ecclesiastical immunities. The struggle was in vain. He had to seek asylum in France, where he died a very short time later. His feast day is November 16.

EDWARD THE CONFESSOR, ST. (1004?-1066). The reign of King Edward in England stretched between that of Canute and William the Conqueror. He was called The Confessor because of his great piety and the austerity of his life. Always recognized as a saintly monarch, he is said to have been able to cure scrofula, "the king's evil," with his touch, perhaps the last of English kings to have this miraculous gift. The ability is ascribed to him in Shakespeare's *Macbeth.* More susceptible to historical proof was his reduction or removal of many high taxes which had long overburdened the English people. His feast day is October 13.

EFFICACIOUS GRACE. According to Catholic theology, that grace which always produces its proper effect because the will, though not constrained to receive it, inevitably does because of the nature of the grace itself.

ELECT, THE. In Calvinistic theology, those whom God has predestined from all time for salvation, regardless of what they might or might not do or be while living. Catholics recognize the elect as those chosen by God either for the grace of faith or the true religion or eternal glory, in which latter case they are elected to receive the graces and merits necessary to attain salvation.

ELECTION. The choice made by God that a man or woman shall be predestined to eternal glory; Calvinistic theology views the process as entirely arbitrary, while other doctrines of election, such as the Catholic, include in it the decree that God intends to give the merits and graces necessary for the attainment of salvation.

ELEEMOSYNARY (Gr.: alms; el'-ə-mos' n-er'-ē). An adjective denoting something freely given, as alms, charity, or the like. In the Old English word *aelmysee,* derived from a Latin term taken from the Greek eleos, or "pity," can be seen the first form of the modern word "alms."

ELEVATION OF THE HOST. The lifting of the Host, the Communion bread, so that the congregation can see and adore it, immediately after its consecration during the Mass. The custom apparently originated in twelfth-century France to refute the teaching that the Lord's body was not present in the bread until after both it and the Communion wine had been consecrated. The chalice containing the consecrated wine is also elevated after consecration, a custom introduced in the late sixteenth century.

ELEVEN THOUSAND VIRGINS, THE, and ST. URSULA. This old legend tells the tragic story of the maiden Ursula and her companions who fled England to avoid capture by the Saxons, only to fall into the hands of Huns at the mouth of the Rhine near Cologne, where they were all massacred. A likelier possibility is that a dozen or so young Christian girls met their death in this way somewhere around the end of the third century in the general area of Cologne. Nothing is known with certainty although the old story is generally held to be a much elaborated account of some actual event.

ELIJAH, ELIAS. The prophet of the Old Testament who appeared at Jesus' transfiguration. Members of the Carmelite order regard him as the founder of their order and their spiritual father, and Moslems as well as Jews adore him also. (1 and 2 Kings and Matthew 17:3,4)

ELISHA, ELISEUS. The Old Testament prophet who succeeded Elijah (1 Kings 19:16-21).

ELIZABETH, ST. Probably the most prominent of the several saints named Elizabeth is the mother of John the Baptist. The story is recounted in Luke 1:5-79.

ELOHIM. The name used by the ancient Hebrews to designate God. The form is plural, a usage that is taken by some to indicate polytheism, by others to emphasize the majesty of Jehovah. The former belief seems strengthened by the fact that the term is interpreted as "heathen gods" in Exodus 18:11, and is translated as "angels" in Psalms 8:5.

EMBER DAYS. In the Catholic Church calendar there are four groups of three ember days, days observed with special blessings and fasting which mark the four seasons of the year. The name itself is derived from the Anglo-Saxon *ymbren,* a "coming around," a circuit or a revolution, which refers to the seasonal changes. The days are the Wednesday, Friday, and Saturday after (1) the first Sunday in Lent (2) Pentecost (3) Holy Cross Day, i.e., September 14 and (4) St. Lucy's Day, i.e., December 13.

EMINENCE. A title for a cardinal in the Catholic Church, as "His Eminence," or "Your Eminence."

EMMANUEL. "God with us," a name or title found in Isaiah 7:14 and again in Matthew 1:23: "Behold, a virgin shall be with child, and shall bring forth a son, and they shall call his name Emmanuel, . . ."

ENCLOSED ORDER. A popular term used to designate a religious order which follows strict regulations regarding the sequestration of its members from the outside world. See ENCLOSURE.

ENCLOSURE. In the Catholic Church, the part of a monastery or convent enclosed as the living place of the monks or nuns, as well as the condition of living there. A variety of rules governs the sort of living called "enclosure;" some are quite strict, for example, those which forbid the nuns of certain orders to leave the enclosure except under extreme duress or exceptional circumstances, or to receive outsiders except as absolute necessity demands. Other more lenient rules and orders allow for more contact with the outside world.

In general, members of religious orders for men may leave their enclosure with the permission of their superior which is usually freely given, and laymen may enter the enclosure. Women, with the exception of rulers, are rarely admitted. Nuns who have taken solemn vows (which see) are far more strictly enclosed, but those who have taken simple vows have more freedom as do nuns of enclosed orders whose active work requires that they meet outsiders within the limits of the hospital or school of the order.

ENCYCLICAL. A letter addressed by the pope to the whole Catholic Church represented by its patriarchs, primates, archbishops, bishops, etc.

END OF THE WORLD. Judgment Day, the day on which Jesus will return to earth to judge the living and the dead, who will rise, is also sometimes called the Second Coming or the Parousia. The time and the manner of the end of the world are uncertain, though the accompanying events are referred to in Matthew 24, 25:31-46, in Luke 21, and especially in Revelation. In Mark 13:32 Jesus affirmed that the day and the hour of the world's end were known only to God.

ENGLAND, CHURCH OF. See ANGLICAN CHURCH.

ENGLISH MARTYRS. Those English Catholics who were put to death for their faith between the schism of Henry VIII, approximately 1534, and 1681, when Charles II, a Catholic at heart, eased the condition of his Catholic subjects.

ENGLISH POPE. Pope Adrian IV, 1156-1159, named Nicholas Breakspear, was the only Englishman ever to be a pope in the Catholic Church.

ENVY. One of the seven deadly sins.

EPHESIANS, THE EPISTLE TO THE. An epistolary book of the New Testament composed by St. Paul, probably while in prison in Rome, and directed to a number of churches including the one at Ephesus. It consists of doctrinal comments on the unity of the Jew and Gentile in Christ, and a variety of practical moral teachings.

EPIPHANY, THE (Gr.: showing; ē-pif'-ə-nē). January 6, a church holiday celebrating the manifestation of Jesus to the Gentiles in the persons of the Three Kings or Magi, the miracle at Cana, and the baptism of Jesus. It is also called Twelfth Day, its eve being Twelfth Night; Old Christmas or Little Christmas; and the Manifestation of Christ to the Gentiles.

EPISCOPAL. As a general term, this word identifies any Christian church organized with bishops in an hierarchical system, and teaching the divine appointment of the bishops through Jesus and the Apostles.

EPISCOPAL CHURCH, PROTESTANT. In the United States, the Episcopal Church is, to most intents and purposes, a branch of the Anglican Church. Its doctrines are set forth in the Apostles' and the Nicene creeds and the Thirty-nine Articles; a Book of Common Prayer only very slightly revised from the Anglican Book of Common Prayer is used as the service book. The separation from the Anglican Church, if it can be called a separation, came after the American Revolution. In 1784 its first bishop, Samuel Seabury, took charge, and in 1789 a general conference approved the name, constitution, and revised version of the Book of Common Prayer, but the church is considered an integral part of the Anglican Communion. Membership in the United States is approximately 3,500,000.

EPISCOPALIAN. A member of the Protestant Episcopal Church in the United States.

EPISCOPATE. The office of a bishop, the period of time during which he holds the office, or the bishops of a country, church, etc., considered as a group.

EPISTLE. In the church service, the first of two scriptural lessons read by the minister or priest, often, but not necessarily, drawn from the epistolary books of the New Testament. An "epistle" is a formal, literary letter.

EPISTLE SIDE. The side of the sanctuary from which the epistle is read, the right hand side facing the altar.

EPISTOLARY BOOKS. Those books of the New Testament which were composed in the form of letters written to various churches or individuals. The Authorized Version includes: Romans, 1 and 2 Corinthians, Galatians, Colossians, 1 and 2 Timothy, Philemon, James, 1, 2, 3 John, Jude, Ephesians, Philippians, 1 and 2 Thessalonians, Titus, To the Hebrews, James, 1 and 2 Peter. The Pauline Epistles (those by St. Paul) are: 1 and 2 Thessalonians, Galatians, 1 and 2 Corinthians, Romans, 1 and 2

Timothy, Ephesians, Titus, Philippians, Colossians, and Philemon. The Catholic or General Epistles comprise the remainder.

ERA, THE CHRISTIAN. The reckoning of time from the year presumed to be that of Jesus' birth; all that time which has elapsed since the birth of Jesus. The letters "A.D." stand for the Latin *Anno Domini,* or "the year of the Lord," while "B.C." stands for Before Christ, i.e., the pre-Christian era.

EREMITE. A hermit, or one who lives like a hermit.

EREMITIC LIFE. The life of a hermit, lived in solitude and usually considerable austerity.

ESCHATOLOGICAL SCHOOL, THE. The Protestant biblical scholars who believe that Jesus felt the end of the world was imminent, and that the Kingdom of God would descend during his disciples' generation. It is based on such scriptural texts as Mark 13:30: "Verily I say unto you, that this generation shall not pass, till all these things be done."

ESCHATOLOGY. (Gr.: discourse or study of the last things; es'-kə-tol'-ə-jē). The part of theological study that is concerned with such things as death, resurrection, the immortality of the soul, the destruction and renewal of the world, and the second coming of Jesus. In the popular form these are called the "last things," and are usually identified as death, judgment, heaven, and hell.

ESSENES. One of the major Jewish sects, this group practiced communal living and observed strict austerity and a highly ethical code. They established a monastery by the Dead Sea, but a number of Essenes stayed in their own villages, where they lived pious and humble lives and set a moral example to the Jews around them. Much speculation has taken place on the subject of Jesus' contact with Essenes, since many of his teachings resemble theirs as revealed in the Dead Sea scrolls, priestly writings of monastic Essenes of Qumran.

ESTHER. A historical book of the Old Testament Apocrypha detailing the plot to destroy the Jews in Persia and its defeat by Esther and her uncle Mordecai. The Jewish festival of Purim is still observed, and is called the Feast of Lots because it was by lot that the enemy's day of massacre was chosen.

ETERNAL CITY, THE. Rome; the name "Eternal City" was adopted, from the classical usage by Ovid and others, to emphasize Rome's importance in the early Christian era.

ETERNAL LIFE. The belief that every human is destined for life everlasting in the next world, whether it be in heaven or hell. The concept may be limited to refer to the eternal life of the soul, and to refer only to life in Heaven.

ETERNITY. All time; forever; having no beginning and no end. In more everyday terms, it often refers to the "time" after death, although strictly speaking, "time" has no meaning in relation to "eternity."

ETHICS, CHRISTIAN. This very complex subject is one of the most difficult to summarize meaningfully. Essentially, though, the system or concept of Christian ethics is based on the life of Jesus and requires that each believer live as far as possible a life patterned morally on that of Jesus. Thus it includes a moral code and an application of that code to practical problems; a system of ethics and values; and a general rule for behavior toward and with one's fellow man. It may be, for some, summed up in the Golden Rule. Others, however, have delved more deeply, theoretically and philosophically, and thus many types of Christian ethics have been formulated, ranging all the way from a concern with Christian perfection through the study of the definition of "the good" to a doctrine of social justice and concentration on social problems.

EUCHARIST (Gr.: thanksgiving; gratitude, yōō'-kə-rist). The Communion, or the Lord's Supper, or the bread and wine used therein. The ceremony commemorates the Last Supper (Matthew 26:26-29) and may be interpreted as a sharing of the sacramental experience or as a perpetual renewal of Jesus' sacrifice of himself for man.

EULOGIA (Gr.: a blessing; yōō-lō-ji-ə). Any object which has been blessed may be called by this name, but it most usually refers to bread which has been blessed, though not consecrated, to be given to those who cannot receive Holy Communion. The term may refer to the Eucharist itself.

EVANGELICAL. In general usage, this term refers to a fundamentalist or conservative church which has as one of its main purposes the sending of missionaries or preachers out into the world to preach the word, i.e., evangelize, and to organize new church groups. More specifically, the term refers to the churches that hold with the gospel of "salvation by faith" and which recognize no rule of faith except the Bible. Often the missionary activities of churches which are not by definition "evangelical" are referred to as "evangelical activities."

EVANGELIST. A traveling preacher, especially one whose purpose is to win converts to the Christian faith or to bring back to the faith those who have drifted away. Originally, the term referred to the "authors" of the first four gospels, Matthew, Mark, Luke, or John.

EVE. The first woman, created by God to be Adam's wife in the Garden of Eden, where she became the first victim of Satan as The Tempter, and led Adam as well to sin (Genesis 2 and 3). It is a particular use of the abbreviation—it isn't an abbreviation for "evening" exactly, since "Christmas evening" is different from "Christmas Eve."

EVIL. Moral badness; wickedness; extreme wrong doing; corruption. By a common application of the term, "evil" is worse than "bad," and often implies a motivation and origin independent of any redeeming forces which might change it or lead to repentance; it implies continuous wrongdoing with awareness of and pleasure in the acts committed. The Catholic Church, as well as other churches, holds that evil is a negation of good, or an absence of good, a privation or emptiness, real only "insofar as it presupposes the good which it limits; . . ." (*Catholic Dictionary,* p. 179).

One massive theological problem arises from the existence of evil in the world; if power and goodness are attributed to God, why is evil allowed? The dilemma is that either God is not all-powerful (which he is said to be) or he is not all-good (another attribute); if he were both all-powerful and all-good, then evil would be obliterated. Since it is not, then God must be either not all-powerful or not all-good. The attempt to justify God's goodness and omnipotence in the face of the problem is termed Theodicy.

EX CATHEDRA (Lat.: from the chair or throne). Usually applied to the pope, who is said to speak *ex cathedra* when he speaks officially to define a doctrine concerning faith or morals to be held by the entire Catholic Church. By extension, the term means to speak from the position of one's authority, officially, not as a simple person but from the office that is the origin and seat of one's responsibility. The term "cathedral" is derived from the fact that it refers to the church where the bishop has his throne, or chair (*cathedra*).

EX OPERE OPERATO (Lat.: from the act itself; eks ō'-pə-rā ō-pə-rä'-tō). The term used to designate the Catholic belief that the sacraments themselves confer grace if the recipient consciously intends the act. Protestants generally hold that without faith the sacramental act is empty. Catholics may contend that the Protestant belief closes the door to the one who is weak in faith, while Protestants often declare that the Catholic belief makes the sacrament effective even if the recipient is not worthy or is without worthy intentions. Neither is a very accurate interpretation of the position of the other.

EXCARDINATION. The permanent transfer of a cleric from the jurisdiction of one bishop to that of another.

EXCOMMUNICATION. The censure of the Catholic Church which excludes a member from Communion, i.e., the Eucharist, though he may attend church services. Acts which lead to excommunication are numerous, but among them are treating the consecrated Communion bread with irreverence, becoming an apostate, physical assault on a cleric, and procuring abortion.

EXEGESIS (Gr.: explanation; ek'-sə-jē'-sis). A critical analysis or interpretation of a word or passage in writing, especially in reference to the Bible. It may also refer to the explaining of the sense of the scriptures.

EXEGETE. One who does work in exegesis, either interpretation of words or explanation of what the scriptures actually say, and who is looked upon as expert in his field.

EXEQUIAL MASS. The requiem Mass said at a funeral and followed by the absolutions and procession to the grave.

EXODUS (Lat.: going out). The second book of the Old Testament; it describes the departure of the Hebrews from Egypt, their wanderings in the Sinai Desert, the delivery by God of the Ten Commandments, and the establishment of a priesthood and a liturgy. In its present form it dates from about 350 B.C., although some authorities place it as early as 1400 B.C.

EXORCISM. The driving out of evil spirits. The act of exorcism can be done only with the special permission of a high church official. In the Catholic Church, a lesser exorcism which doesn't imply that a person is possessed by an evil spirit is used at baptism and in certain blessings, but in general the rite of exorcism is understood as referring to that form used to purge a human of an evil spirit. "Possession" is recognized as a possibility, and it means that a person is occupied by and controlled by an evil spirit. Occurrence is rare in primarily Christian countries, and is extremely rare today compared with its prevalence in earlier centuries. The order of Exorcist and the rite of exorcism were established during early Christian history. The rite has a specific form including prayers, reading of scriptural passages, admonishments to the spirit, recitation of the creeds, etc. Other churches besides Catholic and Anglican have no such set rite, but ministers may practice exorcism of much the same type if necessary.

EXPIATION. The making right through an act, sacrifice, prayer, etc., of some injury or other harm done to someone, including God or oneself. The prototype of the expiatory act was Jesus' sacrifice of himself for man's sins. Expiation is almost identical with atonement and is closely related to propitiation.

EXTREME UNCTION. One of the seven sacraments of the Catholic Church, extreme unction, though generally associated with death, is actually intended to help restore to health a person in danger of death. It consists of anointing with oil and reciting of certain prayers, and is called "extreme" or "last" only because it follows three other rites of anointing: baptism, confirmation, and holy orders, in the order established for the seven. It is so closely associated with the bringing back to health of the body that certain Eastern dissidents apply it as a simple anointing which may be received by anyone to help avert illness, or as an act of devotion. According to Catholic theology it was established as a sacrament in Mark 6:13 and James 5:14-15.

EZEKIEL, EZECHIEL (Heb.: strengthened by God). A prophetic book of the Old Testament which probably takes its name from its author, a priest exiled in Babylon, and which dates from about 600 B.C. It contains prophecies of the destruction and restoration of Jerusalem and Israel and of the coming of a new kingdom, but its stress on individual responsibility and its visionary mysticism are of primary importance. Probably it was written to boost the morale of the Hebrews, for it stresses the importance of ritual practices and rejects the idea that the sins of the fathers are visited upon the children.

EZRA, ESDRAS. A book of the Old Testament, Ezra may be the name of the author, and is at any rate the main figure in the book. It recounts the events following the return of the Jews from the Babylonian captivity and the rebuilding of the temple. The period covered is about one hundred years, between 530 and 450 B.C.

FAITH. According to Hebrews 11:1, faith is "the substance of things hoped for, the evidence of things not seen," and the remainder of the chapter describes what faith is by the means of examples of what faith accomplishes. From this and other early texts has been built a complicated theological structure of what faith is and what it is not. By popular definition, "faith" is unquestioning belief, trust, or confidence with little or no absolutely empirically verifiable evidence; or, in another sense, a set of tenets and doctrines considered as a whole, as "the Catholic faith."

Traditionally and intellectually, "faith" may be regarded as belief in or mental assent to truths about God, or certain eternal and divine "truths." It is not identical with salvation, though it is the necessary first step. St. Thomas Aquinas formulated the basic teachings of the Catholic Church, which assert that faith is "an intellectual act of approving assent to certain supernatural truths or dogmas because of their divine authority." (*Theological Terms,* p. 96) In this view, trust and confidence are directed to the divine authority, and the idea that faith alone unites man and God is rejected, the supernatural virtues of hope and charity also being necessary.

The second major interpretation of faith, which is the view of Martin Luther, holds that faith is "the basic orientation of the total person" (*Theological Terms,* p. 95) which can also be called trust, confidence, or loyalty, and which may include belief. It is a trusting reliance on God's faithfulness, includes hope and charity, and has as its object not any supernatural truth but God himself. Doctrine as such came to be considered an attempt to express faith, rather than the object of faith, and as it became ever more liberal it differed ever more widely from the Catholic position which stressed intellectual assent to historical truth and doctrine, i.e., belief through faith.

129

More recently, in the face of the advances of science and the rejection of metaphysics and literal biblical interpretation, the emphasis on Jesus' virtues and benefits, rather than on his doctrines, has grown. Some theologians, in fact, have rejected doctrines entirely as the objects of faith. Thus "faith" is manifested in a man's life, rather than in his belief in specific doctrines.

FAITH CURE. The cure of physical, usually, or sometimes mental illnesses through prayer and special supplication and intercession by a minister or other individual, with and on behalf of someone who is sick. Generally the faith and the desire of the one to be helped are essential for such a cure to be effected. Physicians do not entirely rule out the validity of "faith cures" in certain illnesses, for the psychological origins of many illnesses are either suspected or verified. The resort to "faith cure" for others, however, is strongly condemned, since it may delay resort to medical assistance through which the illness could be arrested or cured.

FAITH, THE. A synonym for the Catholic Church when written as "The Faith." Within that church, the term refers to the system of belief and behavior taught as revealed truth. The expression may also be used more generally to refer to Christian beliefs as a whole, as in "He has the faith," when it often implies acceptance of a more or less conservative type of Christianity.

FAITHFUL, THE. Baptized Christians, but especially those who attend a church regularly and demonstrate that they have "the faith." Specifically, it designates members of the Catholic Church.

FALDA. A papal garment worn over the cassock, the falda is made of white silk and is fashioned with a train.

FALDSTOOL. A four-legged chair with arms but no back, used as a praying desk to kneel and lean the arms upon, or by a bishop in the Catholic Church when he is not on his throne or is officiating in a church not his own; or in the Anglican Church as a desk from which the litany is read.

FALL OF MAN, THE. Also called simply "The Fall," the term refers to the fall from grace through their sin by Adam and Eve in the Garden of Eden. Having been forbidden to eat of the Tree of Knowledge of Good and Evil, Eve succumbed to the temptation of the Devil in the form of a serpent, and Adam was led to sin by Eve. It is generally held that the "first parents of man" chose the way of rebellion and disobedience through their gift of free will, and that all mankind share in the first sin, called "original sin," because they are all "children of Eve." The Fall is not understood to imply the total corruption of human nature, but only as the loss of certain special gifts such as innocence, eternal life, the vision of God, etc. Read into the story in Genesis is the conclusion that, with free will, man tends toward rebellion and sin rather than toward obedience and virtue.

FALLEN NATURE. The nature of every man when he is born; another name for the condition is "original sin," and it returns biblically to the sin of Adam and Eve. It does not imply that man is corrupt or that "human nature" is by definition bad, although various Protestant denominations have so interpreted the phrase. Rather, it refers to the condition of man after the first sin, that of Adam and Eve, by which he can never again be sinless or totally unblemished as he was at Creation, by virtue of his relationship with the first man and the first woman. The only human exempted from being born with a fallen nature was, according to the teaching of the Catholic Church, Mary the Mother of Jesus. (See IMMACULATE CONCEPTION.)

FALSE WITNESS. Making under oath a statement that is known to be untrue, i.e., perjury. "Thou shalt not bear false witness," is one of the Ten Commandments and is more generally interpreted to mean "Thou shalt not make false statements about another." Often the law is taken to mean that only false defamatory or damaging statements are meant.

FAMILIAR. A servant employed in a monastery or a bishop's household. Also, in supernatural lore, a spirit that serves one closely, often in the form of an animal, as a cat might be held to be housing a witch's "familiar."

FAMILY PRAYERS. The daily gathering together for prayer of a household. This is a custom recommended by almost all Christian churches, but now little observed by their members. It probably had its greatest popularity during the Victorian era.

FAN, LITURGICAL. An accessory at worship services in the early Christian churches where its purpose was to keep flies away from the utensils that held the bread and wine for Communion. Today it survives primarily in the processional ostrich plumes used in certain Catholic rituals.

FARCING. Filling in between verses of a psalm with scriptural texts or other similar material, farcing was common during medieval church services. The name is derived from the verb "to farce," meaning to stuff, or to fill out.

FAST. A period of time, or a practice during that time, when church law requires that only one full meal be eaten during each day, and that that one must be taken after noon. It is more rigorous than abstinence and applies only to those between the ages of twenty-one and sixty, and even then may be waived for reasons of health, heavy labor, or the like. Liquids, except soup, are not limited.

FASTING COMMUNION. Receiving Communion bread and wine as the first food of the day, which, in practice, means eating nothing from midnight until Communion is received. The practice was customary by the time of St. Augustine and is still recommended if not absolutely required, in both Catholic and Anglican Churches.

FATHER. God; a name or title used by Jews and Christians alike. It is also the title by which most priests of the Catholic, and often the Anglican, Church are addressed in English-speaking countries and in the Eastern rites, although it is most correctly reserved to mendicant friars.

FATHER OF HERESIES. Simon, who tried to buy the gift of God with money according to Acts 8:9–24, and who gives his name to the crime of simony.

FATHER OF LIES. The Devil, a designation bestowed in John 8:44.

FATHERS OF THE CHURCH. Authoritative and influential writers on Christian dogma and doctrine who wrote during the first twelve centuries, approximately, of Church history. They wrote from positions of great learning and formed the doctrine of the Church, especially when their opinions were unanimous. See DOCTORS OF THE CHURCH.

FEAST DAY. In the Catholic and Anglican Churches, a special day commemorating a significant religious event, as Pentecost, Christmas, saints' days, or the like. Feast days may be "immoveable," that is, fixed dates on the calendar, as Christmas and the various saints' days which usually mark, when possible, the date of the saint's death. On the other hand, they may be "moveable feasts," which include all those such as Pentecost which are dated from the day on which Easter falls and have no set date on the calendar.

Within these ranks, feast days are divided into "primary," those which observe the main mysteries and the saints' days; "secondary," those derived from other feasts, as for example the feast day of the Stigmata of St. Francis; and "cardinal feasts," those which have a series of Sundays connected with them, as for example Easter.

FEAST OF OUR LORD. Fourteen feast days that commemorate special events in the life of Jesus are observed in the Catholic Church, and, to a greater or lesser extent, in Protestant churches. They are: 1. Birthday (Dec. 25); 2. Circumcision (Jan. 1); 3. Epiphany (Jan. 6); 4. Easter (movable); 5. Ascension (movable); 6. Corpus Christi (movable, honoring the institution of the Eucharist); 7. Exaltation (Sept. 14); 8. Finding of the Cross (May 3); 9. Dedication of the Basilica of St. Saviour or the Lateran (Nov. 9); 10. Holy Name (Jan. 2); 11. Precious Blood (July 1); 12. Sacred Heart (Aug. 6); 13. the Transfiguration (also Aug. 6); 14. Christ the King (the last Sunday in October).

FERDINAND, ST. (1191–1252). King Ferdinand III of Spain successfully battled the Moors in his country, seizing Cordova which they had occupied for several centuries and capping his victory with the conquest of Seville in 1248. Thus Mohammedanism was eliminated as a vital and active force in Spain. His feast day is May 30.

FERIAL DAY (Lat.: from a word meaning a free day). Any day of the week other than Saturday or Sunday.

FERRAIOLA. A brief cape which is worn with the cassock and which reaches halfway to the elbows, a part of the vestments of a priest. The "ferraiolone" is a long black cloak which is worn over the cassock by secular priests at a papal audience.

FERULA (Lat.: a rod; fer′o͞o-lə). In the early church, a staff with a short cross-piece at the top on which a clergyman or a layman might lean during long church services. At this time, no seats were provided in churches.

FIACRE, ST. (d. 670). An Irish or a Scottish religious man who lived in the forests of France, devoting his life to prayer and work among the poor. He is the patron saint of hosiers and gardeners, and his feast day is August 30.

FIDEISM (Lat.: faith; fē′dā-ism). A theological position which holds that faith is the foundation of religious or philosophic knowledge, and that all religious certainty is based on divine revelation. Human reason is deemed incapable of arriving at truth apart from such revelation.

FILIATION. A term used to identify the relationship of the Son, Jesus, to the Father, especially to distinguish it from the relationship of the Holy Spirit to both. The word is derived from the Latin *filius,* a son, and in general usage means derivation from a parent, as in the religious sense Jesus is the begotten Son of God. The Holy Spirit, on the other hand, is held to have "proceded from" God the Father, and, in the Catholic Church, from the Son as well.

FILIOQUE (Lat.: and from the Son). The term designating the proceding of the Holy Spirit from both the Father and the Son. It was the insertion of this term in the Nicene Creed in 589 (Council of Toledo) that angered the theologians of the East, at that time the Greek Church, and which led or helped to lead to a schism between Eastern and Western divisions of the Church in the eleventh century.

FINDING OF THE CROSS. A feast day celebrated on May 3 in commemoration of the "finding of the true cross" in 326. In that year, St. Helen, or Helena, mother of the Emperor Constantine and herself a Christian convert, journeyed to Palestine where she was able to have excavations made near Calvary that led to the finding of those relics believed to be the cross on which Jesus was crucified.

FIRE. The only fire connected with worship is in the use of candles, a practice which perhaps grew out of the processional torches sometimes carried for early Roman officials. "The Holy Fire" is a term used to refer to "new fire" believed by Orthodox churches as well as some others to be miraculously re-lit in the Church of the Holy Sepulchre on Holy Saturday and handed out by patriarchs through chapel windows to the waiting crowd. Its miraculous nature is neither affirmed nor denied by the clergy, but the practice was denounced by the Catholic Church.

FIRMAMENT (Lat.: strengthening or support). The sky, originally believed to be domed, and, according to Genesis 1:6, created to divide the waters from the waters.

FIRST FRIDAYS, THE NINE. In the Catholic Church, "to make the nine First Fridays" refers to the receiving of Communion on the first Friday of every month for nine consecutive months, an action deemed efficacious in and of itself so long as no superstitious importance is attached to the certain number of times or the certain day of observance. According to tradition, the practice was instituted by Jesus in an appearance to St. Marguerite Marie Alacoque (1647–1690), a French nun, and was accompanied by the promise that those who "made the nine First Fridays" would not be allowed to die without full repentance, or the sacraments, or in Jesus' displeasure. Catholics are not bound to believe in the promise or in the manner in which it is said to have been given.

FIRST FRUITS. Traditionally, the first or the best of a harvest was given to the temple, i.e., dedicated to God. "First fruits" may also refer, however, to the revenue collected during the first year of an ecclesiastical benefice which may be paid to the Papal curia or, in the Anglican Church, to the Crown.

FISH, THE. A main, and perhaps the earliest, symbol in the Christian religion. The Greek word for "fish" was ιχθνς, the letters of which are the first letters of the phrase, in Greek, "Jesus Christ, Son of God, Savior."

FISHERMAN, THE. St. Peter, also called Simon, or Simon Peter, and "the Fisherman" because fishing was his occupation before he became a disciple of Jesus. In Matthew 4:19, Jesus addresses Peter and Andrew, "Follow me, and I will make you fishers of men."

FIVE WOUNDS, THE. The wounds of the crucified Jesus, in the palms, feet, and side. During the Middle Ages they were an object of devotion and were frequently represented in church decoration.

FLABELLUM (Lat.: fan). The ceremonial ostrich plume fan carried in some papal processions. See FAN, LITURGICAL.

FLAGELLANTS (Lat.: *flagellum,* a scourge). A name given individuals who beat themselves with rods or whips as a form of penance. In the Middle Ages, the practice was fairly common in Italy, Germany, and northwest Europe, and the whipping was often done in public; some penitential sects, deemed heretical by the Catholic Church, actually organized for the purpose. Prohibited by the Catholic Church in the fourteenth century, a modified form of the practice became more common again after the Reformation, especially with the Jesuits. There are certain recognized legitimate religious reasons for such penance, and in certain monasteries moderate self-flagellation for devotional reasons is not forbidden. Perhaps the best known flagellants today are in the group called Penitentes which exists in New Mexico.

FLIGHT INTO EGYPT, THE. Being warned by an angel of danger from Herod, Joseph took Mary and the baby Jesus and fled into Egypt for safety. They remained there until Herod's death. The story is recounted in Matthew 2:13–23.

FLOCK. A name for the congregation of a church or members of a parish, as the minister, or pastor, is envisioned as a "shepherd" who tends the "sheep" under his care.

FLOOD, THE. The biblical account of the destruction of the world by water is found in Genesis 6:13–8:19. The account of the Deluge may be historically based in a great flood that occurred in the Euphrates Valley in ancient times, although the exact date and extent of damage are still being searched for in archaeological excavations.

FLOWERS. Most Christian churches, both Catholic and Protestant, use flowers for the adornment of the altar and the church for church services. They must generally be fresh rather than artificial. They represent many things: a gift, the honoring of God, purity, life, the wealth and beauty given man in this world.

FONT. The receptacle that holds the water for the baptismal ceremony, and hence often called the "baptismal font." It may be either a part of a permanent construction in the church or a temporary arrangement especially placed for the baptismal service.

"FOOL FOR CHRIST'S SAKE, A." A form of asceticism more common in the East than the West, being "a fool for Christ's sake" was based on the self-humbling of Jesus and was more practiced by the simple than the sophisticated. St. Simeon the Fool, an Egyptian of the sixth century, was perhaps the prototype of such persons.

FOOLS, FEAST OF. A pseudo-liturgical celebration that often accompanied the January 1 Feast of the Circumcision in western Europe. In the Middle Ages it became the occasion for far too enthusiastic merrymaking, eclipsing the religious festival, and the observance was officially suppressed in the fifteenth century.

FORBIDDEN BOOKS, INDEX OF. A list of books comdemned by the Catholic Church as heretical, dangerous to faith, religion, or morals, or otherwise especially objectionable. These books may not be read by church members without a permit from the Holy Office which compiles the Index from books specifically denounced to it, but such permission is easily obtained if a good reason is given for reading the book. A professional need to know its contents, or a need to know what it says in order to prepare an intelligent defense against it, is deemed a good reason; curiosity, however, is not. Few English books appear in the Index, but translations are condemned equally with originals. A recent Index contained about five thousand titles, but as titles are added and dropped from time to time, the list is never in a final form.

"FORBIDDEN TIMES." Those days between the beginning of Advent and Christmas, and between the beginning of Lent and Easter, when marriages may be contracted and celebrated but for which the nuptial Mass may not be used in the Catholic Church.

FOREKNOWLEDGE. God's quality or attribute of having knowledge of past, present, and, as this particular term states, the future. Philosophical difficulties develop when *foreknowledge* is extended to include *foreordination,* i.e., God's determination in advance of all events, thus raising the question of man's freedom. Some modern theologians solve the dilemma by ignoring it, but others prefer to adopt a position first advanced in part by William of Occam (c.1300–1349) that sees the future as indeterminate even by God, and God's perfect knowledge as knowledge of the actual as actual, the indeterminate as indeterminate, the possible as possible, etc., thus preserving both God's foreknowledge and man's freedom.

FOREORDINATION. See PREDESTINATION.

FORGIVENESS. The taking back into favor of a person who has harmed, slighted, disobeyed, or in any way physically or mentally hurt one. Forgiving a person who says or shows he is sorry is deemed just and necessary for true Christian charity, but it does not preclude the possibility of punishing the wrongdoer in the eyes of many moralists. However, pardoning or forgiving usually does entail the abandonment of the desire, need, or duty to punish.

FORGIVENESS OF SINS. The removal of guilt and the stain of sin through true repentence, and, in some churches, the penance of the sinner, and God's act of mercy to do so. Most denominations hold that all sins can be forgiven a penitent sinner; some define the "sin which cannot be forgiven" or "the sin against the Holy Ghost" mentioned in Matthew 12:31–32, Mark 3:28, and Luke 12:10, as the failure or refusal to repent, since without repentance no forgiveness is possible.

FORM CRITICISM. A method of analysis of old writings which begins with the conviction that ancient writers set down oral stories, legends, wise sayings, and the like in distinctly identifiable forms, so that it is possible to pick out a popular aphorism, for instance, from the wise saying of a specific person. Changes in short, illustrative stories may show the stories' development and pattern of transmission through many years, and thus whole developmental patterns may be made identifiable. Form criticism has proved a very promising method of studying the Old Testament, and is held by many to be equally efficient in establishing the earliest and most reliable traditions about Jesus.

FORETELL. To prophesy or predict; an ability to announce or suggest what the future may hold is the ability to "foretell the future." This quality, with "forthtelling," made the Old Testament prophet a man with a serious duty to discharge for his people.

FOUR HORSEMEN OF THE APOCALYPSE, THE. In the vision recounted in Revelation 6:1–8, four allegorical horsemen are seen. The first revealed was mounted on a white horse, and was presented with a crown; he is sometimes said to represent Jesus, more often, a powerful king. The second horseman was mounted on a red horse, and was presented with a sword; he is said to represent war. The rider of the third horse, a black mount, held a pair of scales; he represented famine or plague. Death rode the pale horse, the last of the four. Together they represent the deaths, or the powers, that oppress mankind, when the first is interpreted as a conquering king; otherwise, the first horseman must receive a different reading than the remaining three, and the "Four Horsemen" idea is somewhat mitigated.

FOUR LAST THINGS, THE. Generally, death, judgment, Heaven, and Hell. Eschatology, a branch of theology, is concerned with their study.

FRACTION, THE. In the Catholic Church, the breaking of the Communion bread, or Host, between the Lord's Prayer and the Agnus Dei in preparation for reception of the Eucharist by the priest and then by the people. It is called the fraction "because an essential part of the Mystery is that the Body of Christ is broken and divided and yet remains entire in every fragment." (*Myth and Ritual,* p. 151)

FRANCIS DE SALES, ST. (1566?–1622). Born of an old French family, Francis de Sales studied successfully in his native country and Italy before beginning his life's work as a priest. Throughout his life, preaching and writing with the purpose of giving spiritual direction to others were of the utmost importance to him. Appointed bishop of Geneva in 1603, he was later offered a better French bishopric by Henry IV, but he turned it down in order to continue in the lesser station to which he felt his allegiance was due. He is reputed to have been calm, efficient, and humble, reiterating the fact of his "uselessness" even as he died. His feast day is January 29.

FRANCIS OF ASSISI, ST. (1181–1226). Having spent a wild youth, Francis Bernardone, son of a well-to-do merchant in Assisi, Italy, repented and reformed after several months in jail. The path he was to follow thereafter led him to a place in the hearts of almost all Christians, Protestants as well as Catholics, the heretics and sinners as well as the faithful and good. He is renowned especially for his love of all creatures, a love which grew from his devotion for God and all God's creations. He had a gift with animals, taming the wild and curing the ill. Known as "The Poverello" or "The Poor One," he gave up his wealth and lived a life of poverty entirely devoted to caring for others, but particularly others for whom no one else cared: the contagiously ill, those beyond the law, the very poor.

In 1209 he was joined by some men who became his disciples, forming the order of Friars Minor, one of the present Franciscan orders. Three years later, with his help, Clare of Assisi founded the Sisters of the Poor, or Poor Clares, a women's order. A dozen or so years later a third order was founded for those who wanted to lead a religious life without completely abandoning their secular existence. Some five years before his death, the direction of the order was taken from his hands by reformers, or, more accurately, he willingly gave it up to avoid stirring already somewhat troubled waters. He continued to preach, however, and composed the rule for his order. In 1224 he received the stigmata and died peacefully two years later, one of the best loved and greatest of saints. The work, *The Little Flowers of St. Francis,* is actually a collection of little stories that illustrate the holiness and simplicity of his life, but he himself wrote hymns and poems of great beauty. His feast day is October 4.

FRANCIS, THE RULE OF ST. This rule may be summarized as " 'to observe the holy gospel of our Lord Jesus Christ by living in obedience, without goods, and in chastity.' " (*Catholic Dictionary,* p. 200) There are, in effect, three rules, one for Franciscan friars, one for the Poor Clares (the nuns of the order), and one for the third order, or lay tertiaries. All three originated with St. Francis of Assisi, who founded the parent order in 1209. This, the Friars Minor, is the largest of three independent groups of friars, the others being the Capuchins and the Conventuals. There is also the women's order, the Sisters of the Poor or the Poor Clares, and the lay organization for men and women who choose to follow a religious life while remaining in the world, but all follow a modified and adapted form of the original rule.

FRANCISCANS, THE. Founded by St. Francis of Assisi in 1209, the Franciscans (friars) are divided into Friars Minor, Friars Minor Capuchin, or simply Capuchins, and Friars Minor Conventual. The Friars Minor follow the original rule; the Capuchins were organized in the sixteenth century to restore a more literal observance of the rule; the Conventuals follow a more liberal pattern of the rule in the accumulation and use of property and wealth held in common. The order for women is called the Sisters of the Poor, or the Poor Clares, and was founded, with St. Francis' help, by Clare of Assisi in 1212. Franciscans stress the doctrine of poverty and missionary work, two main ideals of the founder. They have been responsible over the centuries for the "popularization of such devotions as the stations of the cross and the Christmas crib." (*Catholic Dictionary,* p. 201) A third order, for both men and women, allows individuals to continue their secular lives, or enter a religious community if they choose, and emphasizes the religious life.

Franciscans, from an early habit, were once called the Gray Friars, but now the habit is brown with a rope belt, and only sandals are worn on the feet.

FRANCIS XAVIER, ST. (1506–1552). One of the founders of the Jesuits, with his friend St. Ignatius Loyola, St. Francis Xavier is often called the Apostle to the Indies, as his missionary work was done in India. He was reputedly a worker of many miracles and a converter of hundreds upon thousands of souls. His feast day is December 3.

FRANKINCENSE (Old Fr.: luxuriant incense). An aromatic gum resin from various trees of the balsam family that grow in Asia, East Africa, and particulary Arabia. It was burned as incense, and is especially mentioned as one of the gifts brought to the baby Jesus.

FRATICELLI (from It.: brothers; fra-ti-chel′lē). The name given a rigorous, often heretical group that existed from the thirteenth through the fifteenth centuries in Europe; in France the group was called *Frerots*. They observed a rule of extreme poverty, and they held that sin deprived clergymen and rulers of their powers and jurisdiction, and that all popes after John XXII (1316–1334) were spurious. The groups were suppressed vigorously by the Catholic Church.

FREEDOM OF THE WILL, OR FREE WILL. The human will considered as having the quality of liberty to choose as it wishes without compulsion or preset conditions. A free will is held to be God's gift, the gift, in fact, which enabled Adam and Eve to choose evil instead of good. Those who believe in freedom of the will may be termed libertarians; the concept is opposed to that of determinism, which holds that all actions are preset, or predetermined, by a sequence of causes, and that man's choices only have the appearance of having been made freely.

Historically, and similarly in modern theology and philosophy, the definition of freedom of the will is far more complex. It entails the asking of such questions as: If man lost, in Adam's fall, the ability to will the good, then in what sense is his will really free? If God has foreknowledge, and to a greater or lesser extent predetermines the course of each life, then is it not true that man only seems to have any freedom of choice?

The Freudian as well as many contemporary sociological views hold that man is shaped as much by the conditions in which he is raised as by his heredity, (which is, itself, rarely "neutral") and is thereby narrowly limited in the number and variety of choices available to him, making his will something much less than free. Other philosophies, however, emphasize man's condition as one of constant decision-making and uphold the freedom of his will to make the decisions freely.

FREEDOM OF WORSHIP. The right of men to worship God according to the dictates of their own conscience, or, if such is the case, not to worship at all. In practice, certain restrictions have had to be applied to this basic freedom. Worship which is excessively noisy may in some cases "disturb the peace," and other forms may encroach upon the freedom of others, but within all reasonable limits the existence of this freedom is an identifying characteristic of the United States and various other nations of the world.

FRIAR. A member of one of the "mendicant orders," i.e., Domini-cans, Franciscans, Carmelites, and Augustinians, whose head-quarters is a friary, but who works in some active form outside its walls, or in some contact with the outer world, as a teacher, preacher, missionary, or the like. By contrast, a *monk* lives and works within a monastery, though neither friars nor monks may own personal property. Today, a friary as well as a monastery may hold property, but originally a friary could not while a monastery could. The law was modified in 1545 at the Council of Trent.

FRIARS MINOR, and FRIARS MINOR CONVENTUAL. See both FRAN-CISCANS and FRANCIS, RULE OF ST.

FRIARS PREACHERS. Another name for the Dominican friars.

FRIARY. The community and house of any of the orders of friars, though now the term most usually refers to a Franciscan house.

FRIDESWIDE, ST. (d. c.735). The woman who is the patron saint of the city and university of Oxford, England.

FRIENDS, SOCIETY OF. The Quakers, a small but important reli-gious order within general Protestantism, was founded in the mid-seventeenth century in England by George Fox. The Friends are distinctive in their worship. They meet together in silence, and whoever among them feels moved by the inner spirit to pray, praise, rebuke, or otherwise speak forth, does so. Certain mem-bers may be called "ministers," but they have no ordained ministry, and meeting houses are distinguished by their simplicity. Neither do they have a profession of faith, although belief generally fol-lows the Apostles' Creed; rather, they recognize the "Inner Light," or Holy Spirit, a perception of Divine presence within each individual heart and mind, which is also the source of the rule of faith. Although they regard the Scriptures with reverence and honor, they do not regard them as rule.

Friends refuse to take oaths or bear arms, although usually not such a strong position is now taken in this regard as was once the case. At one time, their speech was distinguished by its use of "plain speech," i.e., "thee," "thou," "thine," etc., and they were frequently the object of the jokes of their more worldly neighbors. Their nickname "Quakers," in fact, was given them because they were said to tremble or quake during the emotional experience of their meetings.

Emphasis on morality and humane endeavors have probably won the Friends more general respect than that granted most other religious denominations. Their position on any issue almost invariably represents that of the most distinterested humane thought, and, in war time, this has occasionally led to their condemnation by patriotic groups with more nationalistic tendencies. At present membership in the United States Society of Friends is about 126,000; the headquarters is in Philadelphia, Pennsylvania, long known as the "Quaker City."

FRONTAL. The piece of material which hangs over and covers at least the front side of an altar, although it may also cover the sides and the back as well.

FRUITS OF THE HOLY GHOST, or HOLY SPIRIT. As described in Galatians 5:22–23, the Fruits of the Spirit are: love, joy, peace, longsuffering, gentleness, goodness, faith, meekness, and temperance, and "against such there is no law."

FULL OF GRACE. A term frequently used to describe the Virgin Mary in Catholic worship, as in "Hail Mary, full of grace." It does not mean that Mary was filled with grace to the fullest possible extent, but rather that she was endowed with grace sufficient to be Jesus the Son of God's mother. That is, she possessed enough grace to fulfill her calling or perform her purpose, and, as the calling and purpose were great, so must the grace have been. In general, though, whenever anyone is said to be "full of grace," the meaning is "grace sufficient for the fulfilling of a calling."

FUNDAMENTALISM. The name given the viewpoint that rejects all efforts to liberalize faith or belief, or to interpret the Bible in other than a literal sense, or to question at all its infallibility. Fundamentalism is highly orthodox Protestant in nature, affirming such basic doctrines as the Bible's literal infallibility, the doctrine of the Trinity, the virgin birth of Jesus, the bodily resurrection, and the doctrine of atonement. The position taken on the Old Testament is usually as literal, and often fundamentalists accept the Creation in seven days, the account of the Fall, and other matters from Genesis and other books as "fact as written." Probably the best known among fundamentalist opposition to anything which seems to contradict the Bible's word is the fairly recent and continuing dispute with the evolutionists.

"Fundamentalism" took its name from *The Fundamentals,* religious tracts published between 1912 and 1914, that had as their purpose to define and defend orthodox Protestant doctrines. Nowadays, fundamentalist theologians who object to the identification of fundamentalism with absolute opposition to any sort of critical enquiry prefer to be called "conservatives" or "evangelical conservatives." They feel that the Bible and its beliefs and facts can be logically defended, and that doubters are welcome as they, the fundamentalists, can answer any questions in a rational, factual, and intellectually acceptable manner.

# G

GABRIEL (Heb.: man of God). The archangel of the Annunciation and the Messenger of Divine Comfort. In the hierarchy, his place is next after Michael; his feast day is March 24.

GALATIANS, THE EPISTLE TO THE. A book of the New Testament, highly personal in tone, and directed by St. Paul to various churches in Asia Minor which, he felt, were defeating his purpose by emphasizing the need for Christian converts to follow the Law of Moses, i.e., to follow the Jewish faith in order to be able to follow the Christian.

GALILEE. The northern province of Palestine. The term "galilee" also designates the large porch at the entrance to a church, although the origin of the latter usage is obscure.

GANG DAYS. An ancient term for Rogation Days in the Catholic Church. The major Rogation Day, April 25, was marked in pagan times by processions and ceremonies designed to help encourage the gods to give a good harvest. In earlier Christian centuries, the custom was adopted, and informal processions might encircle, i.e., go around, each village, from which the term "gang" or "going" perhaps developed. For details see ROGATION DAYS.

GARTH (Old Norse: a yard). The open space enclosed by the walls of a cloister.

GATES OF HELL. Considered in the most rigid sense, the gates of Hell are the gates which form the entrance to the Underworld. The term, however, is a commonly used synonym for the power of evil or for the evil influences from Hell, as "the gates of Hell closed behind him," might mean that after a specific time he lived his life in an entirely evil way.

146

GAUDETE SUNDAY (Lat.: rejoice; gô-dā'-tā). The third Sunday of Advent. The name is derived from the first Latin word of the introit.

GEHENNA. The valley near Jerusalem that served as the city's refuse dump and incinerator. The term was used by Jesus to signify Hell, and may refer to a place of punishment and burning.

GENERAL CONFESSION. In various Protestant churches, this expression refers to the confession made, silently or orally, by the entire congregation. In the Catholic Church, it refers to the confession which may precede such major events as first Communion and Ordination, and which entails the repetition of all one's previous confessions or of those during a certain period of time. It demands great detail, and is discouraged except for a very important occasion, as above, or in the event that the previous confessions were willfully false or incomplete or were invalid for some other reason.

GENESIS (Gr.: origin). The first book of the Bible and of the Pentateuch, deriving its name from the fact that it covers the creation of the world and the story of early events. Traditionally ascribed to Moses, current criticism holds it to be the work of multiple authors.

GENESIUS, ST. St. Genesius of Arles, France, was a fourth-century martyr who apparently held some sort of clerical position before his death; he has had a considerable following over the centuries. Even for the existence of St. Genesius of Rome, supposedly a comic actor who was converted while performing before Diocletian and became a martyr for his faith almost on the spot, there is no real proof. The feast day of both is August 25.

GENEVA BIBLE, THE. A 1560 English revision of the Great Bible and Tyndale's Bible, it derived its name from the fact of its publication in Geneva, Switzerland. It contains the entire Bible, excluding the Apocrypha, and was the result of efforts of Protestants, persecuted in England by Mary Tudor, who fled to the continent, among them John Calvin, John Knox, and Miles Coverdale.

GENEVIEVE, ST. (422?–512). The patron saint of Paris, St. Genevieve persuaded the people of Paris not to flee from Attila the Hun's approach, as she was sure the city would be spared though the Huns might level everything else. She was proved correct, as Attila turned aside to attack Orleans, and was thereafter defeated. At a later date, she secured food for the city while it was under siege, and is credited with saving the entire population from starvation or surrender. Renowned for her courage and ability, St. Genevieve was honored as the city's patron; her feast day is January 3.

GENTILE. In early biblical usage, "gentile" or Hebrew *goyim* was a term of contempt for any person not one of the Chosen People. After St. Paul became the Apostle of the Gentiles, the expression came to refer to one who was neither Jew nor Christian. Most recently it refers to any non-Jew, but popular usage makes it refer to Christians.

GENUFLECT. To bend, and to straighten again, the right knee, allowing the body to lower itself comfortably and to return to an erect position. It is an act of reverence performed when passing before an altar which holds the Blessed Sacrament; often when crossing in front of an altar in a Catholic or Anglican church; and at various points during the worship service of the Mass. The genuflection replaced the low bow or curtsey during the sixteenth century. The alternate spelling of "genuflection" is "genuflexion."

GEORGE, ST. (d. c. 303). All that is known about the patron saint of England is that he probably suffered martyrdom, perhaps while a soldier, in Asia Minor. However, tales of glory grew about his name almost from the beginning, and by the fifth century monasteries and churches were being built in his honor. In the fourteenth century, King Edward III of England founded the Knights of St. George, otherwise known as Knights of the Garter, for whom St. George is the patron, and in the fifteenth century St. George's Day was accorded a position of great importance in the Church calendar. St. George's red cross appears on the flag of Great Britain.

The legend of St. George and the dragon, the most popular of the stories told about him, was perpetuated in *The Golden Legend,* a thirteenth-century collection of saints' lives. A mighty dragon, the inhabitant of a lake in a pagan country, could not be killed and so had to be appeased with a steady offering of sheep. However, when sheep were few, maidens had to be substituted, and it happened that the king's own daughter had drawn the unfortunate lot on the day that St. George passed by. Making the sign of the cross, the knight slew the dragon with one blow. After the king and his people had turned to the Christian faith and asked for baptism, St. George went on his way, accepting no reward but giving the entire great sum to the poor. His feast day is April 23.

GEORGIA, or GEORGETTE, ST. (d. early sixth century). One of the popular virgin saints, St. Georgia lived near Clermont, France, where she went into the country to pray and fast. When she died, having led a life of great purity, her body was accompanied during the funeral and to the cemetery by a flight of doves believed to be angels, for the birds were said to ascend back into Heaven after the burial. Her feast day is February 15.

GERMAIN, ST. (495?-576). St. Germain, made the bishop of Paris in about 555, exerted considerable influence on the French king, Childebert, whom he was said to have miraculously restored to health, and they founded in Paris the well-known abbey of St. Germain-des-Prés. Although St. Germain continued in importance during the rule of Childebert's successor, Clotaire, he was less fortunate with Clotaire's sons, and excommunicated the king for adultery. St. Germain was buried in the abbey he founded; his feast day is May 28.

GERTRUDE, ST. (626-659). Abbess of a Belgian convent, St. Gertrude was noteworthy in her own time for bringing Irish monks to the continent to instruct the nuns in Scripture and to evangelize the area in Brabant in which the convent was located. She was a popular saint in the Middle Ages in Belgium, Germany, and Poland, and was especially invoked for the finding of a suitable place to stay overnight while traveling, and against rats, mice, fever, and insanity. Her feast day is March 17, a day on which she is somewhat eclipsed in many English-speaking countries by St. Patrick.

GETHSEMANE (Ara.: oil press; geth-sem'-ə-nē). The site of Jesus' agony and betrayal, a garden on the Mt. of Olives; the term generally refers to a place of agony, especially of a spiritual nature.

GHETTO. Although modern usage has expanded the meaning of this word to include the quarter of a city in which any minority group is forced, or forcibly influenced, to live, or, in fact, to include any area that forms the residential area for a minority group, the original usage applied only to the portion reserved for Jews. The origin of the word itself is doubtful, but it may have come from the Italian *juidecca,* "Jewry."

GHOST, SEVEN GIFTS OF THE HOLY. According to Isaiah 11:2, these are wisdom, understanding, counsel, strength, knowledge, and the fear of the Lord: piety, the seventh, is included as essential to the others.

GHOST, THE HOLY. The Holy Spirit, a term referring to the third person of the Trinity; the later term, Holy Spirit, is now preferred because of the unpleasant and not entirely religious connotations "ghost" has accumulated over the centuries. The Old English "gast," or "ghost," meant simply "a spirit."

GIFT OF TONGUES. The ability to speak in any language; the "gift of tongues," as referred to in the Bible, is usually bestowed in order to allow a disciple to spread God's word or Jesus' story to foreign lands whose language he could not speak. See especially the story of Pentecost, Acts 2:1-13, when the gift of tongues was bestowed. The term also designates the condition of speaking unintelligibly during some sort of ecstatic state.

GIRDLE. A long rope, tasselled at the end, used to belt the alb. It is made of linen or hemp and is usually white; its symbolic meaning is sacerdotal purity. An alternative name is *cincture.*

GLASTONBURY THORN. A variety of the common thorn tree which often has a second blossoming season around Christmas time, at least if the two preceding months are mild. Legend has it that the thorn developed from the staff of Joseph of Arimathea, which he thrust into the ground during his journey to England after Jesus' crucifixion. The name is derived from the spot where the original tree stood. It was destroyed by Cromwell's men in the seventeenth century, but slips had been taken from it and all Glastonbury thorns have sprung from that tree.

GLEBE (lat.: *gleba,* soil). Land that is part of a parochial benefice and which forms the endowment for the support of a parish priest.

GLORIA IN EXCELSIS DEO (Lat.: Glory be to God on high; glôr'ē-ɔ in ek-sel'sis-dā ō). The Greater Doxology, or Angelic Hymn, this song of praise to the Trinity is taken from Luke 2:14, "Glory to God in the highest, and on earth peace, good will toward men." There are additions and alterations.

GLORIA PATRI (Lat.: Glory be to the Father; glôr'ē-ɔ pä'trē). An ancient hymn also called the Lesser Doxology, used throughout the Christian churches of the west, probably since the seventh century. Its verse is: "Glory be to the Father (*gloria Patri*), and to the Son, and to the Holy Ghost. As it was in the beginning, is now, and ever shall be; world without end."

GLORIFY. To honor, or give glory to, or acknowledge the glory of, as "we glorify Thy Holy Name."

GLORIOLE. A halo.

GLORIOUS MYSTERIES. This term usually refers to "The Five Glorious Mysteries of the rosary," that is, the resurrection, the ascension, the descent of the Holy Ghost, the assumption of the Virgin Mary, and the coronation of Mary in Heaven.

GLORY. Spiritual splendor or perfection; the term is sometimes used as a synonym, though now probably obsolete, for Heaven, as "to enter Glory," "gates of Glory," or "gone to Glory," i.e., deceased.

GLOSS. Writing in the margin, in footnotes, or interlinearly to clarify or explain a text, especially an old or perhaps obscure text. Bible glosses were fairly common, and the term later came to apply to commentary on the biblical text.

GLOSSOLALIA. The "gift of tongues" or "speaking in tongues."

GLUTTONY. One of the "seven deadly sins," gluttony consists of overindulgence in food and drink, and becomes truly serious when the overeating damages the health, or the overdrinking results in complete drunkenness.

GOD. Although the Bible gives no definition of God, many attributes are named. Perhaps first and foremost is that God is spirit; he is eternal, perfect, all-powerful, all-knowing. Theology holds that God exists not as one person but as three in the Trinity: The first, God the Father; the second, God the Son; the third, God the Holy Spirit or Holy Ghost. Nevertheless, they are not three separate persons, but one, co-eternal, equally powerful, perfect, and knowing. The concept of God has many puzzling aspects for theologians and laymen. That an absolute deity, unchanging and incomprehensible creator and destroyer, should be approachable through personal prayer and apprehension is but one of them. In practice, most believers probably consider "God" first as the creator of everything, himself eternal and uncreated; second as the concerned "Father" to whom the prayers of his "children" always reach; and third as the more remote controller and director of all the events of the universe. See ATTRIBUTES OF GOD.

GODPARENT. An individual who, at a baby's baptism, assumes at the parents' request a responsibility for the child's faith. In actuality, a godmother or godfather often feels a more far-reaching responsibility toward the godchild, extending into the fields of the youngster's education and overall well-being.

GOD'S ACRE. The yard around a church, or a cemetery.

GOD'S WORD. The most usually encountered interpretation of this phrase equates it with the Bible or with preaching or speaking of the biblical message, as "He preaches God's word." However, the term has three possible meanings. It may be the Word as preached, when it is held to be "a positive command which does not permit man to assume the attitude of a spectator or to enjoy mere disinterested research. . . . It is not subject to our power, but is effective whenever, wherever and however it will." (*Protestantism,* p. 205 f.) Second, the Bible is held to be the revealed Word of God. Third, it may be interpreted as God's activities working toward the salvation of mankind.

GOLDEN RULE. The commandment formulated by Jesus (Matthew 7:12) as "Therefore all things whatsoever ye would that men should do to you, do ye even so to them." The antiquity and universality of some form of the rule are noteworthy, for example, it was expressed by Confucius, Plato, and Aristotle.

GOOD BOOK, THE. The Bible.

GOOD FAITH. The condition of believing sincerely and conscientiously that what one does or thinks is right, good, and innocent, even if it is, in fact, otherwise.

GOOD FRIDAY. The Friday preceding Easter; the day on which the death of Jesus by crucifixion occurred and is commemorated. The origin of the name is obscure. It may be a modern form of "God's Friday," or a reference to the crucifixion as a sacrifice which led to the redemption of man and was, therefore, "good." Many churches mark especially the period between noon and 3 P.M., often called the Three Hours, when Jesus hung on the cross.

GOOD FRIDAY OFFICE. In the Catholic Church, the special Good Friday service which is composed of four parts; the readings, the prayers, the adoration of the cross, and the Communion service.

GOOD SAMARITAN, THE. According to Luke 10:30-37, a Samaritan was the only person who would help a traveler who had been beaten and robbed. Traditionally, residents of Samaria were held in contempt by the Jews.

GOOD SHEPHERD, THE. A symbol of Jesus as "the good shepherd," the shepherd who is willing to die for his flock, was used by early Christians and appears in the catacombs. The concept itself is derived in part from John 10:11, although the idea of shepherd and flock as symbols of a man and those individuals under his care is even older. Often Jesus is pictured as a shepherd, perhaps with a lamb in his arms; the idea has been a popular one in religious art.

GOOD THIEF, THE. One of the two thieves crucified with Jesus who confessed his belief in Jesus as savior. See DISMAS.

GOOD WORKS. The good things done by one such as prayers, fasts, help given others, etc., as well as the good deeds performed more or less in the process of carrying on one's secular life. Protestant and Catholic theology sometimes are at odds over the necessity of good works to salvation or justification. "Justification by faith" was a tenet of Luther which meant that faith alone was necessary to secure the change of a soul from a state of sin to a state of grace. Good works, though not necessary, would presumably follow. Catholic theology, on the other hand, explains, "Good works are not the cause of justification. We are made just by the sanctifying grace of infused charity, but if we love God efficaciously above all things we necessarily act accordingly, and thus good works are necessary to salvation. But good works must also precede justification in an adult." (*Catholic Dictionary,* p. 213) According to James 2:14, "What doth it profit, my brethren, though a man say he hath faith and have not works?" and in 2:17, "Even so faith, if it hath not works, is dead, being alone." St. Paul, however, put the emphasis on faith.

GOSPEL (Old English: *God spell,* good news, tr. of good tidings). The books of Matthew, Mark, Luke, and John are "the Gospels," but more generally, the teachings and history of Jesus and his Apostles may be called "the Gospel," whether located in these specific four books of the New Testament or others.

GOSPEL, APOCRYPHAL. Any of a group of some fifty early writings that narrates events in the life of Jesus but which was composed anywhere from a hundred to several hundred years after the events recounted and which therefore lacks authenticity. The Pseudepigrapha contains both the Apocryphal Gospels and the Apocrypha. While both Catholics and Protestants reject the Apocryphal Gospels as spurious, the Apocrypha is accepted as canonical by Catholics and as valuable by Protestants. For details on two, see NICODEMUS, APOCRYPHAL GOSPEL OF, and THOMAS, APOCRYPHAL GOSPEL OF.

GOSPEL SIDE, THE. The left hand side of the sanctuary facing the altar; it is from this side that the gospel is said or sung.

GOSSIP (Old English *Godsibb,* God-relation). Originally, this term designated the sponsor at baptism and was so used in parts of England until the early part of the nineteenth century.

GRACE. "The free, unmerited favor and love of God," as well as the concept of the influence of God operating in man to uplift and strengthen him (*American College Dictionary*). Any gift freely given by God to man may be referred to as "grace" whether it is relevant to his salvation or not, although most frequently the term applies to the gift that leads to moral or spiritual strengthening. The Catholic Church distinguishes among the types of grace, for which see: ACTUAL GRACE, BAPTISMAL GRACE, COOPERATING GRACE, EFFICACIOUS GRACE, ELEVATING GRACE, HABITUAL GRACE, ILLUMINATING GRACE, INTERIOR GRACE, NATURAL GRACE, PREVENIENT GRACE, SACRAMENTAL GRACE, SUFFICIENT GRACE, AND SUBSTANTIAL GRACE.

GRACE, STATE OF. The condition of being in God's favor. It may refer to the condition after penance and absolution or to the state of the elect or justified.

GRACE, TO SAY. To repeat a prayer before, or sometimes after, a meal. The usage is from the Latin meaning of the term *gratiae,* thanks, from which "grace" is derived.

GRADINE. Any shelf at the back of an altar on which candlesticks, a cross, or the like may be set.

GRADUAL. The two verses from the psalms, Scripture, or religious song sung after the reading of the epistle during the church service.

GRAIL, THE HOLY. A medieval term for the cup from which Jesus drank at the Last Supper. Legend surrounds it. Not only are the King Arthur tales and other medieval romances built around the search for it, but also shorter stories have existed which account variously for its whereabouts. In the 1100's, Joseph of Arimathea was believed to have taken it to Glastonbury, England, filled with the water in which the dead body of Jesus was bathed, and it has also been said to be in the Cathedral of Valencia, Spain, and in Montserrat and Genoa, Italy. The true repository, if one exists, is not known.

GREAT BIBLE, THE. Cranmer's or Cromwell's Bible, an English version edited by Miles Coverdale at the order of Thomas Cromwell and published in 1539. It was called "great" because of its size, and, though edited by Coverdale, is not to be confused with the earlier Coverdale's Bible. Those two issues published first are called "Cromwell's Bible," while the later editions are called "Cranmer's Bible" because they carried a long preface by the Archbishop. For a number of years, the Great Bible was the official Bible for England.

GREAT RELICS. The relics recognized as the "great relics" by the Catholic Church are the point of the spear which pierced Jesus' side, the veil with which a woman wiped his face when he was walking to Calvary and on which an impression is said to remain imprinted (called the Veronica), and a piece of the true cross. These relics are kept in St. Peter's, Rome.

GREAT SCHISM, THE. The controversy that divided the Catholic Church between 1378 and 1417 is also called the Schism of the West. It arose out of the Roman populace's pressure to have the man who was to be called Urban VI made pope at the death of Pope Gregory XI. He pleased no one as pope, and the cardinals declared the election null and void, choosing in his place Robert of Geneva, now usually, though not entirely correctly, known as Antipope Clement VII, who fled to Avignon, France. The problem was resolved at the Council of Constance, 1414–1418, which succeeded in ousting two rival popes and securing the resignation of the other, Gregory XII, since considered canonical, to bring about the naming of Martin V. Among important business which was neglected during the schism and the split papacy, part in France, part in Italy, was internal reform of the Catholic Church, long recognized by the best churchmen as a necessity. Thus, in effect, one of the most far-reaching results of the Great Schism was the Reformation.

GREAT WEEK. The liturgical name for Holy Week, the week before Easter.

GREEK FATHERS. Sts. Athanasius, Basil, John Chrysostom, and Gregory Nazianzus are often the first-named Greek Fathers, or Doctors, of the Church. Also included, however, are Cyril of

Jerusalem, Gregory of Nyssa, Cyril of Alexandria, and John Damascene. Since all except John Damascene are from the fourth and fifth century, the name of this eighth century Father is sometimes omitted. See DOCTORS OF THE CHURCH.

GREEN. The liturgical color used for vestments on Sundays and ferial days from the octave of the Epiphany until Septuagesima and from the octave of Corpus Christi until Advent. These seasons, Epiphany and Trinity, approximate most of January and February and most of the summer and fall. The color symbolizes hope.

GREEN THURSDAY. Maundy Thursday, a name derived perhaps from the ancient custom of giving penitents green branches on that day to signify the end of their penance and their acceptance back into the full communion of the church from which they were excluded during Lent.

GREGORIAN CHANT. See PLAIN SONG.

GREGORY OF NAZIANZUS, ST. (329?–389?). Born in Arianzus in Cappadocia, Gregory was the son of a Christian convert who became bishop of Nazianzus and urged his somewhat reluctant son to be ordained a priest. Gregory evidently had a genuine gift for oratory, but he much preferred a life of peaceful and quiet seclusion. He and Basil, the founder of the Rule for monks still followed in Greek monasteries, were close friends, and together with Basil's brother, Gregory of Nyssa, sought satisfaction in the religious life. Gregory of Nazianzus was the gentler and more affectionate, it would appear, while Basil was far more outgoing and probably more brilliant. Though Gregory acted as bishop of Nazianzus and, briefly, as archbishop of Constantinople, his real joy lay in either the monastic life or life on his own estate, where he was able to spend his last few years. As well as being a devoted and frequently self-sacrificing churchman, St. Gregory was a gifted writer, the author of forty-five discourses, much poetry, and over two hundred excellent letters which show him at his literary and humane best. He contributed to the theology of the Trinity, especially, and is one of the Greek Doctors of the Church. His feast day is May 9.

GREGORY OF NYSSA, ST. (d. c. 394). Together with Gregory of Nazianzus (see preceding entry) and Basil, Gregory of Nyssa made up the group called the Cappadocians, from the country of their birth. The brothers, Gregory of Nyssa and Basil, were perhaps more energetic, at least to outward appearances; the former was bishop of Nyssa and archbishop of Sebaste in Lesser Armenia. He wrote much and opposed Arianism determinedly. His feast day is March 9.

GREGORY OF TOURS, ST. (538-594). Author of *History of the Franks*; it is to Gregory of Tours that much is owed for his account of France during the time of the early Merovingian kings (the Merovingian history began with Meroveus, a half-legendary ruler whose grandson, Clovis I, founded the first French monarchy in 481). He was bishop of Tours, but is more widely remembered for his contribution to history. His feast day is November 17.

GREGORY THE GREAT, ST. (540?-604). Especially remembered for his organization of the liturgical chant, still called Gregorian chant, and for sending St. Augustine to Canterbury, England, to evangelize that country, Gregory I, also known as the Great, is memorable for a number of other reasons, as well. He belonged to a wealthy and noble family, but in his middle thirties sold all his possessions, had several monasteries built with the proceeds, and entered one of them. After being a monk, a papal ambassador, and again a monk, he was chosen pope at the death of Pope Pelagius, and occupied that position until his death. He fought heresies strenuously, and was intent on enforcing church displine and reuniting various schismatic groups. He expanded the influence of the church and set an example for the behavior of churchmen with the austerity and devotion of his own life. The feast day of this Doctor of the Church is March 12.

GREY FRIARS. A name given to Franciscan friars in England during medieval times on the strength of the color of the habit. Franciscan habits are now brown.

GRILLE. The grating that divides priest from penitent in the confessional. Its use is obligatory under canon law. The name is also used to designate the grating which separates enclosed nuns from visitors, whether it be a structure only a few feet square or a room divider.

GROTTO OF THE NATIVITY. The cave in Bethlehem in which one account says the birth of Jesus took place. The cave is accepted as an authentically holy place.

GUTENBERG BIBLE. Also called the Mazarin Bible from a copy that was found in the library of Cardinal Mazarin, this was the first book printed by Johann Gutenberg on his newly invented movable-type printing press. It dates from 1456, and is a large folio size book with two columns of forty-two lines each in Gothic type. It is also sometimes called the Forty-two-line Bible.

GUARDIAN ANGEL. The personal angel appointed by God to watch over an individual from birth till death. The guardian angel has the particular function of keeping his charge out of trouble, suggesting good thoughts, and helping in prayer. It is probably accurate to say that guardian angels were once taken far more seriously than is presently the case.

# H

HABAKKUK (Heb.: to embrace; Hab'-ə-kuk). A prophetic book of the Old Testament dating from about 600 B.C. Habakkuk puzzles over why the wicked Hebrews are not punished, and foretells both their punishment by the Chaldeans and the punishment of the Chaldeans as well.

HABIT. The clothing, a type of uniform, of a member of a religious order. Most habits are long and full, although a modern tendency is toward the above-ankle-length habit for women who teach, do hospital work, etc. Common colors are black, brown, or white, though a few orders use bright tones such as the blue of one Benedictine order or the blue and red of Redemptorist nuns.

HABITUAL GRACE. A supernatural quality inherent to, and fixed in, the soul by which men are made the co-heirs of Jesus and truly friends with God. According to Catholic theology (see GRACE), habitual grace is not the same as the indwelling Holy Ghost, for the grace is created and finite, nor is it a "garment" or an imputation of Christ's merits to Catholics as it is in Protestant theology.

HADES. Traditionally, Hades is the place of departed spirits, or the place of the dead. In Christian thought, however, it is used synonymously with Hell, to refer to the place where the souls of the damned dwell.

HAGIOGRAPHY (Gr.: *hagio,* saintly or holy, and derivative of *graphein,* to write; hā'ji-og'-rə-fē). The study of the lives of saints, or the writings of saints' lives.

HAIL MARY. See AVE MARIA.

HAIR SHIRT. A garment made of the hair of an animal, often a

160

goat, worn next to the body as a form of self-mortification. It may be only a belt, or it may be a complete vest or shirtlike covering. In the past, hair shirts were worn by many pilgrims, penitents, and the very devout; they are now worn mostly, if not entirely, by members of religious orders, some of which require them.

HALFWAY COVENANT. A seventeenth-century decision of New England Congregationalists, or Puritans, is called "the Halfway Covenant" because it permitted grandchildren of members to share in the covenant even if the parents themselves had not been converted. The original membership rule allowed only the children of adults who had been converted to the faith to share, not the grandchildren of converted adults, unless, of course, their parents also were converted. There were many objections to this decision, which amounted to liberalizing membership requirements, on the grounds that it was inconceivable that children living in an unconverted household should share in the salvation of the elect. Many members who objected even went so far as seceding from the church in defense of their belief in theocracy and the intimate family circle as the "fortress of Godliness."

HALLELUJAH (Hebrew: *hallelu,* praise, and *yah* or *jah,* Yahweh or Jehovah). An exclamation of joy, or a song of praise to God, meaning literally, "Praise God!"

HALLOWED. Holy, blessed, or made sacred; also, to bless, honor, or regard as holy. In origin, the word is related to "holy" and to the German "heilege."

HALO (Gr.: disk of the sun). A circle or disk of light of supernatural origin around and just over the head. In pre-Christian times it represented majesty and power, and it has come to represent exceptional virtue and grace. Halos are usually reserved to Jesus, Mary, and Joseph (and perhaps angels) in Protestant churches, while the Catholic Church extends the usage to the Agnus Dei, the Holy Ghost, any representation of God, and the saints. "Nimbus" is an alternative term, but infrequently used.

HANC IGITUR (Lat.: hänk-i'-gi-tŭr). The prayer during the Mass that is said when the priest spreads his hands over the bread and wine of the Communion to show that Jesus sacrificed himself for man and took upon himself man's sins.

HARMONY SOCIETY. A religious society founded in Germany in the eighteenth century by George Rapp, leader of German Separatists, so called because of their withdrawal from the established church of the time. The members of the Harmony Society combined economic endeavors with their religion in communal settlements, held all property in common, and practiced strict celibacy.

Settlements in the United States included Harmony, Pennsylvania (1805), New Harmony, Indiana (1815), and Economy, Pennsylvania (1825). Foreseeable difficulties which proved in the end to be unsurmountable included: survival in a near wilderness; the laziness of some members; and the near impossibility of enforcing celibacy in a mixed community. None of the communities remains today in its original economic-religious form, and even the name of Economy has been changed to Ambridge. Harmony and New Harmony are towns of about a thousand inhabitants; the latter was sold in 1825 to Robert Owen who attempted to establish a communistic colony which was even shorter-lived than the "Rappite" experiment.

HARROWING OF HELL. The popular old English name to refer to Jesus' descent into Hell; it is also the name of a medieval mystery play depicting that event.

HEARTH PENNY. A medieval English term for the penny tax placed on every household for the expenses of the Holy See. "Peter's pence," another term for the same thing, now applies to voluntary contributions for the purpose.

HEATHEN. Anyone who follows a religion other than Christianity, Judaism, or Islam. It is often used synonymously with "pagan," although the latter more frequently refers to the heathen of ancient times. As religions were often spread most rapidly in cities, and only lastly into the countryside, both words have their origins in terms that mean country, or wasteland, dwellers, or the country itself.

HEAVEN. Originally, a place somewhere in the sky where God lived and where the souls of the saved went after the body's death. In a more modern sense, "Heaven" often means a state or condition of perfect and eternal happiness into which the pure or blessed souls enter after the body's death and which is characterized by the vision of God, companionship with Jesus and the angels, and, usually, a full understanding of creation and all things.

HEBREWS, EPISTLE TO THE. An epistolary book of the New Testament that was originally attributed to St. Paul. Its aim was to prevent backsliding into, or a too great reliance on, Judaism in the young churches of Jewish converts to Christianity. It also stresses the superiority of Christians over Jews and emphasizes the doctrine of justification by faith.

HEDGE PRIEST. An illiterate and pseudo-priest who wandered about the countryside of Europe and England several centuries ago. Such a "priest" had no ecclesiastical office or permanent church, and was of very low social and economic status.

HELENA, ST. (248?–328). The mother of Constantine the Great, converted to Christianity in 313, later went to Jerusalem and Palestine where she is said to have ordered excavations that located the relics of the true cross. Her feast day is August 18.

HELL. The condition or the place of eternal punishment considered to be the destiny of souls of those who die unrepentent of their sins. Traditional theology holds that punishment consists of deprivation of the vision of God and the infliction of physical pain, and that such punishment is eternal. The Devil, or Satan, is the "ruler" of Hell; Hell has usually been portrayed as a place of flames, although this picture varies somewhat from person to person. Perhaps a more modern viewpoint is that Hell is more a state of mind than a place. At any rate, it is only infrequently located now somewhere deep in the earth, as it once was, and has, with its opposite state, Heaven, become far more spiritual or mental than physical.

HELL-FIRE. Punishment of an extreme nature, perhaps to test courage or competence in some way. The term, of course, is derived from the ancient and persistent image of Hell as a place where punishment is by some form of fire or heat.

HEPTATEUCH (Hep'-tə-to͞ok'). The first seven books of the Bible, i.e., Genesis, Exodus, Leviticus, Numbers, Deuteronomy, Joshua, and Judges. The term is derived from the Greek for "seven" and "book."

HERESY. Any religious belief which is in opposition to the official doctrines of an established church. In practice, most churches, and especially the Catholic, have tended to brand as heresy only the conflicting beliefs which relate to matters so fundamental as to lead to schism were the contrary beliefs allowed to grow freely. Some early Christian heresies, for example, related to belief in the divinity of Christ, the nature of grace, the nature of the Trinity, and the forgiveness of sins. Much blood was shed by equally sincere and devout believers over the various sides of these and similar questions. Many churches passed through a period in their history of rigid and punitive attitudes toward the slightest deviation from doctrine, but in general, as churches grew older and more firmly established with fewer threats to their existence, so their attitudes became more tolerant. And as churches lost or surrendered their power of life and death over members to civil authorities, their ability to act decisively in what were deemed heresy cases was lessened. A clergyman may still be expelled or excommunicated from his church for heresy, as, in theory, may a layman, but it is more common now for the clergyman or the layman to give up membership in the church.

Those who hold contrary religious faiths, for example Christians, Jews, and Moslems, do not generally look upon the others' beliefs as heresy, since heresy by definition originates within a specific church framework. The word itself is derived from a Greek term meaning a taking, or a choosing, and implies the decision, for himself, by a member of a church, about theological truths which are actually within the province of the orthodox churchmen and authorities. See: ALBIGENSIANISM, ARIANISM, CATHARISM, DOCETISM, DONATISM, MANICHAEISM, MONOPHYSITISM, NESTORIANISM, PAULICIANISM, and PELAGIANISM.

HERMAS. An Apostolic Father of the Church, author of writings called *The Shepherd,* a small book of moral teachings and admonitions to penance that was valued almost as scripture in the early Church. By the fourth century, however, the work of Hermas was more and more neglected. Today even the identity of the author and the date of composition are uncertain, though most critics put the latter at about A.D. 150 or a little earlier.

HERMIT (Gr.: desert). A recluse who lives a solitary life, devoting himself entirely to worship and the love of God. "Hermit" may be reserved to refer to a member of an eremitical, or "hermit" order of the Catholic Church. Such religious orders were once fairly numerous and included Carmelites, Carthusians, and the Hermits of St. Augustine and of St. Paul. Today they are rare, and hermit-like living of a permanent type is rare; retreats offer a hermit-like existence but of a very temporary nature. As the Greek derivation of the word shows, desert hermits were the most numerous in ancient times, and their life was one of extreme simplicity, even deprivation and solitude. The true hermit usually eats only once a day, observes perpetual silence, and rarely receives visitors.

HEXAPLA (Hek'-sə-plə). Any volume containing six (Gr.: *hex,* six) versions of the same text arranged side by side in parallel columns, but especially one of the Bible or of the Old or New Testament. The term usually refers to an edition of the Old Testament made by Origen, a Christian philosopher born in Egypt about 185, in which the first column was Hebrew, the next was a Greek transliteration, and the remaining four were Greek versions. Only fragments of this work exist today.

HEXATEUCH (Hek'-sə-tōōk'). The first six books of the Old Testament, that is, Genesis, Exodus, Leviticus, Numbers, Deuteronomy, and Joshua. The name is derived from the Greek *hex,* six, and *teuchos,* book.

HIERARCHY, THE CELESTIAL. The arrangement of the nine groups of celestial, or supernatural, beings: angels, archangels, virtues, powers, principalities, dominations (dominions), thrones, cherubim, and seraphim. Angels and archangels are identified as God's ministers; virtues and dominations as God's servants; principalities and powers as God's agents of strength; and thrones, cherubim, and seraphim as those turned toward God in worship, for they are the closest to the heavenly throne.

HIERURGIA (Gr.: sacred act hī'-ēr-ur'-jē-ə). Any holy or sacred rite or act; specifically, the Mass in the Catholic Church.

HIGH ALTAR. The main altar of a church, traditionally centered in the East arm or at the East side and elevated three steps.

HIGH CHURCH. An Anglican church which is close in ritual and practice to the Catholic. This may include the use of incense, bells, and chant during the worship service as well as genuflexion and making of the sign of the cross. "High Church" may be contrasted to "Low Church" which omits most ritual and symbolism and which emphasizes the Protestant nature of Anglicanism.

HIGH MASS. The "Missa Solemnis" characterized by: A celebrant assisted by a deacon or subdeacon; a choir; servers or acolytes; the use of incense; the singing of various portions of the service and recitation of the whole of the Mass, including what is sung by others. For comparison, see LOW MASS.

HIGHER CRITICISM. See BIBLICAL CRITICISM. In general terms, "Higher Criticism" refers to the asking and answering of questions about the text, significance, meaning, etc., of the Bible, excluding only questions about the authenticity of the text.

HILARY, ST. (310?–c.367). St. Hilary was born in Aquitaine and was converted at about the age of thirty-five to Christianity. He achieved renown as a defender of orthodox belief, best represented by Athanasius, against Arianism, one of the prevalent heresies of the day. He was exiled for a short period of years by the Emperor Constantius, but returned and was chosen bishop of the diocese of Poitiers. He has been credited, probably incorrectly, with composition of the Athanasian Creed. His feast day is January 14.

HILDA, ST. (d. 680). She is the founder of the famous Whitby Abbey in Yorkshire, England, as recounted in Bede's *Ecclesiastical History of England;* one of the preservers and originators of art and literary works, it was at Whitby that the first of the English poets, Caedmon, lived. St. Hilda's feast day is November 18.

HILLEL. A rabbi who lived shortly before the birth of Jesus and who represented a liberal tendency within Judaism as opposed to that of his contemporary, Shammai. His teachings are frequently spoken of as rivals of Jesus', although substantiation for this opinion is meager.

HISTORICAL JESUS. That picture of Jesus and his life which can be called factual, although "The term is somewhat ambiguous because it may mean the actual Jesus or what can now be known about the actual Jesus." (*Theological Terms,* p. 119) Albert Schweitzer's book, *The Quest of the Historical Jesus* (1910), was very influential in this field, for he pointed up the personal bias of historians operative in the nineteenth century re-creation of the man Jesus and his life. It has generally been agreed that the Gospels provide very little sound historical evidence for conclusions regarding anything except the years of Jesus' ministry; even for that period they reveal surprisingly conflicting views of events and about such matters as Jesus' own view of himself. Modern scholarship is still struggling with this problem.

HOLY (Anglo-Saxon *halig,* from *hal,* meaning sound or whole or happy, and akin to German *heilig;* used to translate the Latin *sacer* and *sanctus*). Sacred; belonging to or coming from God; spiritually perfect and sinless; "consecrated" and "hallowed" refer to something or someone that has been made sacred or holy.

HOLY CITY, THE. An honorary name for Jerusalem, or, occasionally, Rome.

HOLY CROSS DAY. September 14 in the calendar of the Catholic Church. It is the feast of the Exaltation of the Cross and marks the dedication of a basilica on the site of the Holy Sepulcher in Jerusalem, itself commemorating the discovery, between 325 and 347, of relics of the True Cross.

HOLY DAY. A religious holiday, one on which attendance at church is obligatory; every Sunday is a Holy Day. See HOLY DAY OF OBLIGATION.

HOLY DAY OF OBLIGATION. In the Catholic Church, this term designates a day of important religious celebration which does not invariably fall on Sunday, which is itself always a Holy Day. Attendance at Mass is required on every Holy Day of Obligation, as it is on Sunday, and other Sunday obligations also obtain. In 1963, Holy Days of Obligation were January 1; Ascension

Day (May 23); the Assumption of the Blessed Virgin Mary (August 15); Feast of All Saints (November 1); and Christmas.

HOLY FAMILY, THE. Jesus, his mother Mary, and his father Joseph.

HOLY FATHER. A title for the pope.

HOLY GHOST. The third person of the Trinity, also called the Comforter (John 14:16) and, especially in modern times, the Holy Spirit. Theologically, the Holy Ghost is held to be "consubstantial," that is, of one and the same substance, and coeternal with the Father and the Son. It was the Holy Ghost which descended upon the Apostles at Pentecost, and which is sent on missions of aid and inspiration by the Father and Son.

HOLY INNOCENTS. This feast day, celebrated on December 28, is also called Holy Children or Childermas. It commemorates the slaughter of the children two years old and under carried out at Herod's order when he was attempting to get rid of the infant Jesus.

HOLY LAND, THE. Palestine. It is so called because it was this land which was promised to the children of Abraham by God.

HOLY NAME OF JESUS. A feast day of this name is observed on the Sunday following January 1, or on January 2 when the first Sunday is January 1, 6, or 7. Honor is paid by all Christians, however, to the name of Jesus, which is reserved to Jesus, the Christ, except in Spanish-speaking countries where it is often given as a baptismal name. It is derived from the Hebrew Jehoshua (Josue or Joshua) and means "(Jahweh) God is salvation."

HOLY OFFICE. In the Catholic Church, a body, previously known as the Inquisition, established to protect faith and morals, root out heresy, and defend orthodoxy.

HOLY OF HOLIES. The innermost part of the Hebrew temple built in the form of a cube to symbolize the wholeness of God. In it is kept the Ark of the Covenant.

HOLY ORDERS. The sacrament, or the rite, of ordination which marks the entry of the candidate into the rank of Holy Orders, that is, into the priesthood or the ministry. Thus, to "take Holy Orders" is to be ordained. The three highest orders of both the Catholic and the Anglican Churches are termed "Holy Orders"; in the Catholic Church these are priests, deacons, and subdeacons, and in the Anglican Church, bishops, priests, and deacons.

HOLY PLACES. The places in Palestine associated with the life and death of Jesus, among them being the Upper Room, Gethsemane, Calvary, the Via Dolorosa, and the Grotto of the Nativity.

HOLY ROLLER. A minor Protestant religious sect which gained some notoriety during the first half of the twentieth century by its violent form of worship. Religious enthusiasm and emotion were demonstrated by shouting, loud singing, and bodily contortions and movements supposed to be as extreme as the enthusiasm was intense. The group was evangelical to an extent, and fundamentalist, but never attained any significant membership beyond the South and Midwest, where it was never large.

HOLY ROOD. The cross on which Jesus was crucified; "rood" is the Anglo-Saxon term for "cross." Also, any representation of this cross.

HOLY SATURDAY. The Saturday in Holy Week, just before Easter Sunday.

HOLY SEE. The episcopal see of Rome; also, the pope, together with those associated with him in the government of the Catholic Church's headquarters.

HOLY SEPULCHER. The site of the burial of Jesus after the crucifixion and before the resurrection; also, now, the church which stands upon this spot.

HOLY SOULS. According to Catholic theology, the souls of the just, or the saved, awaiting in Purgatory the time of their transition to Heaven.

HOLY SPIRIT. See HOLY GHOST.

HOLY STONE. The name given, according to tradition, to the large flat piece of sandstone used to scour a ship's deck for the Sunday worship service held there.

HOLY THURSDAY. Maundy Thursday; the Thursday in Holy Week, before Easter Sunday. Holy Thursday was also the older name for Ascension day.

HOLYTIDE. A holy season; any period that is longer than one day spent in worship.

HOLY WATER. Water which has been blessed by a priest. The Catholic faithful dip the tips of their fingers into a basin, or font holding the holy water, and cross themselves before Mass and usually afterward as well. Symbolically, the action represents the cleansing of the spirit before the worship service; before re-entering the world after it, it is a reminder of that cleansing.

HOLY WEEK. The week preceding Easter including Palm Sunday which commemorates Jesus' entry into Jerusalem; Holy Thursday which commemorates Jesus' washing of the disciples' feet and also the Last Supper; and Holy Saturday, which terminates Lent at noon. Monday, Tuesday, and Wednesday are designated simply "days in Holy Week."

HOLY YEAR. In the Catholic Church, a year when "the Holy See grants an extraordinary plenary indulgence to all throughout the world who shall visit Rome in order to venerate the tombs of the Apostles and the see of Peter, practically all other indulgences being suspended." (*Catholic Dictionary,* p. 235) A Holy Year originally occurred in 1300 and every hundred years thereafter. It was then changed to every fifty years, then to every thirty-three years, and now occurs every twenty-five years.

HOMILY. A short, informal talk on a passage from the Scriptures. It is the oldest form of the sermon, or preaching.

HONORÉ, ST. (sixth century). A bishop in Amiens, France, St. Honoré was honored with a church in Paris in the thirteenth century, and his name is still well known as that of the Rue St. Honoré in that city. His feast day is May 16.

HOOD. The covering for the head of a monk or friar. It is part of the habit and may be either pointed or rounded. It is often erroneously called a cowl, which is a sleeved garment with a hood attached.

HORNS OF THE ALTAR. The corners of any Christian altar. The term is derived from the Latin *cornu,* a projection, with which "horn" is cognate. It originally referred to the projections on an altar in the temple at Jerusalem.

HOSANNA (Heb.: Save, we pray!). A cry of praise to God.

HOSEA (Heb.: salvation). One of the books of the Old Testament, designated as the work of one of the minor prophets of about the eighth century.

HOSPITALERS. Members of a religious and military order which, through the years since its founding in the eleventh century, has been variously called the Order of the Hospital of St. John of Jerusalem, Knights of St. John, Knights of Jerusalem, Knights of Rhodes, Knights of Malta, and Knights of the White Cross.

The order was founded in a hospital in Jerusalem that had been opened to care for pilgrims to the Holy Land. Members took part in the Crusades, and the order accumulated considerable wealth and power which enabled it to found branches throughout Europe. In 1187, when the Saracens took Jerusalem, the order transferred to Acre, then about a century later to Cyprus. By that time it had become almost entirely military; it took Rhodes in 1310, and after the dissolution of the rival order, The Knights Templars, was able to dominate the Mediterranean.

The order was defeated defending Rhodes against Suleiman I in 1522, but in 1530 was given Malta by Emperor Charles V, and the island soon became its headquarters. The Knights of Malta, as it was thereafter called, successfully defended the island against the Turks until the final defeat of the latter at the Battle of Lepanto in 1571. From then until 1798, when Malta was seized by Napoleon, members were concerned primarily with charitable hospital work. When Napoleon was defeated, the order was rendered almost completely inactive; the office of grand master was reinstated in 1879, but there is little resemblance between today's Knights Hospitalers and the old Knights of Malta.

HOST. The Eucharistic bread. The term may also be applied to both the consecrated bread and wine.

HOT CROSS BUNS. Small round buns made of simple ingredients

and marked with a cross, often, now, in white frosting. They were originally eaten on Good Friday, for, being plain food, they were appropriate for a day of penance. Since then, probably no later than two or three hundred years ago, they have become less plain and now usually contain raisins, candied fruit, and the white cross.

HOURS, CANONICAL. See CANONICAL HOURS.

HOUSEL. A medieval name for the Eucharist, perhaps derived from a form of "holy."

HOUSELING-CLOTH. A medieval term for a white linen cloth that was attached to altar rails to be held up under the chin of a communicant to catch any of the Communion bread, should it be dropped. The expression is derived from Housel, a name for the Eucharist.

HOUSE OF GOD. The church building, especially the sanctuary; also, Heaven, or the condition of the souls of the saved after the body's death, as "In my Father's house are many mansions."

HUMERAL VEIL. A wide scarf some eight feet in length that is a portion of the vestments of a subdeacon at High Mass. Its name is derived from the Latin *humerus,* shoulder, and it is worn over the shoulders like a shawl. The usual color is white, but it matches other vestments at Mass.

HUGH OF GRENOBLE, ST. (1053–1131). This saint, for fifty years bishop of Grenoble, was renowned for his austerities and kindnesses. He was also instrumental in founding the Grande Chartreuse, with St. Bruno, an abbey which was the main house of the Carthusians until they were expelled from France in 1903. His feast day is April 1.

HUMILITY. A moral virtue that is considered necessary if all the rest are to follow. False humility and self-denigration are foreign to true humility which by definition allows a man to recognize and appreciate his limits, no matter how broad or how narrow they may be, though not to be proud or self-assertive.

HUSS, JOHN (1369–1415). A Czechoslovakian religious reform-er who held many of the same views as John Wyclif, an English reformer of about the same time, by whom he was influenced. In 1403, Wyclif's doctrines, including the assertions that Jesus was man's only overlord; that the clergy should not own property; that many Church doctrines (and especially transubstantiation) were false; and that the Scriptures were the supreme authority, were condemned by the University of Prague. Huss opposed the university's action, but in 1409 was made rector there, primarily through his support of the rulers of the country, Emperor Wenceslaus and Queen Sophia.

He was not supported by the clergy, however, and won their hostility, particularly that of Baldassarre Cossa, Antipope John XXIII, who excommunicated him. Nevertheless, Huss attended the Council of Constance (1414–1418) with the protection of a safe conduct from Emperor Sigismund, a German king and the brother of Emperor Wenceslaus, and hoped to be able to present his views and help initiate Church reforms. Instead, he was convicted of heresy, in spite of the safe conduct, and was subsequently burned at the stake. After Huss' death his followers continued his work, which included demanding changes in the Communion, freedom of preaching, civil punishment for mortal sins, and limitation of property ownership by the Church.

HYMN (Gr.: a religious song). A song of religious character and message suitable for church singing. It is sometimes made up of many verses, and a large body of modern hymns are verses set to music. Others are psalms or other Scriptures for which music, some of it closely resembling plain song, has been composed. The origin of some compositions has been lost in antiquity. To generalize, Protestant churches use more of the popularized, verse-type hymns, while the Catholic Church uses more of the older, Latin-based, or psalm-based hymns. Of modern origin is the broadening of the concept "suitable for church singing" to include jazz composition or other music in the modern idiom.

HYPERDULIA. In the Catholic Church, the special homage paid to Mary as the mother of Jesus and thus greater than the saints who receive the *dulia.*

HYPOSTATIC UNION. The technical theological term referring to the union of God and man in the person of Jesus. The two natures are held to be inseparably joined yet still distinct.

# *I*

ICON (Gr.: image). Technically, any image, but used almost exclusively to refer to the flat religious paintings used in Eastern churches in the place of statues. In Greek, Russian, and other Eastern churches, icons receive much more attention than do statues in Western churches, often being incensed, kissed, and carried reverently in processions. Our common word "iconoclasm" originally meant the belief, deemed heretical by the orthodox, that veneration of icons was unlawful, and it may still be translated "image-breaker."

IDOL. Any image, thing, or person other than God which is worshipped. "Graven images" such as religious statues, the crucifix, etc., are not idols for they are not worshipped.

IDOLATRY. The worship of anything or person other than God, i.e., the worship of an idol.

IGNATIUS, ST. (50?–109?). One of the early martyrs of the Christian faith, Ignatius was the third bishop of Antioch. While on his way to Rome, where he was condemned to fight the lions in the amphitheater, he addressed many letters to the early churches, and a number have survived; that to the Romans is one of the best examples of early Christian writings. His feast day is February 1.

IGNATIUS LOYOLA, ST. (1491–1556). The founder of the Society of Jesus, or Jesuits, was a Spanish courtier before entering the Church. He and a small group of friends took the vows of chastity and poverty, and he remained general of the order until his death. Although his first interests were foreign missions and the education of boys, he was also a leader in the Catholic Reform

174

movement, a mystic, and a writer of considerable skill. His work called the *Formula,* and, in a revised form, the *Constitutions,* is the charter of the Jesuits to this day. His feast day is July 31.

I.H.S. The possible meanings of this monogram are rather numerous. It has often been said to refer to the Latin phrase *In Hoc Signo (Vinces)*, "in this sign," that is, the cross, "conquer." It may also represent the first letters of the Latin *In Hoc Salus,* "in this," that is, the cross, "salvation," or *Jesus Hominum Salvator,* "Jesus, Savior of Men." When written IHS it may represent a monogram of the name Jesus in Greek, or, in the same language, the initial letter of Jesus and of Christ with a cross in between.

IMAGE. A sculpture, painting or other representation of a person or thing related to religious belief. The term is applied especially to statues and is often used to refer to an idol.

IMAGE OF GOD. The likeness to God in which man was created according to Genesis 1:26 ff has given theologians much cause for puzzlement over the years. Traditionally, man was held to be created in the physical image of God. However, modern belief in general holds that the "image" is in man's spirit, intellect and reason which are like God's rather than in physical resemblance to the Deity, but this is not by any means a unanimous opinion. Catholics, Protestants, and Protestants among themselves disagree over the extent of the loss of this "image of God" in the Fall, a dispute which is far from settled.

IMMACULATE CONCEPTION. The Catholic doctrine that Mary the mother of Jesus, from the moment of her conception or from the moment of her soul's creation, was preserved exempt from all stain of original sin. The doctrine of the Immaculate Conception does not imply that Mary was conceived in any way other than the normal human manner, nor does it have anything to do with the virgin birth, although Protestants often confuse the two. The doctrine was long gaining acceptance, although the event was commemorated as early as the tenth century. Thomas Aquinas, among others, would not agree that Mary was exempted from original sin, and it was not until 1854 that it was finally proclaimed as an article of faith. The feast day of the Immaculate Conception is December 8.

IMMANENCE. This technical term refers to the concept of a God who is indwelling and near, in the creation and the universe, ever preserving, activating, and moving man's life and soul. The concept termed "transcendence," on the other hand, may refer to God as transcendent, that is, to a degree separate from, above, remote from the world, though nonetheless the source of being. This latter idea, though it does not rule out the possibility of God actively participating in and affecting man's daily life, tends to lead to a view of God as totally distant and unknowable.

IMMANUEL (Heb.: God with us). A name often applied to Jesus, as in Matthew 1:23, and a name by which Isaiah referred to the Messiah (Is. 7:14).

IMMERSION. Baptism by total, or nearly total, submersion or dipping of the candidate in water.

IMMORTALITY. The quality of being free from death. Only a living being that was capable of resisting all external forces (indestructible) and that was free from internal destructive forces (incorruptible) could be immortal. To the best of human knowledge, no such being exists.

IMMORTALITY OF THE SOUL. The freedom of the soul from death; its survival after the death of the body. This basic doctrine has the support of many arguments, including that of having been proved syllogistically.

IMMOVABLE FEAST. Any religious feast day set for a certain date, as Christmas is December 25, in contrast to the movable feasts such as Easter.

IMPENITENCE, FINAL. Remaining impenitent for grievous sins at the time of death. This is often interpreted as "the sin against the Holy Ghost," and as "the unforgivable sin," since forgiveness without repentence is usually deemed impossible.

IMPOSITION OF HANDS. The laying on of hands, most often a term used to refer to the bishop's placing of his hands on the head of a candidate for confirmation. It may also refer to the laying on of hands by a minister, priest, or bishop in other ceremonies and rites such as ordination, absolution, or prayer. It follows Jesus' practice and in general is to convey a spiritual gift, power, or aid toward recovery from spiritual, mental, or physical weakness.

IMPRIMATUR. The license of a Catholic bishop or delegate which authorizes a book to be printed. In Latin the word means "let it be printed," and the possession of an imprimatur implies official Catholic Church sanction.

INCARNATION. The taking on of human nature by God the Son, i.e., the Word made flesh, so that the man so created was a true human being with body, soul, and will.

INCENSE. The use of incense in the Catholic Church Mass and in some Anglican churches occurs only during solemn, sung services. Such smoke symbolizes prayer, and the rising of prayers to God. Use of incense probably originated as early as 500; the incensing of altar, the people, etc., is recorded in the ninth century.

INDEX, THE. The *Index of Forbidden Books.* See FORBIDDEN BOOKS, INDEX OF. Another *Index,* the *Index Expurgatorius,* is a list of passages from books, the deletion of which makes the book from which it is taken freely readable.

INDULGENCE. According to Catholic teaching, an indulgence is "The remission before God of the temporal punishment due to those sins of which the guilt has been forgiven, either in the sacrament of Penance or because of an act of perfect contrition, granted by the competent ecclesiastical authority out of the Treasury of the Church to the living by way of absolution, to the dead by way of suffrage." (*Catholic Dictionary,* p. 252). Three characteristics of indulgences that often disturb non-Catholics are (1) the recollection that during corrupt medieval times, many priests grew wealthy from selling indulgences; (2) the feeling that an indulgence is somehow permission to sin; (3) the use of time periods in the granting of indulgence, as a cardinal may grant two hundred days remission, a bishop fifty days, etc. In answer to these, the Catholic replies that now it is deemed the sin of simony to traffic in indulgences and any who practice it incur excommunication; it is necessary to be in a state of grace to gain even the smallest indulgence, so that it is far from being permission to sin; and the time periods are a holdover from older times when actual penitential discipline was the rule, and the Church itself does not define the time periods in modern terms.

INFALLIBILITY. The doctrine of the Catholic Church which states that it is preserved free from the possibility of error in definitive teachings about faith and morals. Infallibility involves preservation and interpretation of truths, not inspiration or revelation of new truths or dogmas. The "infallibility of the Pope" is exercised when the Pope speaks *ex cathedra;* it was declared to be dogma only in 1870.

INFANT. Any child before the age of reason, usually seven years old, or any adult without complete mental faculties.

INFANT, THE. The baby Jesus is referred to whenever "Infant" or "The Infant" is capitalized.

INFANT, UNBAPTIZED. According to the teaching of the Catholic Church, the soul of an unbaptized infant does not go to Heaven because it has not had original sin remitted through baptism, but the soul does enjoy perfect natural happiness in limbo, lacking the vision of God, but loving and knowing Him without grief. Most other churches teach that the souls of unbaptized babies go to Heaven.

INFIDEL (Lat.: not faithful). One who does not believe in the religion most prevalent in his area; usually, a non-Christian to the Western world.

INFINITE, THE. A term for God; one whose being and perfection have no limit, i.e., are not finite or circumscribed.

INFUSION. A method of baptism by the pouring of water onto the head; also called "affusion," the more correct term.

IN HOC SIGNO VINCES. See I.H.S.

INNOCENCE, ORIGINAL. The state of man before the Fall; man without sin or the knowledge of good and evil.

INQUISITION. An ecclesiastical tribunal instituted for the purpose of discovering heresy and endowed with the power to punish heretics. In past centuries, the Catholic Church used the inquisitorial method to discourage heresy, and the surviving body, the Holy Office, or Sacred Congregation of the Holy Office, though it has vastly reduced powers, still exists in part to judge heresy.

The Spanish Inquisition, undoubtedly the best known, was not the first inquisition. The Holy Roman and Universal Inquisition was originated in the thirteenth century for the purpose of dealing with heresy in any part of Europe, but its French branch was particularly vicious. A more lenient attitude distinguished the special Roman Inquisition begun in 1542 as the doctrinal tribunal for the world, and it in time became the aforementioned Holy Office. The Spanish Inquisition, set up by King Ferdinand and Queen Isabella in 1478 to act against lapsed converts from Judaism, Christian Moors in danger of apostasy, and others, was influenced by and cooperated with civil authorities, punishing people for bigamy, perjury, forgery, and other offenses not strictly heretical. It often acted in defiance of Rome, where complaints of its severity were soon received. Nevertheless, it spread to South America, and in Spain it was sufficiently active to prevent the rise of Protestantism until the seventeenth century, its last revival there not occurring until the early nineteenth century.

**I.N.R.I.** The initials of the Latin words *Jesus Nazarenus, Rex Judaeorum,* i.e., Jesus of Nazareth, King of the Jews.

INSPIRATION OF THE SCRIPTURES. In general, the Bible is taken as the Word of God, but within this acceptance there exists a wide range of differing opinions. The Catholic view is that the book was supernaturally inspired so that each writer has, in a sense, "held the pen for God." This is also the fundamentalist or conservative Protestant viewpoint, which, indeed, usually goes much further than the Catholic in defense of the literal truth of the Bible, maintaining that every word in it is sacrosanct. Other views hold that the Bible is divinely inspired, but that some parts are more divinely inspired than others. Luther, for instance, established an inner standard and criticized the prophets as being in error, the reliability of the Book of Chronicles, the canonical acceptance of Esther, and the equal value of the Synoptic Gospels. Modern biblical criticism has made it more difficult to defend the view that every word was from God, but admitting errors and contradictions once, opens the door to distrust of the entire work, and even liberal Protestants are reluctant to do this though they feel that the Bible is the creative work of religious geniuses rather than of divine origin. The view of the Bible as witness to the Word of God but not entirely infallible in every text is one compromise which helps the book retain considerable authority without denying the finds of scholars.

INSTRUMENTS OF THE PASSION. The articles employed in Jesus' death, such as the cross, hammer, nails, and spear.

INTERCESSION. The praying by one person for another, that is, when one intercedes on behalf of another. Such concern of human beings one for another is recommended by St. Paul in the form of "supplications, prayers, intercessions, and giving of thanks." (1 Timothy 2:1)

INTERMEDIATE STATE. The state of the soul between the death of the body and the final judgment What this state is, whether conscious, purified, reformed, or something other than any of these, has been a matter of considerable debate.

INTINCTION. A manner of receiving Communion in which the Eucharistic bread is dipped into the wine and so administered. This practice was common in the West from the seventh to the eleventh century, and survives today in the East.

INTROIT (Lat.: entrance). The beginning of the service in the Catholic and Anglican churches, consisting, in the former, of a psalm verse, an antiphon, and part of the Proper, or variable part, of the Mass, and in the latter of a hymn or psalm that is sung or played. The choir may sing it during the procession from the sacristy, or while the celebrant says the preparatory prayers. Other Protestant churches besides the Anglican may now begin their worship services with the Introit also, usually a hymn by the choir.

INVENTION OF THE HOLY CROSS. The discovery of the relics of the Cross by St. Helena is commemorated on May 3.

IRRESISTIBLE GRACE. The essentially Calvinistic tenet that God's grace is irresistible, and that man, though free from physical necessity to respond to it, is literally forced to do so by the grace he is given. Catholic theology counters the idea with the tenet of "cooperation," and the possibility of the free will of man to accept or to reject God's grace.

ISAIAH (Heb.: Yahweh is salvation). Isaiah, one of the great prophets of the Old Testament, lived and wrote this book of the Bible in the sixth century before Christ. The book is especially honored for passages on the Prince of Peace, 9:2–7. Chapters 40–66 are now believed by scholars to have been the work of another writer often called the Unknown Prophet; they contain the famous Messianic prophecy and the Song of the Suffering Servant.

ITALA VETUS (Lat.: old Italian). The Old Latin version of the Bible used in the Western Church until St. Jerome's *Vulgate* of the fourth century replaced it. The New Testament in the *Vulgate* is very close to that in the *Itala Vetus,* which is, itself, almost a verbatim setting over into Latin from Greek. Most of the rest of the *Vulgate,* however, St. Jerome himself translated.

IVES, ST. (1253–1303). A Breton, St. Ives was an ecclesiastical lawyer and judge renowned for his fairness. He lived modestly and cared for the poor and the orphans in his family's manor. His feast day is May 19.

JACOBA (JACQUELINE), ST. (d. 1273). A member of the Roman nobility, Jacoba was a close friend of St. Francis of Assisi. Though she never entered the religious life but stayed in the world and raised two sons after her husband's death, she was energetically devout. Her feast day is February 8.

JAHVEH. A Hebrew name for God, also spelled Yahweh; probably a more correct rendering than "Jehovah" of the Hebraic JHVH, those letters used to represent the name of God which could not be spoken.

JAMES, EPISTLE OF. An epistolary book of the New Testament which was apparently written to counterbalance St. Paul's idea of justification by faith. James stresses the need for works and includes the well-known "be ye doers of the word, and not hearers only," and "faith without works is dead." It also contains the source for the sacrament of extreme unction.

The author of this book may have been the apostle James the Less, or he may have been James, the brother (or kinsman) of Jesus and head of the Church in Jerusalem. In turn, these two may or may not be one and the same. At any rate, it has not been held to be the work of James the Greater, the brother of John.

JAMES THE GREATER, ST. (d. A.D. 42). A brother of John the Apostle and son of Zebedee, James is called "the Greater" because he became an apostle of Jesus earlier than James the Less. He was the first apostle, or among the first, to die a martyr. He is the patron saint of Spain, where he is called Santiago. His feast day is July 25.

JAMES THE LESS, ST. (first century). This James is called "the Less" because he did not become an apostle of Jesus as early in

the latter's ministry as did James the Greater. He is reported
to have been the son of Alphaeus, and also the brother of Jesus
(Gal. 1:19); although an alternative reading substitutes "kinsman of Jesus," there still exists the possibility that James the Less
was the son of Alphaeus and the author of the Epistle of James,
and that another James entirely was Jesus' kinsman and the head
of the Church in Jerusalem. The feast day of James the Less is
May 1.

JANUARIUS, ST. (d. 305). Probably the most popular patron of
Naples, St. Januarius, a bishop, died a martyr's death by beheading during the persecution of Diocletian. His body and two
phials of his blood are now in Naples; the liquefaction of the
blood three times each year is held to be miraculous. The dates
are September 19, the saint's feast day; December 16, the date
of the eruption of Vesuvius in 1631 from which Neapolitans believe St. Januarius preserved them; and the first Sunday in May,
the anniversary of the removal of the saint's relics from their
first resting place to the present spot. The liquefaction consists
of the blood changing from a more to a less solid state to a more
or less liquid state with a noticeable increase in the amount appearing to take place at the same time. This ranks, perhaps, as
the most famous continuing miracle of the Western world. The
feast day of St. Januarius is September 19.

JEHOVAH. The modern rendering of the ancient Hebraic name
for God, which could not be spoken or written because it was
so holy, but which was represented by JHVH or YHWH, or any
of several similar consonant constructions called Tetragramma-
tons, or "four letters." "Jehovah" is made from JHVH by in-
serting between the consonants the vowels of the word Elohim
or Adonai (God) somewhat arbitrarily to achieve a pronounceable
word.

JEREMIAH. A prophetical book of the Old Testament named for
its author who lived and wrote around 600 B.C. It is distinguished
by its gloom, for the author held little hope for his nation and
emphasized the value of personal righteousness in the face of the
nation's wickedness, which he denounced. In English, a "jere-
miad" is a lamentation or a woeful complaint.

JEHOVAH'S WITNESSES. A highly evangelistic and Bible-centered Protestant sect which was founded in 1872 in the United States by Charles Taze Russell; followers were first known as Russellites. The members call themselves primitive Christians and consider each to be a minister. Belief centers around acceptance of the Second Coming as imminent. Present membership is about half a million. Jehovah's Witnesses have encountered difficulties with the federal government, for their belief that the Kingdom of Christ will soon replace all earthly authority has led them to deny the authority of federal law.

JEROME, ST. (347–419?). One of the Latin Doctors of the Church, St. Jerome is justly famed for his biblical editing and translating which resulted in the *Vulgate*, or common edition, the earliest version of the entire Bible extant and still an official Latin version of the Bible for Catholics. Jerome was a scholar before a vision led him to reject pagan studies and devote himself to religion. He studied first in solitude in the desert, then under St. Gregory Nazianzen, and it was at the request of the pope that he began his work on the Bible. His feast day is September 30.

JESSE WINDOW. A stained-glass window showing the individuals of Jesus' family tree. The name is derived from Jesse, the father of David.

JESUITS. The largest of the Catholic religious orders, the Society of Jesus is especially noted for the fine quality of the members' training and education. The order was founded by Ignatius Loyola in 1534, with the concept that members should be "soldiers of Christ," and with the purposes of establishing foreign missions and educating boys and young men. Another duty, however, was to be at the pope's call for whatever work needed to be done, and in the past this was often the order's primary function. During the sixteenth and seventeenth centuries much jealousy was aroused among princes and other orders toward the Jesuits because of this closeness with the Holy See. Stories of commercialism, secrecy, scandal, and the like eventually were spread, and during the eighteenth century the princes successfully worked for the suppression of the order in Portugal, France, and the Spanish dominions. In 1773, Pope Clement XIV was forced to dissolve it. However, it survived in Russia and Prussia because both Catharine the Great and Frederick the Great refused to publish the papal brief ordering suppression, and it was reestablished more or less by popular demand in 1814. Since that time it has flourished and enjoys an excellent reputation, perhaps especially for its schools and colleges; among the latter in the United States are Fordham, Loyola, and Georgetown.

JESUS (Heb.: God is salvation). The given name of the baby born to Mary and Joseph; the Son of God, called "Christ," i.e., "anointed" or "Messiah," and held by Christians to be the incarnation of the second person of the Trinity. The historicity of Jesus has been questioned since the nineteenth century, but generally accepted are at least the basic facts of his life. He was born to Mary and Joseph at a time of considerable unrest in Jewish history. Although the year is called A.D. 1, historical events indicate that it was, by this reckoning, more likely to have fallen between 8 and 4 B.C. Little is known of Jesus until he was approximately thirty years old, at which time he began his ministry. John the Baptist, a messianic prophet, had been in the wilderness, urging Jews to repent and prepare for the coming of the Messiah. Jesus, also, was baptized by John, and after a period of meditation began his work of preaching and teaching. He continued in this way for some three years, posing something of a problem to the Pharisees and scribes who adhered strictly to the Mosaic law and were rigidly orthodox. Through the agency of such as these, Jesus was arrested as a troublemaker, the event which terminated in his crucifixion. See also HOLY NAME OF JESUS.

JOACHIM, ST. (first century). According to tradition, St. Joachim was the husband of St. Anne and the father of Mary, Jesus' mother.

JOAN OF ARC, ST. (1412–1431). The Maid of Orleans, the daughter of a farmer, successfully turned the tide of the Hundred Years War, and had the Dauphin, now King Charles, been more energetic, would probably have pushed her military accomplishments even further. As it was, she succeeded in leading troops against Rheims and having the king crowned there. St. Joan was captured by the Burgundians, sold to the English, tried and found guilty of heresy and sorcery, and burned at the stake. Throughout her military career, she never ceased to maintain that she had been inspired by the visions she had seen and the voices she had heard, of St. Michael, St. Catherine, and St. Margaret. The results of the first trial, which had been highly irregular, were set aside in a new trial some twenty-five years later. She was canonized in 1920; her feast day is May 30.

JOAN, POPE. See POPE JOAN.

JOB (Heb.: One persecuted). The Book of Job in the Old Testament dates from approximately 350 B.C. It poses the question: Why are the innocent made to suffer? The book is largely philosophical drama in poetic form, and is believed to have been influenced by Greek tragedy, although it was not, of course, meant to be acted out. The answer to its question, barring a contradictory "happy ending" that reverses Job's punishment, is that man is presumptuous to ask the question in the first place; that why the innocent suffer is a question that cannot be answered by man and that man must not question the ways of God.

JOEL (Heb.: God is strength). A very short and early prophetical book of the Old Testament dating from about 750 B.C. It is famous for a description of a plague of locusts and a prophecy of a Messiah (2:28–32 and 3).

JOHN, EPISTLES OF. The First, Second and Third Epistles of John in the New Testament are usually attributed to St. John the Apostle. 1 John discusses blending of the mystical and the practical in a religion; 2 John is a very short, seemingly personal, letter which admonishes the receiver to be wary of those who do not recognize the historicity of Jesus, and is the Bible's shortest book; 3 John is a protest against some church's failure to receive a missionary as it should have.

JOHN, GOSPEL OF ST. The one of the four gospels of the New Testament which is not considered synoptic, i.e., it is the one which differs from its companion gospels. The Gospel of St. John is now believed to have been written between A.D. 100 and 125, too late for St. John the Apostle to have been the author. The book emphasizes the divinity of Jesus and shows a Greek influence in the doctrine of the Logos, or Word. It is mostly philosophical, whereas Matthew, Mark, and Luke are biographical and are very similar to each other. In John, the emphasis is placed on the mystical nature of Jesus as evidenced in the events of his life; the continuing influence of Jesus is stressed, and his existence as God and man is spelled out for the first time. St. John the Apostle, originally believed to be the author, is called the Divine, the Beloved Disciple, or the Theologian, and was once thought to be the only one of the apostles not to die a martyr. He is believed to be the author of the Epistles of St. John and, also, by some, of Revelation.

JOHN BEFORE THE LATIN GATE, ST. Celebrated on May 6, this feast commemorates a reputed event in the life of St. John the Apostle. It is said that St. John escaped unhurt from submersion in boiling water before a Roman gate.

JOHN DAMASCENE, ST. (c. 675–749). St. John Damascene, or John of Damascus, was a Syrian by birth. After having been raised in the caliph's court in Damascus, he entered a monastery and lived there the rest of his life, writing works which opposed the iconoclasm of the day and his large doctrinal masterpiece *The Fountain of Wisdom*. He is one of the Doctors of the Church; his feast day is March 27.

JOHN OF EGYPT, ST. (d. 394). St. John was originally a shoemaker, work which he left to follow a hermit who made him do a great deal of hard labor. Some years after the hermit's death, John entered a walled cell on a rock near Lycopolis and lived therein the life of a desert hermit for the rest of his life, about forty-eight years. His feast day is March 27.

JOHN OF GOD, ST. (1495–1550). The life of St. John, born John Ciudad, was nothing if not complex. He ran away from his home in Portugal while still a young boy in the hope of finding works of charity to do in Madrid. But he never reached the city; instead, he was found, lost, exhausted, and famished, and became a shepherd for a farmer in Spain. Over the years, he did well, and the farmer offered him his daughter in marriage, a proposal which drove John, terrified, into the army. There, living a camp life, he lost his piety, but he regained it later when he believed the

Virgin saved him from the hanging to which he had been sentenced. Instead of being hung he was dismissed from the service. Thereupon he returned to the farmer, only to flee again when the man renewed the offer of his daughter's hand. His return to his native Portuguese village, where he found that both of his parents had died, his father as a Franciscan, seemed to give his erratic course some direction. He began to devote himself to the poor, to prisoners, to the destitute and the unfortunate, wherever they were to be found. He began with no funds at all, selling firewood to raise money, but help came finally from various individuals, and according to St. John, from angels as well. In 1537, he began the institute which was formalized in 1550 and approved by the pope in 1586, the Brothers of St. John of God or the Hospitalers of St.-John-of-God. His feast day is March 8.

JOHN OF THE CROSS, ST. (1542–1591). One of the later Doctors of the Church, John Yepes, born in Avila, Spain, is recognized as one of the outstanding mystics and poets among Catholic churchmen. He was a close friend and the confessor of St. Theresa of Avila, and, with her, led a reform movement within the Carmelite order, of which he was a member, which resulted in the founding of the Discalced Carmelites. His feast day is November 24.

JOHN THE APOSTLE. ST. (first century). Also called John the Divine, (theologian), John the Evangelist or the Beloved Disciple, John was the brother of James and the son of Zebedee and the author of 1, 2, 3 Epistles of John. He undoubtedly was not the author of the Gospel according to St. John, since the date of that work is between 100 and 125 and St. John died in about 100, according to tradition, or, according to some scholars, as early as 70. He is, by the orthodox, generally held to be the author of Revelation, but again this seems unlikely to scholars, although the author of that book of the Bible was definitely named John. It was to John that Jesus committed Mary, and John throughout the gospels appears with Peter and James as a leading figure. He probably died a martyr's death, for his name appears among the martyrs on an early list and is omitted from a list of apostles who did not die martyrs (Matthew, Philip, Thomas, and Levi), but traditional accounts say that he was the only apostle to die a peaceful death. His feast day is December 27.

JOHN THE BAPTIST, ST. (first century). This ascetic preacher, son of Elizabeth and Zacharias, urged Jews to repent and prepare for the coming of the Messiah, and it was he who baptized Jesus, his cousin, before the latter began his own ministry. St. John died by beheading at the urging of Herodias and Salome; his full story, and his relationship to Jesus, is told in Luke 1 and 3 and other gospels as well. His birthday, June 24, is his official feast day, but the day of his death is commemorated on August 29.

JONAH. This book of the Old Testament is, in essence, a moral tale recounting religious and ethical lessons. It is primarily remembered for its account of Jonah in the whale's stomach, which may or may not be taken literally, but which is sometimes also interpreted as a type of the death and resurrection of Jesus. The book dates from about 275 B.C.

JOSEPH OF ARIMATHEA (Ar-i-mɔ-thē'ɔ). The man who provided a decent tomb in which the body of the crucified Jesus could be buried. The story is recounted in Matthew 27:57-61 and the other gospels as well. Nothing beyond this is known of the man, but many legends have grown up around his name. For some of these, see GLASTONBURY THORN and GRAIL.

JOSEPH, ST. (first century). All that is known of the father, or, as he is often called, the foster father, of Jesus is recounted in the gospels, especially Matthew and Luke. He was, evidently, an older man, a carpenter by trade, and a member of the house of David. Nothing is mentioned of him after the account of the young Jesus in the temple, but it is assumed that he died before Jesus, since Mary was commended to the care of St. John the Apostle by Jesus as he hung on the Cross. St. Joseph's feast day is March 19.

JOSHUA. This historical book of the Old Testament, the final one in the Hexateuch, dates probably from about 350 B.C., though some of the Hexateuch was written as early as 950 B.C. It is famous for its account of the fall of the walls of Jericho.

JOYFUL MYSTERIES. See JOYS OF MARY.

JOYS OF MARY, THE. Usually numbered at seven, though sometimes as few as five or more than twelve, the Joys of Mary are the Annunciation, Visitation, Nativity, Epiphany, Finding in the

Temple, Resurrection, and Ascension. An old English carol notes seven more homey joys: Suckling the baby Jesus; Jesus curing the lame; curing the blind; reading the Bible; raising the dead; and the last two of the above list.

JUBILATE DEO (Lat.: Rejoice unto the Lord; jōō′bə-lä′tā-dā′ō). The opening Latin words of the hymn known by this name, and also the One Hundredth psalm, usually called simply the "Jubilate," which opens "Make a joyful noise unto the Lord, . . . "

JUBILATE SUNDAY. In the Catholic Church calendar, the third Sunday after Easter, named after the first word of the introit.

JUBILEE. A celebration of some sort; specifically, in Jewish history, a year-long celebration held every fiftieth year, when bondsmen were freed, mortgaged lands were restored to owners, and other similar legal releases were granted. In Catholic theology, a jubilee year occurs now every twenty-fifth year, and during it sin is remitted on certain conditions. (See HOLY YEAR) The origin of the word is probably in the Hebrew *yobel* which is the word for ram, since a ram's horn was blown to announce the year.

JUDE. The Epistle of St. Jude is an epistolary book of the New Testament attributed to Jude the Apostle. It is only twenty-five verses in length and is a warning to the faithful to beware of false moral teachings and heresy. Jude was really named Judas, but was called "Jude" or "Lebaeus" or "Thaddeus" to avoid confusion with Judas Iscariot. It was he who asked Jesus the unanswerable question at the Last Supper: Why was it that Jesus manifested himself to them and not to the world? (John 14:22) According to one tradition, Jude, with the apostle Simon, became a martyr in Persia. Their feast day is October 28.

JUDGES. A book of the Old Testament which was probably written as early as 850 B.C. to recount the history of the Hebrews after Joshua's death and during the rule of the judges. It is especially famous for its story of Samson.

JUDGMENT, PARTICULAR. The judgment made on each soul immediately after the death of the body. Traditionally, Protestants believe that the soul is then sent to Heaven, or Hell, while Catholics include Purgatory. The particular judgment is not changed at the Last Judgment, but is confirmed. The intermediate state of the soul between the death of the body and the Last Judgment has always interested certain theologians; see INTERMEDIATE STATE.

JUDGMENT DAY. The "last day" when all the dead shall rise to be finally judged with the living, and the destiny, Heaven or Hell, of each confirmed once and for all. It is also called the Final or Last Judgment, Doomsday, or some similar name that indicates its nature.

JUDITH (Heb.: Jewess). A book of the Apocrypha which tells the story of the beautiful and wise Judith who succeeds in gaining the favor of the enemy Holofernes in order to be admitted to his tent, where she beheads him.

JULIAN OF LEMANS, ST. (d. 250). The story of St. Julian is a mixture of fact and legend, and it is almost impossible to tell which is which. He was, evidently, the first bishop of Le Mans, and he was certainly a powerful influence in converting to Christianity a sizeable portion of France that was still pagan. Some, however, feel that his time was earlier and identify him with Simon the Leper who is mentioned in Matthew 26:6. His feast day is January 27.

JUSTICE. Justice, in the Christian context, probably refers most frequently to a characteristic of God which contains ideas of impartiality, righteousness, fairness, correctness, and the administration of rewards and penalties precisely as deserved. "Justice" may also refer to the defining name of the fair relationship which exists between man and man, and as such, St. Thomas Aquinas regarded it as one of the cardinal virtues. It may also refer to the righteousness of man that has been lost through sin, although it probably occurs less frequently in this context than in either of the other two.

JUSTIFICATION. The bringing back of a man into a proper relationship with God; the "saving" of a man or a soul. Catholics see this as a literal making just of the sinner through the receipt or infusion of grace that obliterates sin, regenerates the soul, and makes it worthy of God. Protestants see justification not as the infusion of grace to make the soul worthy of forgiveness, but rather as the act of divine forgiveness itself, given because of the merits of Jesus, so that an unworthy man no longer has his sins counted against him. In effect, it might be said that the Catholic position demands more cooperation from the individual and leaves him in a literally better condition than he started out, while the Protestant demands somewhat less of a man, emphasizes his perpetual unworthiness, and maintains that nevertheless he is forgiven.

JUSTIFICATION BY FAITH. The doctrine of some Protestant denominations that faith alone justifies, or saves, a man, and that the justifying faith is merely a certain confidence in the divine mercy. The necessity of good works is entirely ruled out, and James 2:24 and 26, which includes the phrase, "Faith without works is dead," is ignored. The doctrine was advanced by Luther and Calvin, who were reacting to the Catholic Church of their day which seemed to place too great stress on the supernatural power of the sacraments and too little on faith. The modern argument for justification by faith is quite similar, though modified somewhat. Catholics feel, on the other hand, that justification by faith "vitiates the Justice of God, who ordained human life so that good works merit salvation, and destroys the intrinsic importance of the sacraments." (*Theological Terms,* p. 137)

JUSTIN MARTYR, ST. (100?–165?). One of the Apostolic Fathers, Justin was born in Palestine a pagan, and was converted to Christianity after finding the Epicureans, Stoics, Peripatetics, and Pythagoreans all unsatisfactory. He was converted by an old man in Ephesus, but had, just prior to this, found more peace for his soul in Platonism than he had in any of the other philosophies. He left two main works, one called the *Dialogue,* which is a conversation with Tryphon, a Jew and the *Apology,* a defense of Christian doctrine. He was apparently denounced by the Cynic, Crescens, whom he had defeated in argument, and was beheaded with six other Christians at the order of the prefect of Rome. His feast day is April 14.

# K

KAIROS (Gr.: kī'-rōs'. A word for "time" that occurs in the New Testament, now, it is believed, interchangeably with *chronos*. Once, however, *kairos* was thought to designate a "fulfilled time" or a very special time, perhaps that at which one era became another; for example, the coming of Jesus, obviously, was such a moment in history to many. This aspect of the word, interesting as it is, has for the most part had to be abandoned because of the findings of scholars of the Bible.

KENOSIS (Gr.: to empty). This term refers to a special theory of Jesus' incarnation which has been called the "kenotic theory." It holds that God the Son, the divine second person of the Trinity, was "emptied out" of the man Jesus at the Incarnation. Thus, omnipotence, omniscience, and omnipresence, all characteristics of God, were not characteristics of the incarnated Son. This theory answered, to the satisfaction of some, certain questions about Jesus' obviously limited knowledge and power. The term is found in one English rendering of Philippians 2:7 as: Christ "emptied himself, taking the form of a servant, being born in the likeness of men." The Authorized Version, however, has "made himself of no reputation."

KERYGMA (Gr.: to proclaim; ke-rig'-mə). The complexities of interpretation of this term are numerous. Most simply, it may be said to refer to both the *proclamation* of the news of Jesus' life, death, and resurrection, with the promise of salvation through belief and penitence, and the "Good News" itself, or to either one of these considered singly. The Kerygma has been called an appeal to sinners to repent and turn to a new life and an argument to accept the sinful self as justified; it is said by some to be less dogma than a call to faith which can and must be constantly reinterpreted for the age. Theological debate continues concerning the nature of the Kerygma.

KINGDOM OF GOD. This phrase has been variously interpreted as the spiritual rule of God on earth; the future kingdom of Heaven; or, by some, as the Christian church on earth. Generally, the Kingdom of God is not purely a heavenly place, but an earthly condition which began with the coming of Jesus, exists partially as a spiritual power now, and will be perfected and fullfilled later. There are many who interpret the phrase otherwise, however. Some consider that the Kingdom of God arrived entirely with Jesus, and that to be in and with Jesus is equivalent to being in that Kingdom; others feel that the Kingdom of God must be a total defeat of evil and that it is therefore entirely a thing of the future. It is believed by almost all, though, to be a spiritual rather than a primarily physical condition, and perhaps, in the well-known words, "within you."

KING OF GLORY. God or, rarely, Jesus, who is, however, often referred to as the King of Heaven.

KINGS, BOOKS OF. First and Second Kings are historical books of the Old Testament dating from about 550 B.C. Both were written to prove that God rewarded those who worshipped him and punished those who did not. 1 Kings deals with the period between the death of David and the accession of Ahaziah, and is famous for its stories of the building of Solomon's temple, the visit of the Queen of Sheba, the dividing of the Kingdom, and Elijah's prophecies. 2 Kings continues through the fall of the kingdoms of Israel and Judah, 721 B.C. and 586 B.C. respectively, and is famous for its account of the fall of the kingdoms, Sennacherib's raid, and the miracles of Elisha.

KISS. A kiss is always a mark of honor when given the cross or some other religious item or individual. In the Catholic Church, the kiss of peace, or Pax, is a survival from early liturgy and betokens brotherly love. After kissing the altar bearing the Eucharist, the priest places his hands on the deacon's arms and they bow their heads a little, left cheek to left cheek, as the priest says "Peace be with thee," and the deacon replies, "And with thy spirit." Use is very limited in the modern church, but the phrase

"Kiss of Peace" continues to convey the special early meaning that it had when the Agape, or Love Feast, was a common Christian ceremony.

KNEELING. A position on the knees assumed by many when praying. It is one of implication or humility, and is standard practice in the worship services of both Catholic and Anglican.

KOINONIA (Gr.: koi-nō'-nē-ə). This term is a defining name of ideal Christian-to-Christian love or communion. Affection, sympathy, compassion, and concern characterize this relationship at its best. An alternate expression is *agape*.

KYRIE ELEISON (Gr.: Lord, have mercy upon us; kir'-ē-ā ə-lā'-i-s'n). A prayer or invocation which is used in the Mass after the introit, as well as the music for the prayer; it also occurs as a response in the Anglican Communion service.

# L

**LADY.** When used alone, or as a form of address, "Lady" refers to Mary, the mother of Jesus. See OUR LADY.

**LADY ALTAR.** In the Catholic Church, an altar dedicated in honor of the Virgin Mary, and usually provided with her statue or picture.

**LADY CHAPEL.** The chapel in a large church, or perhaps a set-off portion of a smaller building, which contains the Lady Altar, and which is dedicated to the Virgin Mary.

**LADY DAY.** The feast of the Annunciation, celebrated March 25.

**LAETERE SUNDAY.** (Lat.: Rejoice ye; lĭ-te′-rā). The fourth Sunday in Lent, so called from the opening word of the introit, "Rejoice ye with Jerusalem." It is also called "Mothering Sunday" and "Refreshment Sunday," perhaps because of an old custom of taking gifts to parents on this Sunday in mid-Lent, or of visiting the mother church. The Anglican gospel for the day is from John 6, a chapter dealing with the feeding of the multitude and Jesus as the Bread of Life.

**LAITY.** The people or members of a church considered as distinct from the clergy.

**LAMB.** The traditional Hebrew sacrificial animal, a symbolism which was transferred whole to Christianity where Jesus is the Lamb of God, or "Agnus Dei," who sacrificed himself for mankind. The concept is articulated in John 1:29.

**LAMENTATIONS.** A book of the Old Testament dating from about 586 B.C. and erroneously attributed to the prophet Jeremiah. Lamentations mourns in poetic form the fall of Jerusalem.

**LAMMAS DAY.** An Old English name for "Loaf Mass" Day, August 1, when the early harvest was celebrated with the baking and blessing of loaves of bread.

LAMPS. In the Catholic Church, lamps consisting of a hanging glass vessel filled with olive oil or beeswax in which a burning wick floated were used as tokens of honor to God. Other oil, or an electric bulb with a suitable fixture, may be substituted by permission. One always burns in front of the Eucharist and usually before the high altar.

LANCE, THE HOLY. The spear with which Jesus' side was pierced at the crucifixion.

LAST JUDGMENT. See JUDGMENT DAY.

LAST SUPPER, THE. The Passover meal shared by Jesus and his twelve disciples in the Upper Room on the evening before his crucifixion. At it was instituted the Communion service, with the bread and wine representing, or being, the body and blood of the Savior, and the service commemorating the Last Supper itself.

LAST THINGS. Death, judgment, Heaven, and Hell are usually identified as the Last Things. See ESCHATOLOGY.

LATERAN, THE. St. John Lateran, or the Church of Our Most Holy Savior, is the cathedral church of the pope as bishop of Rome and is called "the Mother and Head of all churches of the City and of the World." Next to it on a site first occupied by the Lateran family of Rome, the palace of the Lateran served as the papal residence for one thousand years between the fourth and the fourteenth centuries, and is now a museum.

LATIN CHURCH. The Catholic Church using the Latin liturgy and subject to the pope, the bishop of Rome. It is also called the Roman Church or Western Church, and perhaps most frequently the Roman Catholic Church.

LATRIA (Lat., fr. Gr.: worship; lə-trē'-ə). In the Catholic Church, the full worship paid to God alone. See DULIA and HYPERDULIA, for contrasts.

LATTER-DAY SAINTS, THE CHURCH OF JESUS CHRIST OF. The Church of Latter-Day Saints, or Mormon Church, was founded in the United States by Joseph Smith in the early nineteenth century and was based on his revelations from the Book of Mormon which he claimed to have discovered at Palmyra, New York, in 1832. Because of persecution, the Mormons moved west from New York to Ohio, then to Illinois, then finally to the valley of the Great Salt Lake in Utah (1847). The settlement was economically successful and independent under Brigham Young, and probably encountered its major difficulties due to its practice of polygamy, which came to an official end in 1890. At present the church has some 1,700,000 members in the United States.

LAUDS (Lat.: praises; lôds). The second hour of the Divine Office of the Catholic Church, Lauds is the dawn office and is sometimes called dawn prayers. As the day is divided into three-hour periods, it would technically be said at 3 A.M. In practice, however, it is usually combined with Matins, the first hour, which opens the new day shortly after midnight. It derives its name from "Laudete," or "Praise ye," the opening word of Psalms 148, 149, and 150, which once formed an invariable part of this service.

LAVABO. A term referring to the priest's washing of his fingers after offering the oblation in the Mass in the Catholic Church.

LAW. Taken at its simplest, "law" or "a law" is a rule of reason that is established or imposed to the end that good order will exist in a community. Theologically, the case is not so simple. *Law* is first of all distinguishable from *Gospel,* in so far as the Old Testament emphasizes the Law and the Law means the eternal will of God for every human life, while the Gospels emphasize God's graciousness and mercy which inspire faith and hence obedience to and accomplishment of the true intent of the Law. This distinction is made by St. Paul.

Further, Canon Law consists of the body of laws laid down by the Catholic Church. The Divine Law is the law that commands observance and forbids disturbance of the natural order of things; it is the Natural Law when perceived through reason. Eternal Law is the law of God directing the universe to its end. Human Law is ecclesiastical or civil and subject to error and correction, especially if it conflicts with Natural or Divine Law. And Natural Law itself is the set of rules of conduct supposed to be inherent in the human condition, based on man's inate moral sense, and discoverable through the use of reason.

LAWRENCE, ST. (d. 258). Lawrence, the archdeacon of Rome and controller of the ecclesiastical wealth, was seized during the persecution ordered by the Emperor Valerian. He sold all the Church's goods and gave the money to the poor, thus having nothing to render up to the authorities when he was ordered to do so. Convinced that he was hiding money and treasures, they commanded him to be burned to death over a slow fire, hoping that he might reveal where the things were hidden. He accepted the torture and died therefrom. His feast day is August 10.

LAY BROTHER or LAY SISTER. A man or woman who is a member of a religious order in the Catholic Church, but more in the manual than the academic capacity. Lay members often do most of the harder labor, and are, in a sense, servants. They do not take holy orders and they are not bound to the Daily Office in choir as are the choir monks or choir nuns.

LAYING ON OF HANDS. See IMPOSITION OF HANDS.

LAYMAN or LAYWOMAN. A member of a church, but not a member of the clergy; one of the laity. The words "lay" and "laity" are derived from the Greek *laos,* meaning "people."

LEANDER, ST. (d. 601?). An influential churchman who worked in the interests of orthodoxy in Spain. St. Leander opposed the Arian heresy and was a close friend of Pope Gregory the Great. His feast day is February 27.

LECTOR. Also called a Reader, the Lector is the second of the minor orders, which also include Doorkeeper, Exorcist, and Acolyte, of the clergy in the Catholic Church. Once stages through which every candidate for the priesthood had to pass, the minor orders have duties which are now performed mostly by laymen (i.e., those of the Lector and Acolyte) or clergymen (Exorcist) and not by a member of the minor orders. Lectors have been used since the second century to sing or read the lessons or epistles; the duties of the man performing this function have expanded again, now, in many Catholic churches with the increased emphasis on the use of English interpretation.

LEGATE (Lat.: to send). A representative, usually called a papal legate, of the Holy See, having a certain degree of authority beyond that of mere messenger.

LENT (Old English: *lencten,* the spring season). The forty days, excluding Sundays, from Ash Wednesday through the Saturday before Easter, which are observed as a time of penitence, sacrifice, and preparation for the commemoration of the death and the celebration of the resurrection of Jesus. Usually some form of personal sacrifice is made by the faithful during this period, and traditionally no meat is eaten during the time. Lent is the principal fast of the Catholic Church.

LENTEN VEIL. During Lent, a cloth curtain was hung between the altar and the congregation in medieval churches to symbolize the expulsion of sinners and penitents from the church during that period. This was a symbolic survival, even at that time, of a very ancient discipline in the early Church, and, itself, probably survives today in the veiling of statues and other images during the Passion Tide, the final two weeks before Easter.

LEONARD, ST. (d. 559?). St. Leonard has long been popular as the bringer of a peaceful mind, and, sometimes, even of deliverance, to prisoners. He is one of their patron saints and is still invoked in Europe, where many churches bear his name. His life is mainly legend. Supposedly, he was a French lord and warrior who was converted to Christianity, and, somewhat late in life, received the tonsure. The Frankish king, Clovis, gave him some forested land where he could live in solitude, and also the privilege of visiting prisoners and freeing those whom he personally chose. Many converts were released by him and became his disciples. His feast day is November 6.

LEONIDAS, ST. (d. 204?). The father of Origen who was one of the greatest of early theologians; a martyr to his faith. His feast day is April 22.

LEO I, ST. (400?–461). The accomplishments of St. Leo, Pope Leo I, called the Great, were many during his years as pontiff. In fact, this Doctor of the Church fought on two fronts, one spiritual and the other physical. His time was one of several strong

heretical movements. Manichaeism, for example, either a heresy
or a rival religion, flourished; Nestorianism and Monophysitism,
respectively, held that Jesus was not born divine, and that he was
wholly of a divine nature; St. Hilary of Arles (d. 449) disputed
the supremacy of the pope over other bishops. St. Leo successfully struggled against these offshoots from orthodoxy, each of
which posed a serious threat to the Church, and wrote the definitive statement on the nature of Jesus which was accepted by
the Council of Chalcedon in 451.

On the other front, St. Leo achieved the withdrawal of Attila
the Hun from the vicinity of Rome without a sacking of the city,
and, later, persuaded the invader Genseric not to slaughter the
Roman populace or destroy the city's monuments.

In spite of what must have been an extraordinary personal
presence and a brilliant mind—he left ninety-six discourses and
almost one hundred and fifty letters—almost nothing is known
of St. Leo's private life or personality. His feast day is April
11.

LESSON, THE. A reading from the Bible during the church worship service. Churches follow various customs; some have two
lessons, one each from the Old and the New Testaments, while
others have one from the epistles and one from the gospels of the
New Testament. The Catholic Church may include readings from
the Fathers of the Church or other ecclesiastical writings as well.

LEVITATION. A free-floating of a body that normally would not
be so elevated. This supernatural capacity, according to the Catholic Church, has been granted over two hundred persons, usually
during prayer, and the floating has generally been gentle and at
the height of about two feet. The word has only been used in the
past hundred years in this context and has been applied especially
to St. Joseph of Cupertino (d. 1663) and St. Alphonsus Ligouri
(d. 1787). Only certain of the cases seem to be supported by
sound evidence; if they are valid, the event testifies only to the
fact that prayer is a raising of the mind and heart to God, according to Catholic theology.

LEVITICUS. The third book of the Pentateuch, dating in its present
form from about 350 B.C., though some of it is probably two or

three hundred years earlier. It sets forth a legal system of laws and codes, and a religious system of rites and sacrifices, which nevertheless emphasize righteousness and good intentions more than ritualistic details. It was originally attributed to Moses and derives its name from the tribe of Levi.

LIBERAL PROTESTANTISM. Liberal Protestantism apparently grew out of the optimism of the nineteenth century. Its beginning was in Germany, but it spread quickly throughout the Protestant world. In general, it emphasized the fatherhood of God, the importance of Jesus as a good moral example, the goodness of mankind and its perfectibility, and the capability of reason to encompass and explain away the supernatural, the metaphysical, and other so-called irrationalities. Liberal Protestants encouraged biblical criticism, feeling that science and truth could only help strengthen faith and the basis for faith. The movement tended to reject the ideas of original sin and eternal damnation, and many adherents went so far as to question the divinity of Jesus. It had its greatest growth and popularity prior to World War II, by which time many of its optimistic tenets had become highly suspect and the rationality of many of its belief had been called into question.

LICH GATE. (Old Eng.: *lic,* corpse). The roofed gateway to a churchyard, beneath which the coffin is set to await the minister who is to conduct the burial service.

LIGHT. Any light symbolizes the presence of God, as the burning bush did to Moses or the pillar of flame did to the Israelites, but specific lights have specific meanings. Candles, for example, may symbolize Jesus as the light of the world; other lights may represent his divine and human natures, and still others the seven gifts of the Holy Spirit or the seven sacraments. In general, a clear light probably may be said to represent purity.

LIGHT OF GLORY. The feeling, or inspiration, which one receives that makes the mind and soul strong and elevated enough to confront God. Jesus has also been called the Light of Glory.

LIGHT OF LIGHTS. A title sometimes given Jesus.

LIGHT OF THE WORLD. A title given Jesus in John 8:12.

LIMBO. Derived from the Latin word for "edge," limbo is a place and state of rest for certain souls after death; it is characterized by perfect natural happiness, enjoyed without the Beatific Vision. It is the teaching of the Catholic Church that the souls of the just who died before Jesus' time remained in a Limbo of the Fathers (Abraham's bosom or Paradise, as in Luke 16:22 and 23:43) until Heaven was opened for them; children and adults who die unbaptized, though excluded from Heaven, go to a Limbo for Children, if, in the case of the adults, they are free from grievous sin. There they enjoy natural happiness, knowing and loving God, but not having the vision of God which is accorded in Heaven.

LION. A winged lion is the symbol of St. Mark. As a Christian symbol, the lion dates from about the fifth century; a lion also is used to represent God's redemptive powers, symbolism derived from Daniel 6:16.

LIQUEFACTION. A becoming liquid of solid matter, a quality allegedly possessed by certain blood relics, as that of St. Januarius.

LITANY (Gr.: prayer). A prayer in which minister and congregation recite alternately, with the minister reciting or singing an invocation and the congregation responding.

LITTLE HOURS, THE. Prime, Terce, Sext, and None, the shorter hours of the Divine Office in the Catholic Church.

LITURGY (Gr.: a public duty or work). The prayers, acts, and ceremonies of official public worship in the Catholic or Anglican churches, especially the Eucharistic service. When Liturgy is capitalized, reference is to the Mass or, as it is sometimes called, the Holy Liturgy, though in actuality it consists of the entire public worship: Mass, Divine Office, and administration of the sacraments. However, in the Eastern Church, the expression "to make the Liturgy" is often used instead of "to hear Mass."

LIVING, A. In the Church of England, a parochial benefice, i.e., a church and the right of the clergyman to revenues from the endowment.

LOGIA. A group of sayings supposed to have been uttered by Jesus and existing in a collection or document possibly compiled by Matthew and separate from anything now in the New Testament. There is no very convincing evidence for the existence of any such collection, although many biblical scholars feel that Matthew and Luke must have had a common source for the sayings of Jesus included in the two Gospels. References to the Logia, however, are felt to have been made to parts of the New Testament, not to independent material.

LOGOS (Gr.: discourse or reason; word). "The Word" of John 1:1, was used in early Christian times for the mind, or reason, of God that was perfectly embodied in Jesus, who was often called "The Word." It represents the Greek idea of a divine mind, a Jewish concept of the eternal wisdom that contains the law, and "the Near Eastern idea of a pre-existent heavenly man who represents the embodiment of all human perfection." (*Theological Terms*, p. 147)

LONGINUS, ST. (first century). From at least the fourth century, the name of the soldier who pierced Jesus' side with the lance was believed to be Longinus, and he is identified with an early bishop of Cappadocia. His feast day is March 15.

LORD, THE (Old Eng.: "Loaf" + "ward," or "loaf-keeper," that is, one who feeds dependents). God or Jesus, probably, in modern usage, more frequently the latter. "Our Lord" always refers to Jesus, whereas "The Lord" may commonly refer to God, as well as to Jesus.

LORD'S PRAYER, THE. The prayer taught by Jesus to his apostles (Matthew 6:9-13 and Luke 11:2-4). It is also often called the "Our Father" from the opening words.

LORD'S SUPPER, THE. The Communion or Eucharistic service. The name for this sacrament is derived from the fact that the rite was instituted by Jesus at the Last Supper, the Passover meal with his apostles in the Upper Room.

LOST SOULS. The souls damned in Hell. According to Catholic theology, the names of numerous persons in Heaven are known, but not one particular individual human being has ever been said to have been damned.

LOUIS, ST. (1215–1270). Louis IX was one of the best kings ever to reign in France, according to both history and popular report. He was not only a devout Christian but also an efficient administrator. During his rule many of the finest cathedrals were built and many lasting reforms were introduced, for example, the distribution of tax money was improved, private warfare was curbed, and the right of appeal to the crown was extended. Peace and prosperity marked his time, and, even during his own life, he was looked upon as a saint. As leader of the seventh and eighth crusades, however, he was not notably successful, and he died of the plague at the beginning of the latter. He was canonized in 1297; his feast day is August 25.

LOURDES. A town in the Pyrenees Mountains of France, the location of the most famous shrine for present-day pilgrims, that of St. Bernadette. The shrine consists of a church, a grotto, and appropriate and beautiful grounds. Over a million pilgrims journey there each year, several thousands of whom come in the hope of some miraculous cure for a physical ailment, often a crippling one. Records kept by the Lourdes Medical Bureau (a body of physicians to which a doctor of any nationality or belief is welcome) contain several hundred notations of cures which medical science cannot explain, although the Bureau does not certify any cure as miraculous.

LOVE. The intense fondness or deep devotion known as love is, in a religious sense, close to or identical with the virtue of charity, which is said to enable a person to love. Man is commanded to love God, and to love his neighbor as himself, and the words "God is love" are familiar to most Christians. The love of God is said to extend to every creature and never to be withdrawn; the existence of all creation, in fact, is dependent upon the love of God which wills it. Probably the best known biblical passage on love, or charity, is 1 Corinthians 13.

LOW CHURCH. Any Anglican church which manifests more characteristics of Protestantism than of Catholicism is so designated. In low church practice, such ritualistic customs as genuflexion, making the sign of the cross, and kneeling are reduced to a minimum, and the use of incense, the stations of the cross, and any use of Latin are absent. Whether an Anglican church is "high," "low," or "broad" is determined by the minister and, to a large degree, the congregation which is likely to feel strongly either one way or the other. The very high church Anglican service is scarcely distinguishable from the Catholic Mass, which is the name by which it is usually called, while the very low church closely resembles the Methodist or perhaps Lutheran service.

LOW MASS. A modified form of High Mass, and the common way in which Mass is celebrated in the Catholic Church. The celebrant is usually assisted only by one acolyte, there is no choir, and prayers are therefore spoken by the celebrant. There is no incense and two candles only burn on the altar, a third being added during the canon. Low Mass has been in use since the Middle Ages in Western churches, but is still not used in those of the East. See also SUNG MASS.

LOWER CRITICISM. See BIBLICAL CRITICISM.

LUCIFER. (Lat.: Light-bearer). The proper name of Satan, the chief of the fallen angels, probably so called because Jesus likened his appearance when falling to lightning (Luke 10:18).

LUCY, ST. (d. 303?). An early Christian virgin martyr, whose story may well be all legend. According to her biography, she refused to marry, and was renounced by her suitor, a pagan noble. She was condemned to a brothel when she refused to renounce her Christian faith, but she could not be moved from the tribunal where she had declared her belief. A yoke of oxen failing to drag her away and a fire to burn her, she was killed by being pierced in the throat by a dagger. Her feast day is December 13.

LUKE. The gospel written by Luke, the Greek version dating from A.D. 90, perhaps taken from an Aramaic original as early as A.D. 65, is distinguished by the physician's gentle humanitarianism and his fine poetry. The gospels of Matthew and Mark as well as some unidentified source were doubtless the sources for St. Luke, but as he was a companion of St. Paul on some missionary journeys he probably had a good firsthand knowledge as well. Luke was also the author of the Acts of the Apostles, usually called simply Acts, and is reputed to have died a martyr. His feast day is October 18.

LUST. One of the seven deadly sins.

LUTHER, MARTIN (1483–1546). The German leader of the Protestant Reformation, Martin Luther began his ecclesiastical career as an Augustinian friar, and was ordained a priest in 1507. Three years later on a trip to Rome, he was shocked by the spiritual laxity he found there, and he returned home to Wittenberg with a desire to reform both church doctrine and practice. The dispensation of indulgences was especially abhorrent to him, and he protested in 1517, posting his famous ninety-five theses on the door of the castle church. A year later he still refused to recant; that, plus his support of a rising German nationalism and conflict with papal messengers culminating in his rejection of a papal bull of condemnation, led eventually to his excommunication (1821). He lived most of his life in Wittenberg, Germany, where he and his wife, a former nun, raised six children.

Luther was conservative compared with Calvin, Zwingli, and other reformers, and the Lutheran Church is considered, in a certain sense, closer to Catholicism than any other Protestant denomination except the Anglican. This may be because Luther did not set out to shape a new church but only to reform some parts of the one of which he was a member. The story of his life relates that the failure of his own intense and devout spiritual efforts and exercises contributed to his eventual emphasis on justification by faith, and that his disgust with abuses of church privilege led to his desires for reform.

LUTHERANISM. Two of the principal tenets of Lutheranism are justification by faith and belief that, in the Eucharist, Jesus is present in a bodily sense, "in, with, and under" the elements of bread and wine, although their substance is not altered. This belief in consubstantiation is in conflict with Catholic transubstantiation and the Protestant extreme which states that the Eucharist is only symbolic or commemorative. Baptism is held, by Lutheranism, to be essential to salvation, though no form is specified, and no special form of liturgy is required; the unity of the church existing in its doctrine is set forth in the Book of Concord and

The Augsburg Confession, the official statement of belief. The Lutheran church is the established church in Germany, Denmark, Iceland, Sweden, Norway, and Finland, and was begun in the United States at Wilmington, Delaware, in 1638. Lutheran groups in the United States now have a total membership of close to 9,000,000.

LXX. The symbol representing the Septuagint.

# M

MACARIUS THE YOUNGER, ST. (d. 408?). One of the Egyptian desert hermits, St. Macarius was a sugar-plum merchant before he became a solitary. It is not surprising, then, that he is the patron saint of candy-makers and pastry cooks, or that one of the customs of his feast day, January 2, is the making and giving of gifts of candy.

MACCABEES, 1 and 2. Two historical books in the Apocrypha which give a colorful account of the resistance of the Jews, led by Judas Maccabaeus and his brothers, to a Syrian attempt to suppress the Jewish religion and nation between 185 and 135 B.C. These books are included in the Western Canon; on the other hand, 3 and 4 Maccabees are omitted from both the Apocrypha and the Canon, although they are included in the Pseudepigrapha.

MACE. A staff, usually short and heavy and made of metal, which is carried as a symbol of authority in processions and certain ceremonies of the Catholic Church.

MADONNA (Lat.: My Lady). Mary, the mother of Jesus; also the representation of her, as a statue or painting.

MAGDALEN. From the fact that Mary Magdalen, in the New Testament, is thought to have been a prostitute, "Magdalen" has come to be used as a term for a penitent prostitute or for a member of a religious order devoted to the reclamation of prostitutes and other criminals. Members of penitential orders were also once called Magdalens.

MAGI, THE (Old Persian: Magician; member of a priestly class). The wise men of the Bible who came from the East bearing gifts

209

for the baby Jesus (Matthew 2:1-13). Traditionally, there were three: Gaspar, representing the black races; Melchior; and Balthasar. Together they represent the gentiles to whom Jesus' divinity was manifested in the Epiphany of January 6.

MAGNIFICAT, THE. The song, or canticle, of Mary, that is recorded in Luke 1:46-55, beginning "My soul doth magnify the Lord." It occurs after the Annunciation and the departure of the angel Gabriel. The Magnificat is one of the most important canticles in Catholic worship, and is especially used at Vespers.

MAJOR ORDERS. The main religious orders, or ranks, in the Catholic Church, those of priest, deacon, and subdeacon; they may also be called Sacred or Holy Orders. Bishops are within the degree of priesthood, while archbishops, etc., are degrees within the episcopate.

MALACHI (Heb.: messenger of Jehovah). The book of the last of the minor prophets of the Old Testament, Malachi is also the last book in the Old Testament. Malachi reproves the priesthood and the people, and according to one interpretation, prophecies the coming of Jesus (Malachi 4:2).

MALACHY, ST. (1095–1148). A priest and bishop in Ireland, St. Malachy met with misfortunes in maintaining his authority in his diocese, but his life was nevertheless marked with virtue and patience and, according to tradition, various miracles as well. He succeeded to some degree in bringing reforms to the church in Ireland which brought it closer to the church on the continent, and he was a close friend of St. Bernard of Clairvaux. One famous prophecy predicting identifiably the popes who would reign from 1143 forward, has been acknowledged not to be St. Malachy's but rather a forgery perpetrated in 1595 for ecclesiastical-political purposes. The "prophecy" is said to be remarkably accurate until 1590, after which it becomes hazy and generalized; the fact that it was "discovered" in 1595, probably the date of its composition, explains this. At any rate, it is no longer attributed to St. Malachy; his feast day is November 2.

MAMMON. Wealth or money regarded as evil, and, in a personified form, as an object of worship; e.g., "He worships Mammon more than he does God."

MANICHAEISM (Man-i-kē-ism). A religious philosophy, sometimes called a heresy, which was based on a doctrine that the forces of good and evil are of equal power and contend with each other for supremacy. Such a philosophy is called "dualistic." To believers, God is the source of good, and matter is the source of evil, and, by extension, all material substance is positively evil. As a consequence, the human body is considered a product of evil, and the begetting of children is wrong, as it imprisons a spirit, i.e., good, in a body, i.e., evil. Manichaeism's main teacher was Manés, a third-century Persian, and the doctrine itself was taught from his time until the seventh century; one of the main converts, for a period of time, was St. Augustine of Hippo. Manichaeans rejected the Old Testament and accepted in the New Testament only those parts which fitted their own teachings, which accounts for its often being designated heretical rather than altogether separate from Christianity. The Albigensian and Cathari heresies are Manichaeistic.

MANIPLE (Lat.: a handful). Originally a linen handkerchief, this vestment is the mark of the subdeacon in the Catholic Church; it now consists of a band of silk worn over the left forearm. Its color is determined by the day; the length is about three feet, and the ends are often marked with a cross. It represents the fruit of good works.

MANNA. Figuratively, "manna" is the spiritual substance upon which the soul feeds. The name is taken from the food, either miraculous or natural, which was provided the Israelites during their time in the wilderness (Exodus 16:15).

MARCELLA, ST. (d. 410). A Roman matron who is credited with having introduced to Rome the austere customs of dress and life which characterized Egyptian anchoresses (female anchorites, or hermits). She is reputed to have known St. Athanasius, who perhaps discussed the Egyptian way of life with her, and to have been a friend of St. Jerome. She was a strong opponent of Origen, supporting instead the orthodoxy which St. Jerome had taught her. Her feast day is January 31.

MARCIONISM. A heresy named for its chief advocate, Marcion, who left the organized Christian church in 144. It held that

Jesus was a manifestation of the holy and good God who was, himself, opposed to the Old Testament God, a deity of questionable morality. Members rejected the Old Testament, and most of the New as well, and believed that all matter was worthless and evil. As a separate heresy it existed for some five hundred years and eventually became part of Manichaeism.

MARGARET, ST. (third century). One of the early virgin martyrs, St. Margaret is reputed to have wrought many miracles in the prison where she was confined and tortured after refusing to renounce her faith, or to marry the prefect of a town in Turkey who sought her hand. Although of good birth, she became a shepherdess when her father, priest of a pagan religion, put her out of his house upon discovering her Christian faith. The prefect saw her in the fields, and the suit, refusal, confinement, and abuse which led to her martyrdom and canonization followed. Her feast day is July 20.

MARIAMNE, ST. (first century). Supposedly the companion of St. Philip and St. Bartholomew, St. Mariamne reportedly helped evangelize a part of Turkey just north of the Taurus Mountains. Her feast day is February 17.

MARIOLATRY. Worship of Mary, the mother of Jesus, which is held to be idolatrous, for only God, Father, Son, and Holy Spirit may be worshiped. Catholic theology refers to this worship as *latria*, while the veneration due the saints is called *dulia*, and that due Mary is called *hyperdulia*.

MARIOLOGY. The study of the theology, history, speculation about, and role of Mary, the mother of Jesus.

MARK. The Gospel according to St. Mark is almost without doubt the earliest and certainly the shortest and fastest-moving of the three Synoptic Gospels. It is believed by many scholars to have been a source for both Matthew and Luke, which, together with Mark, make up the Synoptic Gospels. Mark covers only the last three years of Jesus' life, those of his ministry. It is generally attributed to John Mark, Peter's companion in Rome, and is dated, in its Greek version, between A.D. 70 and 100, although an Aramaic version may have been composed as early as A.D. 40. St. Mark the Evangelist is usually identified as the "John" named in Acts 13:5,13 and the "Mark" of Acts 15:39, since John was his Jewish name and Mark, or Marcus, his Roman one; further, Acts 12:12 speaks of "John, whose surname was Mark." He was a cousin of Barnabas, and it was in his mother's house that the group around Jesus found a meeting place. Traditionally, St. Mark founded the Church in Alexandria and died a martyr under Trajan. His feast day is April 25.

MARK, LITURGY OF ST. The liturgy of the Church of Alexandria is known by this name.

MARKS OF THE CHURCH. According to Catholic theology, those characteristics which identify the Catholic Church as the true Church of Christ are unity, holiness, catholicity, and apostolicity (descended directly and uninterruptedly in mission and doctrine from the apostles).

MARRIAGE, SPIRITUAL. A spiritual union of Christ, or God, with the church, or of a soul with God in a mystical union.

MARTHA, ST. (first century). The sister of Lazarus and Mary, St. Martha is the patron saint of hotelkeepers. Her story, and her friendship with Jesus, is told in Luke 10:41–42, John 11:1–28 and 12:1–9. It apparently always fell to Martha's lot to prepare the food and to act as the mistress of the house, and no doubt this accounts for her being chosen the patronness of those whose work is feeding and housing others. Her feast day is July 29.

MARTINMAS. The feast of St. Martin of Tours, celebrated November 11, comes at a season sometimes called St. Martin's Summer, and, more familiarly, Indian Summer.

MARTIN OF TOURS, ST. (316?–397?). St. Martin is said to have been the most popular saint in the west, with four thousand churches and five hundred towns in France bearing his name. He was born a heathen, and while yet unconverted, gave half of his cloak to clothe a beggar. It was evidently not long thereafter that he was converted to the Christian faith. He preferred the life of a hermit. He sought out St. Hilary of Poitiers and built a hermitage to live nearby. However, events were against him. After some travel, and a return to France, he founded Ligugé, said to be the oldest monastery in the West, but was forcibly elevated to the position of bishop of Tours by demand of the people. He was nevertheless very effective in that capacity, accomplishing many conversions, good works, and miracles in more than twenty-five years of episcopal service. He traveled widely in France, building monasteries and churches, and converting the heathen tribes and peoples of Touraine, Anjou, Paris, Trier, and Luxemburg. His feast day is November 11.

MARTYR (Gr.: a witness). One who suffers death for his Christian faith is designated a martyr. "The Martyrs" refers to those who died for their faith during the persecutions of the first three centuries of the Christian era; they have been canonized, for the most part. Until about 250, all those who suffered for, or strongly bore witness to the Christian faith, whether or not they died for their beliefs, were called martyrs, following closely the Greek meaning of the word. According to Catholic theology, martyrs are, by the act of their deaths, justified or saved and in Heaven. Even heretics, schismatics, the unbaptized, and those who died for an erroneous belief believing it to be a true one may die as martyrs and thus attain salvation.

MARTYROLOGY, THE ROMAN. A listing of over five thousand names of martyrs and saints officially recognized by the Catholic Church. The list is not exhaustive, and many religious orders, regions, and countries may have their own saints who are just as officially recognized although not given in the Martyrology. The list makes no claim to historical accuracy, but is a useful source of information on the subject.

MARY. The mother of Jesus, often called the Virgin Mary or the Blessed Virgin, was the daughter of Joachim and Anne (according to tradition) and was quite young when she was espoused to an older man, Joseph, a carpenter. Before the marriage she was told by the angel Gabriel (Luke 1:26–38) that, although virgin, she would bear a son who would be the Savior, the Son of God. It is for this reason that Mary is also referred to as the Mother of God. Her story is recounted especially in the Gospel according to St. Luke, but even so it is brief, and she is scarcely mentioned after the birth of the baby Jesus with two exceptions: the search for the lost boy Jesus, when he was found in the temple; and the committal, by the crucified Jesus, of Mary to the care of John.

In Protestant belief and worship, Mary is honored, but plays a minor role. In Catholic theology she is reverenced above the other saints (see HYPERDULIA) and is prayed to as a link binding men to God; during the Middle Ages, especially, Mary was called upon to intercede with her Son for mankind. The chief feast is that of the Assumption, August 15; others are the Annunciation, March 25; the Immaculate Conception, December 8; the Nativity, September 8; and the Purification, February 2.

MARY MAGDALEN, ST. (first century). The woman out of whom Jesus cast seven devils (Mark 16:9) is usually identified with the reformed prostitute whose sins were forgiven in response to her great love (Luke 7:37–50). Mary Magdalen certainly was present at the crucifixion and was the first to witness the resurrection (Matthew 28:1–8). It is the conjoining of the image of the repentant harlot with that of a most favored and intimate member of the circle around Jesus which has had such appeal over the centuries, and which has made the figure of Mary Magdalen so attractive to Christians who feel sinful and in need of forgiveness. Her feast day is July 22.

MASORA (Heb.: tradition; mə-sō'rə). The Masora, or the Masoretic text, of the Old Testament is that collection of annotations and comments and appraisals made by a group of Hebrew scholars, working between about the tenth and the fifteenth centuries, to establish the genuine text of the Old Testament. It was on the basis of exclusion from the Masoretic text that Protestant reformers excluded certain writings from the Authorized Version and relegated them to the Apocrypha. The scholars, called Masoretes, also developed a system of vowels, as the Old Testament Hebrew alphabet had only consonants, and determined accurate readings for each verse by constructing rules which could be followed throughout. The modern Hebrew Bible is still based on the Masoretic text.

MASS. The English form of the Latin *Missa,* used to refer to the principal Catholic worship service, the Eucharistic sacrifice with its liturgy of prayers and rituals. Why use of the anglicization for *missa,* or "the dismissal," developed for the entire ceremony is uncertain, for the term refers specifically to the dismissal of various penitents, and others not deemed admissible, before the ceremony

of the Eucharist, called the offertory, and to the dismissal of everyone after the service. However, similar usages exist in France,
Germany, Italy, and Spain, where the vernacular form of the
Latin is used in just the same way the English vernacular term
is used. Before the sixth century, the Mass was called by a variety
of names, among them, The Offering, but naturalized forms of
*missa* were employed soon thereafter. Four distinct Mass types
exist: High Mass, Low Mass, Pontifical Mass, and Sung Mass,
as well as differentiations according to function, e.g., parochial,
conventual, or requiem.

MASS, THE LITURGY OF THE. The parts of the standard Catholic
Mass are:

The preparation
The incensing of the altar (High Mass)
Introit
Kyrie Eleison
Gloria in Excelsis (feast days and most Sundays)
The collect
Epistle
Gradual (on five occasions followed by a sequence)
Gospel
The Sermon (not a true part of the Mass, but usual)
The Nicene Creed
Offertory-verse
Offertory of bread and wine
Incensing of altar
Offerings and all present (High Mass)
Lavabo (washing and drying of celebrant's fingers)
Prayer to the Holy Trinity
Secret (a prayer said inaudibly by the celebrant)
Preface (a prayer of thanksgiving)
The Canon of the Mass, the fundamental part of the worship
  service, with the consecration of the bread and wine
The Lord's Prayer
Breaking of the Host (consecrated bread)
Agnus Dei
Three prayers preparatory to Communion
Communion of celebrant, then of the people

Ablutions (washing of thumbs and index fingers of the celebrant
to remove the particles of consecrated bread)
Communion verse
Prayers
Dismissal
Blessing
Last Gospel (often John 1:1–14)
The form of the Mass began to appear before the end of the
first century, and by the second century it had taken on much of
its present structure; the Canon, especially, has been almost un-
altered since the seventh century.

The Mass of the Catechumens, those unbaptized adults who
are receiving instruction and plan to be received into the Church,
is that part of the service from the beginning to the offertory. In
early times it was just before the offertory that catechumens,
public penitents, and energumens (insane or "possessed" individuals) were dismissed, and the name continues to be employed;
the remainder of the service was called the Mass of the Faithful.

MASORETIC TEXT. See MASORA.

MATERIALISM. The theory which propounds the reality of matter
in motion, stating that everything can be explained from the
standpoint of *matter* without any necessity to refer to the mind,
spirit, or abstractions of any kind. Materialism is a form of na-
turalism, but not the only form.

MATINS (Lat.: the morning). The night office of the Divine
office of the Catholic Church, Matins is the main, longest, and
oldest of the hours. It is a survival of the ancient Vigils service
and is said about midnight, or, more usually, in a combined form
with Lauds, either at midnight or very early in the morning.

MATTHEW. The Gospel according to St. Matthew, the opening
book of the New Testament, is attributed to the apostle Matthew
and seems to derive much from the Gospel of St. Mark. It is,
however, the only one of the gospels to give the story of the Wise
Men and the Flight into Egypt. Evidently written to convince
the Hebrews that Jesus was the Messiah, as well as to set forth
his ethical teachings, Matthew's gospel was perhaps written in
an Aramaic version about A.D. 55 though the Greek version dates

from some twenty-five years later. With Mark and Luke it makes up the Synoptic Gospels. Very little is known about its author beyond the fact that he had been a tax collector before he became one of Jesus' apostles and, later, an evangelist. Not even the country he evangelized or the date or manner of his death are known. His feast day is September 21.

MATTHIAS, ST. (first century). Nothing is known of the life or death of this apostle who was named to replace Judas Iscariot. Some stories say that he evangelized Palestine, others Ethiopia, and that he died a martyr. An account of how he was chosen is given in Acts 1:15–26; his feast day is February 24.

MAUNDY THURSDAY. The Thursday before Easter in Holy Week. It is the day that commemorates the institution of the Communion service, and the name "Maundy" is derived from the Latin "Mandatum," or "Mandatum, novum," that is, "A new commandment," from John 13:34 "A new commandment I give unto you, That ye love one another; as I have loved you, that ye also love one another." In some Catholic Churches a ceremonial washing of the feet of twelve men by a priest or bishop is part of the service.

MEDAL. A flat metal disk bearing a religious picture of a person, place, or thing. Such medals are worn, not as charms, but as one would wear or carry the picture of any loved person or place.

MEDARD, ST. (d. 560?). One of the missionaries to the French whose name is surrounded more by legend that by facts. The superstition which says that if it rains on St. Medard's day, June 8, it will rain for forty days thereafter, evidently grew from the story of the young Medard's giving one of his father's horses to a poor man, after which it rained violently—on everyone but the young man. St. Medard was bishop of Noyon and was noted during his lifetime for his kindness and generosity to the poor of his diocese. His feast day is June 8.

MEDIATOR, THE. Jesus, who as the Son of God and Son of Man, reconciles man and God. Further, he has often been described as more gentle and approachable than the awe-inspiring God the Father and thus a mediating figure.

MEDITATION. Private, quiet, consideration of a religious or spiritual nature; also, silent prayer.

MEGILLOTH (Heb.: rolls). The five books of the Hebrew Scriptures from the Song of Songs through Esther: Song of Songs, Ruth, Lamentations, Ecclesiastes, and Esther. Each of the five books is written on a separate roll for use in the synagogue.

MEINRAD, ST. (797?–861). After serving as priest and a monk, St. Meinrad, a relative of the royal Hohenzollern family, became a hermit in the forests and mountains near the lake of Zurich. His life was devoted to prayer and worship before an image of the Virgin Mary, and a shrine still exists on the spot. He was killed by thieves who believed he had a treasure hidden somewhere. His feast day is January 21.

MELCHIOR, GASPAR, BALTHASAR, STS. The three Wise Men; the feast day of both Melchior and Gaspar is Epiphany, January 6, while that of Balthasar is January 11.

MELKITES (Syriac: emperor). Historically, the name of the Christians in Syria and Egypt who followed the emperor and accepted the ruling of the Council of Chalcedon (451) on the two natures, human and divine, in one person in Jesus; they opposed the monophysites, who did not accept it. Though this implies that both Catholics and dissidents may be Melkites, the term is only used to apply to Arabic-speaking Catholics of the Byzantine rite in Syria, Palestine, Egypt, and certain other countries. Also spelled Melchites.

MENDICANT FRIARS. Literally, begging friars, this term originally designated the members of religious orders, and the orders themselves, that could own no property, and thus had to beg from the wealthy to supply all their needs. The practice was modified of necessity by the sixteenth-century Council of Trent, and the name now refers to a larger variety of orders; only Friars Minor and Capuchins maintain the original meaning.

MENNONITES. A sect of dissident Baptists, or Anabaptists, that originated in Switzerland but is more closely identified with Holland as the leader from which it takes its name, Menno Simons (1496–1561), was Dutch. Mennonites refused to take oaths, took the Bible as their only rule of faith, and accepted only the sacraments of baptism and Communion. The group spread to Russia and France and settled in the United States at Germantown, Pennsylvania, in 1683, spreading later to the Midwest. There are a variety of Mennonite groups, perhaps the best known one being the Amish.

MENSA (Lat.: a table). The top of an altar; in the Catholic Church, the *mensa* is the flat stone that forms the top.

MERCY. The compassionate flexibility which allows one to temper justice or the rigors of certain laws. In general, it may be said that the Old Testament emphasizes God's justice (e.g., the sinner is punished) while the New Testament emphasizes God's mercy (e.g., the sinner is forgiven).

MERCY SEAT. God's throne; to "stand before the mercy seat" is a synonym for "to be judged by God." In the Old Testament the "mercy seat" was the gold covering of the Ark of the Covenant, the resting place of God (Exodus 25:17).

MERIT. Worth or value; the right to reward, or the condition of deserving good or ill treatment.

MESSIAH (Heb.: anointed). A name often used to designate a king, but applied especially to the great king of the house of David who was to come someday to rescue Israel. The idea was at first entirely temporal and physical, and the Messiah was envisioned as a conquering warrior. But as the qualities of the Messiah expanded, his supernatural powers were emphasized and the more or less realizable idea or ideal became a dream. "The Messiah" always refers to Jesus in the Christian context, and is synonymous with "Christ," or, in a Greek translation of the Hebrew, "The Anointed," which refers back to an ancient custom of anointing with oil the chosen or kingly one.

METHODISM. The religious doctrine and worship originated in England by John Wesley in 1729 won its name "methodism" at first as a nickname from Wesley and his brother and followers' intent to order their lives and study according to rule and method. Preachers of the young group, which remained formally within the Church of England until 1791, spoke in whatever spot they found listeners, and soon a traveling group of lay preachers or "circuit riders" was trained to carry the message to communities scattered throughout England. This message was one of faith, repentance, and full and free salvation. One group which could not accept the doctrine split off to become a Calvinistic branch, while the main body became the Wesleyan Methodist Church after separation from the Church of England. In the 1760's Methodism was brought to America where its first leaders were Philip Embury and Francis Asbury. Besides the biblical message, the denomination was fairly strict morally, opposing dancing, card playing, and drinking; the churches were bare of ritualistic colors and ceremonies, but music remained a portion of the worship service. Ministers and bishops were recognized clergy, and the sacraments of baptism and Communion were preserved along with forms of confirmation, and ordination; the marriage ceremony also retained a modified sacramental form, but penance and extreme unction were abandoned.

The Methodist Episcopal Church, formed in 1784, with a separate branch called the Methodist Episcopal Church South, and the Methodist Protestant Church were the main divisions among many. These three reunited in 1939 to form the Methodist Church, the largest Methodist denomination in the world and the largest Protestant denomination in the United States, with a present membership of about 13,000,000.

MICAH. A prophetic book of the Old Testament, Micah is named for its author who foretells the punishment of the wicked, expresses a hope for universal peace, and prophecies the coming of the Messiah from Bethlehem (Micah 5:1–8); the book dates from about 720 B.C.

MICHAEL, THE ARCHANGEL, ST. St. Michael has been the subject of many popular beliefs and legends, and traditionally is the protector of the chosen people, the defender of Christians, and the guide of souls through the perils and temptations of the earthly journey. St. Gabriel, St. Raphael, and St. Michael are the three archangels named in the Bible. In early Christian times, many cults centered around St. Michael, who often replaced some pagan deity; he was also popular in France, where, in 709, the famous Mont Saint Michel was dedicated to him. His feast day is September 29.

MICHAELMAS. The Old English name for the feast day of the archangel Michael observed on September 29, and celebrated as a holiday with roast goose as the traditional fare.

MIDRASH (Heb.: explanation). The Jewish commentaries written on the Hebrew scriptures between the time of the Exile and about A.D. 1200 are known by this name.

MILLENNIUM, THE. The thousand-year reign of the Christ on earth foretold in Revelation 20. This is accepted generally as figuratively designating a long period of time when Satan will be bound and Jesus' spiritual reign in the church on earth shall occur. Some, however, since the beginning of the Christian era have taken it to refer literally to a thousand-year reign of the physical Christ on earth that will occur just prior to the general Judgment Day. Millennial sects which have arisen since the sixteenth century believe that the end of the world is imminent, and that the Millennium is soon to begin.

MINISTER. According to usual Protestant use, a minister is a clergyman with authority vested in him according to the rule of his specific denomination. He is generally the main clergyman of a church with the responsibility of leading the worship service, preaching, baptizing, and the like. The word is infrequently applied to Catholic clergy, although the word "ministry" is used and "minister" if employed has approximately the same meaning as it does in its Protestant context. One "called to the ministry" has usually entered a seminary, school, or other training center to become a Protestant minister.

MINOR ORDERS. In the Catholic Church, the lower ranks of the clergy through which all candidates for the priesthood once had to pass. At one time, specific duties were attached to each of the four, door-keeper, lector, exorcist, and acolyte, but they are now performed by laymen, in the case of door-keeper, lector, and acolyte, or by a member of the higher clergy, in the case of the exorcist.

MINSTER (Lat.: A monastery). This term, originally applied to a monastery church, has come to refer to any large church or cathedral, often as a suffix, as "Westminster" or "Axminster." The word is frequently confused verbally with "minister."

MIRACLE. An act or event that occurs in apparent contradiction of some scientific law and is thus abscribed to a supernatural cause. The term is not used synonymously with "wonder" in a religious context, although the two are often used interchangeably in popular speech, as in "It is a miracle that he survived." Almost no one would assume from this expression that the speaker believed an actual religious miracle had taken place.

Records of miracles abound in the New Testament, e.g., those of the virgin birth, the changing of water into wine, and walking on the water, and the feeding of the multitude. All of these fit the defining requirement that a miracle should appear to contradict a scientific law. The Catholic definition is somewhat different, as a miracle "is not necessarily a breach of the laws of nature, or even a suspension of these laws, but an effect wrought independently of natural powers and laws and of such a character that man reasonably concludes that God himself . . . is the immediate and direct cause of the effect . . . ." (*Catholic Dictionary,* p. 323).

MIRACLE PLAY. A type of medieval play that dealt with the life of a saint, thus differing somewhat from the mystery play which presented a biblical event or story. These folk dramas were especially popular in the fourteenth and fifteenth centuries though they had begun earlier. Often the term is used to designate any of the very early dramas, generically including mystery plays as well, though only rarely the morality plays.

MISERERE, THE (Lat.: Have mercy; miz'-ə-rā-rā). Psalm 51, beginning with the Latin words "*Miserere mei, Deus,*" i.e., "Have mercy upon me, O God." This is the chief of the so-called penitential psalms in Catholic and Anglican worship.

MISHNA, THE. The oral law of the synagogue that was collected and codified into six orders, or seders, about A.D. 180.

MISSA CANTATA (Lat.: Sung Mass). The Latin term for the Sung Mass.

MISSAL. The book containing all the prayers used in the celebration of Mass, and, by extension, any book of prayers or devotional readings.

MISSION. A district without a church of its own but which is served by a pastor or priest from a nearby, or relatively nearby, church. In a non-Christian locality a mission may have its own church to which a missionary minister is assigned.

To "have a mission," however, is said of someone who is either assigned by his church, or who feels especially called by God, to perform a specific religious duty or service. "Mission work" refers to the work done by missionaries or others in the foreign or domestic fields. Most churches support a number of missionaries in various missions around the world.

MISSIONARY. A person sent out by a church to a foreign and non-converted country or to an area that is still heathen within a Christian country, e.g., a missionary may be sent to an Indian village in Arizona. Occasionally, missionaries are sent by one denomination to convert, if possible, members of another Christian denomination to their way of belief, but this is not common.

MITER (Gr.: A turban). The liturgical hat of Catholic bishops, consisting of two high, stiff parts, a front and a back, which are pointed at the top and joined by soft material so that they can be folded together. The miter began as a soft, low cap; in the consecration of bishops it symbolized the helmet of salvation and the tongues of fire which descended on the apostles at Pentecost. Miters are not worn exclusively by bishops, although they are always thought of in relation to the episcopal rank. At present a softer and lower form is gaining in popularity.

MITHRAISM (Old Persian: friend; (mi'-thrə-i'-zəm). A strong, and perhaps the most vital, rival to Christianity during the first few centuries of the era. Mithra was originally a deity in Iran and India, but the cult spread into the Roman world and by the second century A.D. Mithraites were more numerous than Christians. It was a mystery faith, employing sacramental forms such as baptism and a sacred feast resembling the Christian Communion; morals were strict, loyalty to the faith was emphasized, and self-discipline was considered vital. The central myth was the killing by Mithra of a sacred bull in a cave. Besides this emphasis on animals, Mithraism was mainly for men and lacked the death-and-resurrection theme apparently so important to successful religious faiths.

MIXED CHALICE. Communion wine to which some water has been added. This custom is most ancient, dating back even to Hebrew times when water was often mixed with wine for drinking.

MIXED MARRIAGE. Any marriage between individuals of faiths which are considerably different and which therefore may occasion some conflict, e.g., a marriage between a Jew and a Christian or between a Catholic and a Protestant. Marriage between a baptized non-Catholic and a Catholic, however, is called "mixed religion," and the marriage is not lawful in the eyes of the Catholic Church, although it is valid. Marriage between an unbaptized person and a Catholic is called "disparity" or "difference of worship" and the marriage is considered neither valid nor lawful. Conditions for dispensation to allow the marriage are the same for each, but in neither case does the Catholic Church approve of the marriage. Not since 1918, however, has it considered the marriage of two non-Catholics, one baptized and one not, as invalid.

MONASTERY. From a Greek word meaning "the dwelling of a solitary [individual]" monastery has come to designate the residence and buildings, as church, chapter house, cloisters, and cells, of a community of monks, friars, nuns, or other type of religious order, although the term is usually reserved for the residential complex for monks.

MONASTICISM. A way of life known to all the great religions, with the exception of Judaism, monasticism consists of "the formation of 'a community of monks, bound to live together until death, under rule, in common life, in the monastery of their profession, as a religious family, leading a life not of marked austerity but devoted to the service of God'." (*Catholic Dictionary*, p. 329, quoting Abbot Butler, O.S.B.)

MONICA, ST. (333–387). The mother of St. Augustine of Hippo, St. Monica was raised a Christian but was married to a pagan, a man whom she finally converted. Her son Augustine was also raised as a Christian but became an apostate, a Manichaean, and a licentiate before his reconversion. St. Monica and the young man were together for a while after he reaccepted the Christian faith, but she died, apparently completely happy, only five years thereafter. Her feast day is May 4.

MONK. A man who, through religious vows, binds himself to the monastic life. The life of a monk is nearly solitary, though he participates as his order requires in the daily life of the community. A friar's work, on the other hand, is with people in the active world.

MONOPHYSITISM. The belief that Jesus had but one nature, and was not both human and divine. In practice, Monophysitism held that Jesus' human nature was absorbed entirely into his divine, and that he thus had but one nature, the divine. Monophysites opposed Nestorians who rejected, to a certain degree, the divine nature and emphasized the human. In 451 the Council of Chalcedon articulated the position of the main branch of Christianity on both these points, a position which is held today with few exceptions by all Christians. Eutyches, patriarch of Constantinople, was the originator of the first phase of Monophysitism, often called Eutychianism. Monophysitism grew during the fifth and sixth centuries and by the sixth was very important in Syria, Egypt, and Armenia; the Coptic Church in Egypt, now in communion with the Church in Ethiopia, still holds to this doctrine.

MONOTHEISM. The belief in one God, held by Christians, Mohammedans, Jews, and others, and opposed to polytheism specifically, and also to atheism or pantheism. Monotheistic faith is characteristic of a variety of religions which do not accept the Christian Trinity, of which it was a forerunner.

MONSIGNOR (It.: my Lord; mon-sēn'-yĕr). Literally, my Lord, a title designating certain dignitaries and all prelates of the Catholic Church. One speaks correctly of Monsignor (personal surname), Bishop of (place name), rather than of Bishop (personal surname).

MONSTRANCE (Lat.: to show). The receptacle which contains the consecrated Eucharistic bread, the Host, when it is presented or shown to the people for their adoration during the Mass. The usual shape is a broad base, a stem, and bowl.

MONTANISM. A heresy of the second century whose outstanding adherent was the theologian Tertullian. The Montanists preached an imminent Judgment Day and were exceedingly strict and ascetic in their lives. Their major heretical belief was their denial that the Church could forgive sins, and that a Christian who had fallen from grace could be redeemed. The heresy survived for some two hundred years.

MONTE CASSINO (It.: Mount of Cassino; mōn'-tä-käs-sē'-nō). The "cradle of Western monasticism" that was founded by St. Benedict around 529 overlooking the town of Cassino in central Italy. Monte Cassino was a center of culture and learning for centuries, with a valuable library which was mostly saved although the abbey itself was bombed by the Allies during World War II, having been converted to a fortress by German troops. The rule of St. Benedict, founded on silence, work, prayer, contrition, and respect for the human being, has also survived for centuries and at one time was followed by perhaps 40,000 Western monasteries.

MONTH'S MIND. An ancient Jewish custom, which became a Christian one also, of marking the end of a thirty day mourning period with a worship service or "month's mind."

MORAL THEOLOGY. Another term for "Christian ethics," the applying of Christian theological doctrines to man's moral conduct. It includes the "how" of the application of Christian laws to practical situations as well as a study of moral codes and values.

MORALITY PLAY. A popular type of religious play of the Middle Ages, but especially popular in the fifteenth and sixteenth centuries, depicting the struggle between good and evil in the life of man and teaching a moral lesson from the conflict. *Everyman* is probably the best known and perhaps the finest example we have of the genre. Compare with MIRACLE PLAY and MYSTERY PLAY.

MORAVIANS. A branch of the Hussites founded in the mid-fifteenth century in Czechoslovakia, Moravians are also known as Unitas Fratrum and adherents are called United Brethren, a name not to be confused with the Evangelical United Brethren Church. In America, the group's center is Bethlehem, Pennsylvania. The Moravian Church has a modified form of episcopal government, a simple ritual, the sacraments of baptism and Communion, and the Bible as the only rule of faith. It considers human nature as depraved, but also professes belief in the salvation of all men, a tenet known as "universalism." There are about 63,000 members.

MORTAL SIN. Serious or deadly sin which is committed with full knowledge of the sinfulness involved and thus constitutes a willful rebellion against God's law. According to Catholic theology, mortal sin deprives the soul of supernatural life and sanctifying grace and deserves eternal punishment. Compare with VENIAL SIN. "Mortal sins" may, however, refer also to the seven deadly sins.

MORTIFICATION. Acts of self-discipline or self-punishment. Spiritual mortification is an inner subduing of self-love, while physical mortification is self-inflicted austerity, discomfort, or deprivation. Both are practices of asceticism.

MOSAIC LAW. The old laws of the Hebrews ascribed to Moses, hence the name "Mosaic," in the Old Testament books of Exodus, Leviticus, Numbers, and Deuteronomy.

MOST REVEREND. The style of address used to all archbishops in the English-speaking countries and to bishops, as well, in Ireland. One would properly speak of "The Most Reverend" (personal surname), Archbishop of (place name). It is also part of the official form of address of a cardinal in the Catholic Church and of some prelates and heads of religious orders.

MOTET. A short polyphonic anthem with words usually taken from the Scriptures and usually sung without instrumental accompaniment.

MOTHER CHURCH. The cathedral church of a diocese, or a parish church that has chapels-of-ease for the convenience of members in distant parts of a parish.

MOTHER HOUSE. A self-governing monastery that has established smaller houses that are dependent upon it for their jurisdiction and other aids.

MOTHERING SUNDAY. The fourth Sunday of Lent; See LAETERE SUNDAY.

MOTHER OF GOD. A title for Mary, the mother of Jesus, recognized in orthodox Catholic theology as the Mother of God by virtue of Jesus' having been both God and man. Nestorianism in the fifth century was a heretical movement which opposed this view.

MOTHER SUPERIOR. The title used for the superior, i.e., the woman in authority, in many modern convents of sisters who do not take solemn vows; the term, however, has been widely adopted to designate the superior of any convent. Compare with PRIORESS.

MOVABLE FEAST. A festival or feast day in the Catholic or Anglican church calendar whose date is set from the date of Easter; Ascension and Pentecost are well known movable feasts. Another type of movable feast is set on a certain Sunday in a month (Thanksgiving is a secular feast set on a certain Thursday in a month) or is reckoned from a certain specific date as is the feast day of the Holy Name of Jesus.

MURATORIAN CANON. The oldest extant list of New Testament writings was discovered by Muratori in 1750; this list, compiled in the second century, exists in a fragmentary manuscript of the eighth century, the body of Muratori's find.

MYSTERY. A profound spiritual truth, often beyond, or held to be beyond, the understanding of mere humans. The sacraments were at one time called the Mysteries, and the celebration of the Eucharist is still frequently called the Holy Mystery. In the Catholic Church, there are fifteen "mysteries of the faith" that form the main part of the rosary and are divided into joyful, sorrowful, and glorious. The joyful mysteries are the annunciation, the visitation, the birth of Jesus, his presentation in the temple, and the finding of the young Jesus after he had been lost. The sorrowful mysteries are Jesus' agony in Gethsemane, his scourging, crowning with thorns, carrying of the cross, and crucifixion. The glorious mysteries are the resurrection, the ascension, the coming of the Holy Ghost at Pentecost, the assumption of Mary, and her coronation in Heaven, which replaced the earlier mystery, "Our Lady's eternal felicity . . ."

MYSTERY PLAY. A medieval folk drama which dealt with an event or story from the Bible. Series, or cycles, of mystery plays told main stories of the Old Testament and delved into the New as well. They were often short skits, performed by appropriate town guilds and groups, and were presented on temporary stages set up on a route through a town, or on wheeled wagon-like stages that rolled along the route. The occasion for such a performance, which might include several dozen plays, was a religious festival. Collections which have survived include the Towneley, or Wakefield Cycle; the York; the Chester; and the Coventry plays. Compare with MIRACLE and MORALITY PLAYS.

MYSTIC. One who has experienced God's presence and reality, and, rarely before the Middle Ages, one who has experienced any sort of psychological or psychic phenomena which might be associated with the supernatural, as visions or ectasies. Contemplatives, enjoying acute awareness of God and the divine, are correctly called mystics, a term which does not encompass occult experiences, mysteriousness, loss of contact with reality, or any other vague, misty manifestations of other-worldliness. "A 'practical' character and an 'objective' cast of mind are characteristic marks of the Christian mystic." (*Catholic Dictionary,* p. 338)

MYSTICAL BODY OF CHRIST. The members of the Christian faith bound together with Jesus into a body both spiritual and material, both the church on earth and the redeemed in Heaven (and Purgatory in Catholic faith). The expression is not used to refer to the Communion bread, which is, however, called the Body of Christ.

MYSTICAL INTERPRETATION. The interpretation of Scripture which may also be called allegorical, since a biblical person or thing or event is interpreted as being a "type of" or a pre-existing example of a person, thing, or event to follow. Jonah in the whale, with the "rebirth" after the third day, is a "type" of Jesus' resurrection in this sense.

MYSTICAL ROSE. A title given Mary, the mother of Jesus.

MYSTICAL UNION. The union of a soul with God; the presence of God is felt spiritually, but as a real and direct experience. The degrees of such mystical union are defined by the Catholic Church, and understood usually by non-Catholics, as that of quiet prayer, full union (the soul very conscious of God's inner presence), ecstasy, and spiritual marriage.

# N

NAHUM (Heb.: comforter). A prophetic book of the Old Testament dating from around the seventh century with the name taken from its author. This short book, only three chapters, denounces Nineveh in Assyria and predicts its fall.

NAILS, THE. The nails which were used in the crucifixion of Jesus are reputed to have been found by St. Helena along with the relics of the cross; there are many nails, however, which are now said to be true relics. None are authenticated.

NAME DAY. The feast day of the saint for whom a baby is named is said to be the baby, or adult's, name day.

NARTHEX. A vestibule leading into the nave of a church. This term originally designated the west end, or the porch, of a church in which penitents and others excluded from the nave were allowed to sit.

NATIVITY. The birth, or birthday; in the Catholic Church, only three birthdays are celebrated, those of Jesus (Christmas), his mother Mary (September 8), and John the Baptist (June 24). Most feast days of saints are arbitrarily set or commemorate the known day of death, as death marks an individual's entry into eternal life.

NATIVITY, THE. The birth of Jesus, celebrated December 25, is always meant when reference is made to "the Nativity." A "Nativity play" depicts the story of Joseph and Mary's arrival at the inn in Bethlehem, the shepherds, the Star, and, often, the Wise Men. A "Nativity scene" or creche shows the manger with the baby Jesus, Joseph, Mary, and usually the shepherds, angels, animals, and Wise Men.

NATIVITY OF THE BLESSED VIRGIN MARY. This feast day is celebrated in the Catholic Church on September 8.

NATURAL GRACE. A grace given by God, as life or a natural power, to which an individual has no claim and for which he can take no personal credit.

NATURAL LAW. See LAW.

NATURAL REVELATION. A term used to refer to the revelation of God in all created things, and thus differing from the sort of revelation given in the Bible.

NATURAL THEOLOGY. That theology which bases all doctrines of God on reason and experience, rejects revelation to a considerable extent, and makes no special appeal to faith. This matter has caused much theological debate over the centuries, and in most arguments neither reason nor revelation has been entirely rejected; rather, revelation has often been said to show what man, because of his limitations since the Fall, cannot in *practice* know through his reason though he may know it in theory. In general, Protestant theologians have believed this, while Catholics have believed that, although reason indicates the existence of God, there are certain supernatural truths such as final blessedness for which reason is inadequate.

NAVE. The main body of the church in which the congregation sits during worship services. The name is derived from the shape of the early church which resembled a ship, which is, in Latin, *navis*. In Protestant usage, *"sanctuary"* has come to replace *"nave"* to a very great extent.

NAZARENE, THE. Jesus; he was so called because he was a native of Nazareth.

NAZARENE, THE CHURCH OF THE. A generally conservative Protestant sect, organized in 1908 with headquarters in Kansas City, Missouri. Present membership in the United States is approximately 400,000.

NECESSARY TO SALVATION. The two conditions generally held to be necessary for one to be saved are *belief* and *baptism,* a tenet based on Mark 16:16, "He that believeth and is baptized shall be saved; . . ." Beyond this point of agreement, Catholics and Protestants, and various sects of Protestants, separate over such issues as "state of grace," "faith," "works," and the like.

NEHEMIAH. A book of the Old Testament dating from about 300 B.C.; it describes the rebuilding of the walls of Jerusalem after the Hebrews' return from Exile in Babylon and tells of the religious reforms of Nehemiah.

NEOPHYTE. A newly baptized convert; anyone beginning studies for the priesthood; or a postulant or novice in a religious order.

NESTOR, ST. (d. 250). An early bishop of the Church, Nestor's see was in Pamphylia, a locality under Roman rule. Nestor refused to renounce his faith in Christianity and was condemned and crucified. His feast day is February 26.

NESTORIANISM. A fifth-century heresy which took its name from the man who led it, Nestorius, patriarch of Constantinople. In reaction against Apollinarianism, a heresy which stated that there was only one perfect nature in Jesus, and that that one was the divine, Nestorius and his followers maintained that Jesus was constituted of two separate persons, God the Son who dealt in Jesus the man. This was also opposed to the main stream of orthodoxy, which referred to Mary as the Mother of God and held that God and man were one in Jesus, bound together in a natural unity called a hypostatic union. Nestorius objected to this title being applied to Mary, holding that Mary bore only the man Jesus and not God the Son; Nestorians also maintained that only the man Jesus and not God the Son died on the cross. Nestorius was condemned at the Council of Ephesus in 431 and condemnation of Nestorianism was repeated at the important Council of Chalcedon in 451. The Persian church, nevertheless, upheld the belief, and even today the Nestorian Church, often called Syrians or Assyrians, has a sprinkling of adherents in the Near East, India, and the United States.

NEW COVENANT, THE. The new law taught by Jesus and often set over against the old law, or covenant, of Moses.

NEW FIRE, THE. In the Catholic Church, a lighting with flint and fuel of a fire on or in the porch of a church on Holy Saturday, the day before Easter. From it the Easter, or paschal, candle is lit and is then carried into the church with prayers and lessons following.

NICAEA, THE FIRST COUNCIL OF. The first ecumenical council ever held was convened by the Emperor Constantine with the permission of the pope in A.D. 325. At it the bishops, over three hundred of whom attended, condemned the heresy that the Son of God was not co-eternal with the Father, that he was of a substance other than that of the Father, and that he was created and not begotten. The formula for the Nicene Creed was put together, and the method of determining the day on which Easter was to be celebrated was established.

NICENE CREED. This creed, formulated at the First Council of Nicaea in 325, was expanded into nearly its present form at the First Council of Constantinople in 381. The use in it of the term *filioque* (the usage expressing the belief that the Holy Ghost proceeds from both Father and Son) in the sixth century and thereafter was one of the causes of the break between Catholic and Orthodox Eastern Churches. The Nicene Creed, which follows, also has been adopted and used by Protestant denominations:

### The Nicene Creed

I believe in one God the Father Almighty, Maker of heaven and earth, And of all things visible and invisible;

And in one Lord Jesus Christ, the only-begotten Son of God; Begotten of his Father before all worlds, God of God, Light of Light, Very God of very God; Begotten, not made; Being of one substance with the Father; By whom all things were made: Who for us men and for our salvation came down from heaven, And was incarnate by the Holy Ghost of the Virgin Mary, And was made man: And was crucified also for us under Pontius Pilate; He suffered and was buried: And the third day he rose again according to the Scriptures: And ascended into heaven, And sitteth on the right hand of the Father: And he shall come again, with glory, to judge both the quick and the dead; Whose kingdom shall have no end.

And I believe in the Holy Ghost, The Lord, and Giver of Life, Who proceedeth from the Father and the Son; Who

with the Father and the Son together is worshipped and glori-
fied; Who spake by the Prophets: And I believe one Catholic
and Apostolic Church: I acknowledge one Baptism for the
remission of sins: And I look for the Resurrection of the dead:
And the Life of the world to come.

NICHOLAS, ST. (d. 324?). A bishop of Myra in Asia Minor, St.
Nicholas is without doubt one of the best known and loved of
all the early saints. He is the patron of children and his feast
day was very early celebrated as a children's holiday. English
settlers of New York picked up the custom from the Dutch inhabitants and altered the Dutch *Sint Klaes,* or St. Nicholas, to
Santa Claus. The story, or legend, that accounts for his position
as the patron of children tells that on his way to the Council of
Nicaea St. Nicholas stopped at an inn whose landlord had just
slaughtered three young boys for the little money they had on
them and had, further, cut up their bodies and put them in a
salting tub preliminary to selling them for meat. St. Nicholas
restored the mutilated bodies to life, and, not surprisingly, converted the man who had murdered them. A pleasanter story tells
that St. Nicholas distributed gifts anonymously to poor children
on Christmas eve. His feast day is December 6.

NICODEMUS, GOSPEL OF. An apocryphal gospel, a book of the
pseudepigrapha, that is also called the Acts of Pilate. It recounts
very imaginatively events during the trial, death, and resurrection of Jesus and is the source of the names of the two thieves
crucified with Jesus, Dismas (the Good Thief) and Gestas, as
well as of the name of Pilate's wife (Procla) and the centurion
(Longinus). It is thought to have been written in the first few
centuries of the Christian era and is not considered an authentic
source of information.

NICODEMUS, ST. (first century). A member of the Sanhedrin and
a doctor of the law who, with Joseph of Arimathea, cared for
Jesus' body after the crucifixion. His fuller story is given in John
3:1–21, 7:50–52, and 19:39–40. His feast day is August 3.

NIGHT OFFICE. The office of Matins, or Mattins, the first of the
Divine or Canonical Hours, is usually said "overnight," i.e., at
midnight, or very early in the morning. It is often joined with

Lauds, the second of the Hours, to be said early in the morning. In the Anglican Church, "Matins" is often used to refer to the service of morning prayers just as "Vespers" refers to the evening service.

NIMBUS. A halo.

NINE CHOIRS OF ANGELS. See CELESTIAL HIERARCHY.

NINETY-FIVE THESES, THE. The famous complaints posted on the door of the castle church in Wittenberg by Martin Luther.

NONBEING. In its classical usage, this term designates one of the parts of finite being, held to be composed of *being* and *nonbeing*. Modern theologians and philosophers, influenced one way or another by existentialism, sometimes identify nonbeing as that "nothingness" which modern man sees beneath and around his daily busy life and which he perceives through, perhaps *as*, anxiety. Paul Tillich, for example, "defines God as that power of being which continually conquers nonbeing." (*Theological Terms,* p. 165)

NOTES OF THE CHURCH. See MARKS OF THE CHURCH.

NOTRE DAME (Fr.: Our Lady; Nō'-trə-däm). The French name designating Mary, the mother of Jesus, is often given churches dedicated in her honor, e.g., Notre Dame de Paris.

NOVENA (Lat.: from "ninth," consisting of nine; nō-vē'-nə). In the Catholic Church, a prayer extended over a period of nine days and said for a special occasion or purpose, though in its earliest form it was a prayer for the rest of a deceased person. It may be said publicly in church or in private.

NOVICE. An individual who is undergoing a trial period, usually about a year in length, to test his or her fitness for life and membership in a religious order or congregation. During the time of the novitiate, which usually follows a shorter period called a postulancy, the man or woman dresses in the habit of the order and follows its routine, but he does not yet renounce his property or take final vows, and he may leave or be dismissed if it seems advisable.

NOVICIATE OR NOVITIATE (Lat.: from *novus,* new; nō-vish'-ē-āt). The period or state of being a novice; also, the buildings of a monastery or convent set aside for the use of novices.

NUMBER OF THE BEAST. This reference, taken from Revelation 13:18, "Let him that hath understanding count the number of the beast . . . Six hundred three-score and six," has not been fully identified, although many individuals over the centuries have claimed to have done so. It is quite likely that the number, 666, referred to Nero who was Caesar from A.D. 54–68, blamed the Christians for the great fire that destroyed Rome, and instigated the first persecutions. In Hebrew characters with numerical value, Nero, or Neron Caesar, gives the number 666. At best, however, such a solution is only speculation.

NUMBERS. The fourth book of the Old Testament giving a census of the Israelites, a listing of more religious laws and customs, and a narrative conclusion of the forty years of wandering. It is notable for its story of Balaam's ass. In its present form Numbers dates from about 350 B.C.

NUN (Lat.: old lady; child's nurse; like the Greek *nanna* and Sanskrit *nana,* mother). A woman belonging to a religious order or congregation of the Catholic (or Anglican) Church. Nuns are often addressed as "Sister," although strictly speaking the term applies to *sorores,* sisters, who belong to congregations that have simple vows, rather than to *moniales,* members of orders that have solemn vows. Most of the better known "old orders" such as the Benedictines, Dominicans, and Carmelites, have womens' orders with solemn vows. The nun's life, determined by the order, may be either active with work out in the world, or, perhaps, in the convent but with laymen, children, etc., or it may be contemplative and more or less enclosed. Her habit, or uniform, usually consists of an ankle-length, full-skirted, long-sleeved garment and a concealing headdress; although colors vary, white, grey, and especially black predominate. A modern move to shorten the habit of the nun in active work, especially teaching or nursing, is now underway.

NUNC DIMITTIS, THE (Lat.: now thou lettest depart; nunk dimit'-is). Also called the Song of Simeon, this prayer from Luke

2:29–32, derives its name from the opening Latin words translated as "Lord, now lettest thou thy servant depart in peace. . . ." It is recited or sung daily at Compline in the Catholic Church, and is a fairly popular dismissal verse in Protestant churches.

NUNNERY. A residence of nuns and the nuns themselves. This old term has, for the most part, been replaced by "convent."

# O

OBADIAH. A very short prophetic book of the Old Testament, the work of one of the minor prophets.

OBLATE (Lat.: offered; ōb′-lăt). A person dedicated to a religious or monastic life; the name given persons who join certain religious congregations, e.g., an oblate of St. Benedict. Congregations of oblates generally take no vows, or, at the most, simple vows, and are often organized for the specific purpose of working among the sick or poor.

OBLATION. An offering, but especially an offering that is a sacrifice, or a thanksgiving to God. The thing offered is also considered the oblation, as the bread and wine of the Communion forms an oblation, or as Jesus is referred to as "a full, perfect, and sufficient sacrifice, oblation, and satisfaction, for the sins of the whole world . . ." (*The Book of Common Prayer,* "Prayer of Consecration.")

OBSECRATION. Although the basic meaning of this term is "entreaty" or "supplication," it refers more specifically to prayers which begin with "By," and appeal through some sacred thing to God, e.g., from the litany of the saints, "By thy nativity, deliver us, O Lord."

OCCAM, WILLIAM (d. c.1349). This Franciscan theologian was born in England but spent a considerable portion of his life in France. He attacked the temporal power of the Church, rejected certain of St. Thomas Aquinas' doctrines, and emphasized faith over reason in spiritual questions. He is also called William of Ockham.

OCTAVE. The eight-day celebration of a religious holiday, commencing with the day itself and continuing for seven days there-

239

after, is called the "octave" of that festival. For example, the octave of Christmas extends from Christmas day through January 1; the days between the feast day and the final day of the octave are said to be "within the octave," and the last day, in this case January 1, is called the "octave day." Christmas, Easter, and Pentecost are the only holidays remaining with a true octave, though Epiphany, January 6, still has a recognized octave day, January 13. The term is derived from the Latin *octava,* eighth.

ODOR OF SANCTITY. According to ancient Christian belief, the body of a saint did not emit an unpleasant odor when the person died but rather a pleasing aroma, if any. This was the "odor of sanctity." This faith has survived into modern times; Dostoevsky refers to it at some length in relation to Father Zossima, a character in his *Brothers Karamazov.*

OECUMENICAL. See ECUMENICAL.

OF FAITH. That term used to describe any religious doctrine or tenet which must be believed by members of the religion holding it. It may be said to be of faith that Christians believe in the divinity of Jesus, but in practice the term is used mostly in the Catholic Church.

OFFERING, THE. Something given, and the act of giving. In most Christian churches, "the offering" is the name given the money collected during, or in relation to, the church service, as well as to the act of collecting it. Actually, "offering" may designate the amount pledged over an entire year; or it may refer to a special type of gift, such as one of time, clothing, or food; or it may be "the offering of oneself," as when services, work, or something personal, such as a home, are given or lent, usually for a special cause or to fulfill a specific need.

OFFERTORY. The collection of money taken up at the church service is often called the "offertory" instead of the "offering," and the offertory hymn or offertory prayer is that which is sung or said at that time. In the Catholic Church, the Offertory is the portion of the Mass when the celebrant offers the still unconsecrated bread and wine to God. It marks the beginning of the Eucharistic sacrifice, the heart of the service.

OFFICE. In the Catholic Church, the term refers to services of prayers, the special service for the day, or the prayers and ceremonies for some special purpose. See DIVINE OFFICE.

OFFICE OF THE DEAD. A service of prayers and psalms said for the repose of the souls of the dead; its recitation is especially required on All Souls Day in the Catholic Church.

OIL. Anointing with oil, especially at baptism and of the gravely ill, is a practice of the Catholic Church derived from the ancient Christian church and from the Jewish faith. Olive oil blessed by a bishop on Maundy Thursday is used.

OLD CHRISTMAS. January 6, which was celebrated in Great Britain as Christmas until 1752, is still sometimes called by this name. It was not until that year that England followed the continent in replacing the old Julian calendar with the more accurate Gregorian.

OLD HUNDREDTH. The hundredth psalm, beginning "Make a joyful noise unto the Lord, . . ." and a version of it beginning "All people that on earth do dwell. . ." Old Hundred is the name of the melody to which this psalm was set in an early psalter, and it survives as the tune for the doxology most used by Protestants, "Praise God from whom all blessings flow . . ."

OLD LATIN VERSION. A second-century translation, of the Septuagint Bible into Latin. One of the several texts is called the *Itala Vetus,* a name now often used to designate any Latin text before the Vulgate.

OLD TESTAMENT, THE. The Hebraic, pre-Christian portion of the Bible is composed of thirty-nine books which include ancient Hebrew history and law, prophecy, poetry, wisdom literature, and religious teachings. The traditional arrangement, that followed in the Authorized Version, is: Law, History, Poetry and Wisdom Literature, Major Prophets, and Minor Prophets. Most of the Old Testament was written originally in Hebrew over a period of perhaps a thousand years, the earliest books being those of the Pentateuch, and the latest Ecclesiastes, composed about 150 B.C. Biblical criticism recognizes, also, that Psalms, for example, contains some very early writings as well as some of a later date;

it is also held to be likely that some passages in a number of books were first written not in Hebrew but in Aramaic.

OMNIPOTENCE. Meaning literally "all powerful," this is an attribute traditionally ascribed to God alone. Under examination, this belief that "to God, all things are possible," becomes quite complex, for it raises several difficult questions. For example, can God do what is logically impossible? Or, can God only do all that is possible in a given situation? In general, it is held that God cannot make two self-contradictory statements true at the same time, and that he cannot "make opposites exist, in the same subject at the same time and in the same respect, make a man without a soul, make the past not to have been, or create another God." (*Theological Terms,* p. 167) Theologians generally concur that "omnipotence" means that God can do what is genuinely possible to do, "but as St. Thomas [Aquinas] remarks (I,XXV,3), 'It is better to say that impossibles cannot be done than that God cannot do them.'" (*Catholic Dictionary,* p. 354) Although this may appear a hair-splitting distinction, especially to Protestants, it is probably accurate to say that most of the faithful whether Catholic or Protestant, would take exception to the bare statement that "God cannot do the impossible."

OMNIPRESENCE. The attribute of God generally meaning that he is present in his entirety, and not in parts, everywhere, without localization in time, place, or object. "He was neither large nor small, but so filled space that all of him was in every place . . . This did not mean that God multiplied himself in such a way that one of him was everywhere. There was still just one God, but somehow that entire one was—all of him—simultaneously at every point in space . . . the same thing was true of the way he lived in time, . . ." (*Myth and Ritual in Christianity,* p. 32)

OMNISCIENCE. This attribute of God is defined as his knowledge of everything, and is traditionally expanded to mean everything past, present, and future, without any breaks in time or limitations in space. However, examination by theologians has shown that the concept is anything but simple. Some of the questions raised revolve around "knowledge," which, as usually defined, implies that the knower is affected by what is known; by definition, also, God is unchangeable and "unaffectable," and thus two attributes of the Almighty are apparently mutually exclusive. Other questions turn on the relationship of God and evil: if God knows about evil (he must, for he is omniscient), does this mean that he also wills it? If he wills it, then he must not be all-good; if he is powerless to correct it, then he must not be omnipotent. The matter is of more concern in modern times to Catholic and orthodox theologians than to most of their Protestant counterparts, who tend to regard the questions as unanswerable or irrelevant or both.

ONTOLOGICAL ARGUMENT. (Gr.: being; on′-tə-loj′-i-k′l). A proof for the existence of God first set forth by Anselm of Canterbury in the eleventh century. Fewer objections have been raised to it than to most proofs; it is held to be *a priori,* that is, it follows with strict logic from the accepted meanings of the terms it uses. One objection it has incurred is to its treating of "existence" as if existing added a measure of perfection or greatness to the concept of a thing, whereas in our language or thought a thing that exists in thought alone is, or can be, equal in greatness to a thing that possesses actual existence. The concept of "perfect love," for example, does not become finer when, or if, a "perfect love" exists. In essence, however, the ontological argument for the existence of God has been found to hold up very well. It is, briefly, that God is that which is such that nothing greater or better can be conceived of. Existence is a good. (This is the point most open to dispute.) Therefore, God must contain existence, i.e., God must exist. A second part continues: Either God exists necessarily, because not to exist would mean to be less than perfect, or the very idea of God is self-contradictory (for it would mean to imagine him as both perfect and not entirely perfect at the same time—an impossible condition) and he could not conceivably exist. That is, either God exists necessarily or the idea of God existing at all is inconceivable—the "perfect" must contain existence as an attribute (i.e., it must exist) or the idea of "perfect" loses its meaning. This second part is still open to debate, and such questions as, "Is the idea of God fundamentally inconsistent?" and "Is 'necessary existence' a logical concept?" continue to be asked.

ONTOLOGY. That branch of metaphysics which is concerned with the nature of reality and existence. See also ONTOLOGICAL ARGUMENT.

ORANS (also ORANTE). A representation found in the catacombs of a figure praying with outstretched arms. Symbolically, the soul of the deceased may be the represented entity.

ORATIO (Lat.: speech). A prayer, especially a short one such as that usually called a "collect."

ORATORIO. A religious musical composition usually presented with soloists, chorus and orchestra on a large and dramatic scale but without costumes, action, or extraneous dialogue. Oratorios probably originated in the sixteenth century; St. Philip Neri is generally given credit for founding the Oratory in Rome, where such musical numbers were performed.

ORATORY (Lat.: to speak). A small chapel usually for private prayers; public or semipublic oratories may exist in conjunction with a church, a school chapel, or a hospital, although they are often only open at certain times for the use of the public.

ORDAIN. To appoint or admit to Christian ministry, as "he was an ordained minsiter." Most denominations have their own particular ordination ceremonies.

ORDER. One of the nine ranks of angels in the celestial hierarchy; also, in the Catholic Church, a shortened form of "religious order," referring to such groups as the Benedictines, Cistercians, Dominicans, etc.

ORDER, HOLY or SACRED. Any rank of Christian clergy may be referred to as an order, but correctly, only an ordained minister is said to have "taken holy orders." In the Catholic Church there are both major i.e., holy or sacred, and minor orders.

ORDER, THE SACRAMENT OF HOLY. This is the conferment of priesthood, or the sacrament by which a man is invested with the spiritual power and character to be a priest. Protestants as a whole do not recognize Holy Orders as a sacrament; the ceremony of ordination replaces it.

ORDERS, MAJOR. The major orders, or, with strict accuracy, the holy or sacred orders, in the Catholic Church are subdeacon, deacon, and priest. See MAJOR ORDERS.

ORDERS, MINOR. Porter, lector, exorcist, and acolyte are ranks in the lower clergy in the Catholic Church. See MINOR ORDERS.

ORDINARY OF THE MASS. The essentially unchanging parts of the Catholic worship service which form a framework into which appropriate additions for various religious holidays and seasons may be fitted are: Preparatory prayer, Kyrie, Gloria, the Creed, Offertory prayers, Preface, Sanctus, Canon of the Mass, the Lord's Prayer, fraction, Agnus Dei, Communion prayers, and the conclusion and last gospel. The changeable portion which is added to this framework is called the Proper of the Mass.

ORDINATION. The conferring and receiving of ministership in the Christian church, or being admitted to holy orders.

ORIGEN (185?–254?). The Christian philosopher who edited the Hexapla and who ranks as one of the finest early theologians held, nevertheless, some doctrines totally at odds with the developing orthodoxy of the times. For example, Origen taught that the persons of the Trinity are not equal; that there will be nothing of the material body after resurrection; and that there is no eternal punishment. The Catholic Church's position toward Origen is not one of complete condemnation, for he is believed to have been tortured to death for his faith. Though his errors, as the unorthodox portions of his faith are called, are often attributed to the essential "Greek-ness" of his attitude toward history, cosmology, etc. and not to any vital flaw in his Christian faith, they do prevent his being canonized or designated a Doctor of the Church.

ORIGINAL RIGHTEOUSNESS. Although there is some variation in Catholic and Protestant understanding, this term refers usually to man's condition before the Fall, whether that condition is defined with reference to supernatural gifts, likeness to God, or harmony with God. It is sinlessness, absence of knowledge of evil (and, of course, of any self-conscious awareness of "good") freedom from pain, and the lack of any trait or characteristic which would be *un*righteous.

ORIGINAL SIN. While usually interpreted as a condition of sinfulness, or the sinfulness "born into" each baby, this expression is more accurately understood to be the tendency toward sinfulness which is held by many to be inherent in mankind. Catholic theology teaches that the Fall resulted in the loss of sanctifying grace, a loss which leaves man with the inclination to sin. Baptism remits original sin, but subjection to human and physical disabilities, including death, remains; further, the free will of man still makes possible his choice of a sinful course in preference to a righteous one.

ORNAMENTS OF THE ALTAR. In the Catholic Church, the high altar has traditionally required a crucifix, six candlesticks, three white cloths, a frontal, and a covering (ciborium or canopy); side altars are similarly dressed. Vases of flowers and other ornaments such as images of saints may be added between the candlesticks. In Protestant churches there is no set way of fixing altars, Anglican churches being the exception. A cross, candlesticks, and white altar cloths are often used, while bouquets of fresh flowers are often set at the base. The crucifix rarely if ever is used.

ORPHREY. The embroidered decoration on the back and front of a chasuble; also, the similar decoration on the border and around the opening of a cope.

ORTHODOX (from Greek, *right* or *believer*). Established, conventional, sanctioned by authority. Referring to an individual as "orthodox" in his religious faith means that he adheres firmly to the teachings and dogma of his denomination, neither interpreting for himself nor accepting new or liberal interpretations, no matter how popular they may be, until church authorities have accepted them and included them in church doctrine. More specifically, "Orthodox" is used to designate those who belong to the Orthodox Eastern Church; it may be used as "orthodox" to designate, also, Christians who accept the early creeds, the Apostles, Nicene, and Athanasian, and the definitions and decisions of the Council of Chalcedon convened in A.D. 451.

ORTHODOX EASTERN CHURCH, THE. Also called the Eastern Church, the Orthodox Church, and, less correctly, the Greek Orthodox Church, this denomination broke finally with the Catholic Church in Rome in 1054. It is today still considered to be in a state of schism. The Orthodox Church consists of those churches that recognize the primacy of the patriarchates of Constantinople, Alexandria, Antioch, and Jerusalem, and includes the autonomous churches of Russia, Greece, Rumania, Bulgaria, Finland, Yugoslavia, etc. Orthodox Church doctrine rejects the supremacy and infallibility of the Pope; the doctrine of the Immaculate Conception; the use of indulgences; and all but the first seven ecumenical councils. Use of the Byzantine rite is general, and icons, relics, and images are given more devotion than is usually true in western Catholicism. All of the Orthodox churches agree in matters of dogma, ritual, and liturgy, although practice, as in the use of the sacraments and in the training of the clergy, differ widely. Orthodox Church membership, excluding doubtful figures from Russia, totals about forty million throughout the world, making it the second largest Christian body in existence. By its very nature, however, it lacks the authority and power to speak with a single voice which has given the Catholic Church its position of strength and importance.

OSSERVATORE ROMANO, THE (It.: Rome Observer; o-ser′-vɔ-tō′rä Rō-mä′-nō). The newspaper printed and published in Vatican City, reflecting the views of the Holy See. It was founded in 1860.

OUR FATHER, THE. The Lord's Prayer, often so-called from the opening words, "Our Father who art in Heaven . . ." This is especially true among Catholics, where the Latin phrase of the same meaning, *Pater Noster,* is also used.

OUR LADY. The most common English expression, when writing or speaking informally, to designate Mary the mother of Jesus. It is often used in combination with a modifier, as Our Lady of Lourdes, Our Lady Help of Christians, etc. The first known use was in the eighth century by the poet Cynewulf, and it was for some time common in its longer form, Our Lady Saint Mary.

OUR LADY OF MT. CARMEL. A feast day celebrated on July 16, originally by Carmelites, but since the eighteenth century by Catholics in general, in recognition of the approval given Carmelite rule by Pope Honorius III in 1226. Carmelites take their name from Mount Carmel in Syria traditional place of founding; their order was particularly marked by devotion to Mary, and in the thirteenth century one member, Simon Stock, was given a scapular in a visit by the Virgin. The early festival of Our Lady became, in the seventeenth century, a festival of the Scapular, but it was broadened again in the eighteenth century to include the entire Church in the festival of Our Lady of Mount Carmel.

OUR LORD. Jesus; a synonymous expression used since the twelfth century to refer to Jesus. "The Lord," however, more often refers to God, with such notable exceptions as "The Lord's Prayer."

# P

**PAGAN.** One who does not believe in Christianity, though, more specifically, the term is reserved to refer to one who is neither Christian, Jew, nor Moslem. It refers mostly to nonbelievers of classical, pre-Christian times, while "heathen" is used to refer to nonbelievers of the centuries since the beginning of the Christian era.

**PALATINE.** Relating to the Sacred Apostolic Palace of the Vatican in Rome.

**PALL.** A linen covering for the chalice at Mass; also, a black cloth spread over the coffin at funerals.

**PALLIUM.** A circular band of white, made of wool and worn over the shoulders by archbishops, for whom it is a distinctive vestment. "To receive the pallium" is synonymous with "to be made an archbishop."

**PALM SUNDAY.** The Sunday before Easter on which is commemorated Jesus' entry into Jerusalem, when palm fronds were strewn in his path.

**PALMER.** A medieval name for a pilgrim to the Holy Land, derived from such pilgrims' custom of wearing a palm leaf as a badge.

**PANCAKE DAY.** Shrove Tuesday, the Tuesday before Ash Wednesday, the first day of Lent. The tradition of serving pancakes on this day is very ancient and derived, perhaps, from the need to use up eggs and fats before Lent began, since fasting during that period was obligatory.

**PANCRAS, ST.** (d. 304). A young man who was a native of Phrygia in southwest Asia Minor and who journeyed to Rome where he was beheaded for his refusal to renounce his Christian faith. His feast day is May 12.

PANTHEISM. A religious doctrine that identified God in everything and holds that there is an identity of substance between God and the world, a belief not to be confused with the Christian concept of omnipresence.

PANTOKRATOR (Gr.: all-mighty). A picture or other image of Jesus as the ruler of Heaven.

PAPACY, THE. The office of pope, or the period of office of a pope; the ecclesiastical government that vests authority in the pope; also, the whole series of popes considered collectively.

PAPAL. Of the pope, or of the church government headed by the pope. This adjectival form is familiar in such combinations as "papal state," "papal bull," "papal decree," and "papal robes."

PAPAL BULL. An official edict or decree from the pope. The term "bull" is derived from the same source as "bulletin," a Latin word "bulla," meaning seal or knob and referring to the official seal which was affixed to the document of the sender. In practice, the use of "bull" to refer to the document itself has been narrowed to refer almost exclusively to one from the pope.

PAPIST. A somewhat derogatory term for a Catholic, i.e., a member of the church of which the pope is the head.

PARABLE. A short and simple story used to illustrate a religious or moral lesson. Some thirty parables are recorded in the gospels as having been told by Jesus.

PARACLETE (Gr.: to call, to advocate; par'-ə-klēt). One who pleads or intercedes for another; in religious terms, the Holy Spirit or the Comforter (John 14:16), or Jesus (1 John 2:1), the advocate with the Father.

PARADISE. Heaven, or, in the Old Testament, the Garden of Eden, an "earthly heaven."

PARADOX. In Christian thought, paradoxes such as "he who loses his life shall find it" have been defended as the best way of expressing the truths of God which may appear to be self-contradictions. On the other hand, paradoxes have also been condemned as comfortable evasions of logical thinking and attractive disguises of irrationality.

PARAMENTS. An inclusive term for the vestments of clergymen and religious ornamentation of a variety of sorts.

PARCLOSE. The screen dividing a chapel from the body of a church or separating choir from choir aisles.

PARDON. Forgiveness, as one is pardoned or forgiven one's sin. The name "pardon" is given certain religious festivals of the Catholic Church held in connection with special celebrations, pilgrimages, or the like, when indulgences were customarily given. Perhaps the best known of such "pardons" are in Brittany.

PARISH. The smallest ecclesiastical territorial division in Catholic or Anglican church organization. A parish is a subdivision of the larger diocese; it is usually in the care of a priest, and the main church of the parish, usually the one in the largest, or perhaps only, town, is the one designated for regular services.

PAROCHIAL MASS. The main Mass said every Sunday and on other important religious festivals in the parish church.

PAROUSIA (from Greek, the coming of a royal person; pa-rōō'-zhə). This more general term has come to mean the Second Coming of Jesus, at the end of the world, when the quick and the dead will be judged and the final Kingdom of God will be established.

PARSON. A minister, or a priest of an Anglican church. The term was used widely in nineteenth century America to designate Protestant preachers, whether ordained or not, but in its early usage in medieval England it was the legal and frequently used word for "priest."

PARTICLE. A term for the small piece of Communion bread given to each Communicant.

PARVIS. The open porch at the entrance to a church.

PASCAL BAYLON, ST. (1540–1592). St. Pascal, born of a humble family of Aragon, was a shepherd until he was about twenty-four years old, although he had apparently been quite devout since early youth. As a lay brother of the Franciscan friars, he worked at menial jobs, but later, as mendicant and porter, he was in a position to help with his great generosity all those who needed him. His miracles were reportedly numerous, but perhaps the most widely known is that of "St. Pascal's knocks." According to this story, he concerns himself with the salvation of many, knocking loudly to warn and frighten some into better behavior, knocking softly to reassure and comfort others. It is also said that sounds from his relics or pictures warn his friends three days before they are to die so that their souls can be prepared. His feast day is May 17.

PASCH. (Pasach) The Jewish feast of the Passover or the Christtian Easter may be referred to occasionally by this name. In many liturgical books, the days after Easter are said to be "of the Pasch," and the Sundays up to Pentecost are "after the Pasch." Paschal, of course, is a frequently used synonym for Easter.

PASCHAL CANDLE. The large candle lighted on the Saturday before Easter in the Catholic Church. This Paschal, or Easter, Candle is made of beeswax, a "type" of the flesh of Jesus, deemed entirely pure and unsullied. Its symbolism otherwise is of Jesus as the light of the world and of the newly baptized. It is lighted each Sunday until Ascension Day.

PASCHAL LAMB. The lamb roasted and eaten ritualistically by Jews at the Passover festival was first known by this term. However, Jesus is often called, figuratively, the Paschal Lamb, a title deriving from his role as the victim who sacrificed himself for the atonement of man's sins. See AGNUS DEI.

PASSION, THE. The sufferings of Jesus on his way to Golgotha as well as the crucifixion itself. "Passion Sunday" begins "Passion Tide" and especially "Passion Week," the week preceding Holy Week, which itself is known as "Passion Week" in the East. See STATIONS OF THE CROSS.

PASSION PLAY. A play representing the passion of Jesus. Probably the most famous, that held in Oberammergau, Germany, has become a fully staged, professional dramatic attraction, although it had its inception in a medieval mystery play.

PASSION SUNDAY, TIDE, and WEEK. The Sunday before Palm Sunday is called Passion Sunday. It introduces Passion Tide, which includes Passion Week, the week between Passion Sunday and Palm Sunday, and Holy Week. In Catholic Churches, all images are veiled from Passion Sunday until Easter. See PASSION, THE.

PASSOVER, THE. The Passover, or Pasch, commemorates the deliverance of the Israelites from their long captivity in Egypt. The feast is kept for seven days, beginning on the fourteenth day of the lunar month of Nisan, the first month of the year in the Jewish religious calendar, corresponding roughly to March-April. Unleavened bread is eaten in remembrance of the haste with which the Hebrews departed from Egypt. Lamb, also is a ceremonial dish, as God "passed over" and did not kill the firstborn in the houses of the Israelites whose doorposts were marked with the blood of a lamb, though all the Egyptian firstborn were killed. The story is recounted in Exodus 12:1-15.

PASTOR (Lat.: shepherd). A minister with the care of souls in his parish or other religious territory.

PASTORAL EPISTLES. Paul's letters to Timothy and Titus are so called since they contain instructions for young ministers, or pastors.

PASTORAL LETTER. The communication sent, or message delivered, perhaps through a church bulletin, from a minister to the members of the church of which he is pastor.

PASTORAL STAFF. A shepherd's staff, also called a crozier, about six feet long with a curved top; it symbolizes both the rod of correction and the shepherd's crook of pastoral care. It is a symbol of episcopal office in the Catholic Church and is used by bishops (excluding the pope), cardinals, abbots, etc.

PATEN. The thin metal plate that holds the Communion bread during the Communion service.

PATERNOSTER (Lat.: Our Father; pat'-ĕr-nōs-tĕr). The Lord's

Prayer, so called from its Latin opening: *Pater noster, qui es in coelis, sanctificatur nomen tuum.*

PATRIARCH (from Latin "father" and "to rule"). In biblical terms, "patriarch" refers to Abraham, Isaac, Jacob, and the latter's twelve sons, the "fathers" of the twelve Hebrew tribes. In the Catholic Church, the bishops holding the highest rank after the pope, i.e., the Patriarch of the West, are called patriarchs and include those of Constantinople, Alexandria, Antioch, and Jerusalem, as well as those of the Melkite, Syrian, and Armenian churches.

PATRIARCHATE. Territory under the ecclesiastical jurisdiction of a patriarch, or the position of patriarch itself. In the early Christian church there were five chief patriarchates: Rome, Constantinople, Antioch, Alexandria, and Jerusalem, but of these only that of Rome now survives in its territorial integrity. The others exist more as organizations of Catholics of different Eastern rites, or, in modified form, as federations of Orthodox churches.

PATRICK, ST. (385?–461?). The Apostle of Ireland is undoubtedly, along with St. Nicholas, the best known of the nonbiblical saints. About his life, however, very little is known with any certainty. He was probably born on the west coast of Britain, captured at a youthful age by pirates, and sold into slavery in Ireland. It is said that he heard the call to Christian service, escaped to his home, and later traveled to France where he studied theology. After some years, he returned to the still-heathen land of Ireland which he very successfully Christianized. Some twenty years before his death he journeyed to Rome where he received the pallium, a white circular band distinctive of archbishops, from the pope. His *Confessions* are known to be genuine, and the poem called the "Lorica," a word meaning the shield and breastplate of St. Patrick, is thought to be. It invokes divine help, in part, as follows:

| | |
|---|---|
| Power of God | for my upholding |
| Wisdom of God | for my guidance; |
| Eye of God | for my foresight |

*  *  *

against incantations of false prophets

against black laws of paganism;
against false laws of heresy
against encompassment of idolatry;
against spells of women and smiths and druids;
against all knowledge that is forbidden the human soul.

Many legends surround St. Patrick, probably the best known being that he drove the snakes out of Ireland. His feast day is March 17.

PATRIMONY. Land or other property endowed to a church.

PATRISTICS. Study of the lives and writings of the Fathers of the Church who lived during the first ten centuries. The writings are in Greek and Latin, and at first were comprised chiefly of explanations of the faith to pagans or to Christians who disagreed with the writer. Later they became more varied, including abstract theological thinking, and analysis and interpretation of Scriptures. There are many such writings. Among the authors are St. Clement I, St. Ignatius of Antioch, St. Justin Martyr, Origen, Tertullian, St. Cyprian, Eusebius of Caesarea, St. Gregory Nazianzus, St. Basil the Great, St. John Chrysostom, St. Ambrose, St. Gregory I, and St. John of Damascus. Those of the third, and earlier centuries, i.e., before the First Council of Nicea in 325, are called the ante-Nicene Fathers, and the later ones are called the post-Nicene.

PATRON SAINT. The saint considered to be the special guardian of a person, a place, a church, or the like. Most individuals consider their patron saint to be the one whose name they were given at birth, while the choice of a patron for a town, association, or other similar institution must be formalized through confirmation by the Holy See. By ancient tradition, professions, occupations, and countries have patron saints, and churches are called by the names of the patron saint or "titular," e.g., St. Michael and All Angels, St. Bartholomew's, St. Mary's.

PAUL, ST. (first century). The Apostle of the Gentiles, author of thirteen epistles included as books in the New Testament, is often credited with giving definitive shape and direction to Christianity. His conversion, effected through a miraculous appearance of Jesus to Paul, then called Saul of Tarsus, on the Road to Damascus, and his missionary travels are described in the Acts of the Apostles. Prior to his conversion, he had participated almost fanatically in the persecution of Christians; he died a martyr to his Christian faith, according to tradition at the same time as St. Peter in Rome. The two share the feast day of June 29, but St. Paul's conversion is commemorated on June 30, as well as on January 25.

PAULA, ST. (d. 404). St. Paula provides an example of the type of patrician Roman matron who occasionally gave up all to live a life of piety and poverty. She was a friend and student of St. Jerome and spent part of her wealth erecting a monastery for him and his friends in Bethlehem. Her life was austere, and she demanded similar sacrifices from the nuns in the convent she established, also in Bethlehem. Although she had much unhappiness in her life, such as the loss of all but one of her children, she died happy in her faith and was buried near the cave where St. Jerome had spent his last years. Her feast day is January 26.

PAULICIANISM. The Paulicians formed a heretical sect active from the seventh to the eleventh century, with origins as early, according to some authorities, as the fourth. Their beginnings are obscure, although some speculate that the group was a survival of early Christianity. They accepted a form of dualism, it is believed, perhaps Manichaean in nature; they rejected the sacraments, the use of images, and much of the Bible.

PAULINE EPISTLES. The letters written by St. Paul and now incorporated as books in the New Testament. They include: I and II Thessalonians, Galatians, I and II Corinthians, Romans, I and II Timothy, Ephesians, Titus, Philippians, Colossians, and Philemon. Hebrews, once attributed to St. Paul, is now thought to be a sermon by another writer and not a letter at all.

PAX. (Lat.: peace). In the Catholic Church, the Kiss of Peace; also, a tablet or disc bearing a holy image and used to convey the Kiss of Peace in medieval times and, occasionally, even today.

PAX DEI (Lat.: Peace of God; päks-dā'-ē). The immunity of churches, clerics, members of religious orders, etc. from attack or

danger during time of war is known by this phrase, as is the so-
called "Sunday Truce," long observed in Europe and elsewhere
during wartime and frequently also called the Truce of God, of
which it formed a part.

PAX VOBIS (Lat.: Peace be with you; päks-wō′-bis). This greeting is given to a congregation by a bishop in the Catholic Mass
instead of the priest's *"Dominus Vobiscum,"* that is, "The Lord
be with you."

PELAGIANISM (pə-lā′-jē-ən-iz′m). The heresy taking its name
from Pelagius (355?–425?), a British monk who taught that
there is no original sin, that death is simply a law of human nature, that "grace" is anything such as reason and free will which
leads man to God, and that Heaven is open even to pagans, if they
lead good lives. Pelagius preached in North Africa and Palestine
and, not surprisingly, earned the vigorous opposition of St. Augustine and St. Jerome. Pelagianism was condemned at the Council
of Ephesus in 431, and a remaining modified fragment which
survived in England and France until the sixth century was condemned at the Council of Orange in 529.

PELICAN. A symbol for Jesus, as the pelican is said to feed its
young with its own blood, recalling the Eucharistic sacrifice and
the idea "This is my blood which is given for you."

PENANCE (Lat.: repentance or regret). A suffering, or a task
imposed on oneself, or by an authority, to show sincere repentance
or to make up for some sin or wrongdoing. In the Catholic
Church penance is a sacrament (see ABSOLUTION) composed of the
confession of a sin to a priest, the imposition of a penalty, often in
the form of the recitation of prayers, the giving of alms, or the
like, and absolution. Although a sacrament in the Anglican
Church, also, the following of the above practice varies from
church to church. In both, penance is understood to entail regret for sin because sin is an offense to God, not because one is
afraid of being caught, or of punishment, or of Hell. In ancient
times, penitents were assigned a certain number of days or years,
perhaps even a life, of penance, and during that period they were
excluded from part or all of the church worship service, but
especially from participation in Communion. Prevalent before the

eleventh century, this custom persisted in some places, until the 1700's and may exist in certain missions to this day.

PENITENT. One who is undergoing penance, either imposed by authority or by the individual; also, the feeling of being sorry for and ashamed of one's sins or wrongdoing. *"Penitence"* may be distinguished from *"repentance,"* a full realization of sin and the will to change; *"contrition,"* a crushing sorrow for sin and the will to improve; and *"remorse,"* a torturing sense of guilt.

PENITENTES (Sp.: the repenters; pen-i-ten'-tēz). A secret order of laymen originating from one order of Franciscans, active in the southwestern United States in the nineteenth century. In Holy Week, they practiced flagellation that was concluded with a crucifixion, and, because of such excesses, were condemned by the Catholic Church in 1889. The group may still be active, though to what extent is not known with any certainty.

PENITENTIAL PSALMS. The seven penitential psalms which express penitence and a desire for pardon are numbers 6, 31, 37, 51, 101, 129, and 142.

PENITENT THIEF. The Good Thief, perhaps named Dismas, who accepted Jesus as his savior as he hung on one of the crosses beside him.

PENTATEUCH (Gr.: composed of five books; pen'-tə-tōōk). The first five books of the Old Testament, also called the Torah, the Law, or the Books of the Law of Moses. They are Genesis, Exodus, Leviticus, Numbers, and Deuteronomy. Mosaic authorship is unlikely. Rather, modern scholarship considers the Pentateuch to be the work of several authors, and, in its present form, no earlier than about 350 B.C., although parts may date from around 1000 B.C. *Genesis* covers the creation of the world, the stories of Cain and Abel; Noah; the tower of Babel; Abraham and Isaac; Jacob and Joseph. *Exodus* is the account of the Hebrews' escape from Egypt under Moses, and is, in large part, a book of laws and ceremonies. *Leviticus, Numbers,* and *Deuteronomy* are for the most part made up of laws and codes.

PENTECOST (Gr.: fiftieth). The fiftieth day after Easter, commemorating the descent of the Holy Spirit to the Apostles who were assembled to celebrate the Jewish spring harvest festival, Shabuoth, and the end of Passover time. The Jewish festival is also called the Feast of Weeks and is now celebrated as the time of the giving of the Law to Moses on Mount Sinai. The Christian Pentecost is often spoken of as the "birthday" of the Christian church; the story is recounted in the Acts of the Apostles 21:1-39. In the Christian calendar, Sundays after the holiday are referred to as "after Pentecost" until the beginning of the Advent season. Red is the traditional color of Pentecostal vestments and the great hymn, *"Veni Creator"* was written for the time. Another name for Pentecost is Whitsunday, or White Sunday, because in ancient times those baptized on this traditional day for that sacrament wore white.

PERFECTION, CHRISTIAN. Just what Christian perfection is, and, indeed, whether it is attainable in this life or not, has been the cause of much dispute, especially among Protestant denominations. It is an idea based on Jesus' words, "You, therefore, must be perfect, as your heavenly Father is perfect." Catholic theology early identified Christian perfection as perfect love, possible only for the saints to achieve. Protestant reformers, however, maintained it was not even within the grasp of saints, and, sometimes, that even progress toward it was only transitory, illusory, or impossible. John Wesley reversed this extremely negativistic attitude by asserting the identity of such perfection as pure love, and maintaining that it was within man's range of possibilities. Such pure love, he said, was God's law, and Christian perfection, although it might be long striven for, was, in the end, a gift of grace given instantaneously and accompanied by assurance of having achieved it. In making it attainable, Wesley departed radically from Calvin and Luther, and this departure is often said to constitute one of the outstanding contributions of Methodism to theology. In general, most thoughtful Protestants probably believe that Christian perfection, while possible to achieve, is well beyond the capacities of most ordinary mortals.

PERFECTION, THEOLOGICAL. Also called "divine perfection," this term refers to God's quality of "complete wholeness," as well as "flawlessness." Other phrases such as "absolute" and "pure being" are synonymous with it. This concept is much debated in currrent theology because of certain contradictions implicit in it, e.g., that pure being is the same as nothingness and that "perfection" must include the characteristic of "all-compassionate," which implies being moved by that for which the compassion is felt, though God is by definition unchanging and unmoved.

PERICOPE. A lesson, or a passage, from Scripture to be read in the liturgy.

PERPETUAL ADORATION. Round-the-clock adoration of the Eucharistic elements, the Blessed Sacrament, observed by certain congregations, especially of nuns. It consists of prayers and various devotions and is taken usually in one-hour turns by members. The practice originated in the seventeenth century from the Forty Hours Prayers, adoration of the Blessed Sacrament for forty consecutive hours from the hour at which tradition says Jesus was laid in the tomb until the resurrection.

PERSEVERANCE. The term used technically in Calvinistic theology refers to the preservation by divine grace of the elect from falling into sin. After election, Calvinists held, a person was preserved from committing any act which might entail forfeiture of his state of grace.

PETER, ST. (first century). Held by the Catholic Church in the very highest esteem, Peter (Cephas) named Simon was a fisherman when called by Jesus to follow him. It is written in Matthew 16:16-18 that Peter professed his belief in Jesus as the "Son of the living God," and that Jesus answered ". . . thou art Peter, and upon this rock [Aramaic *Kepha* or *Cephas,* Latin and Greek, *Petra,* rock] I will build my church ; . . ." Although Peter denied Jesus three times, he was the first apostle to see Jesus risen, and he took leadership of the small group of the faithful. He was later bishop of Rome and died a martyr there, by tradition crucified head downward on the same day as St. Paul during the persecutions of Nero. His feast day, June 29, he shares with St. Paul.

PETER CELESTINE, ST. (1215–1296). Founder of the Celestine order, Peter Celestine was one son in a large Italian peasant family. He lived most of his life as a hermit, at first alone, then in the company of a few disciples in a little group upon which he imposed a strict version of the rule of St. Benedict. This was the nucleus of the order which bears his name. At eighty, he was elected pope in an attempt by ecclesiastical authority to fill that office, but five months later he resigned. Boniface VIII, his successor, had him confined for fear that his active presence might bring about a schism, and he died in his cell a year later. His feast day is May 19.

PETER CHRYSOLOGUS, ST. (fifth century). Designated as a Doctor of the Church, Peter Chrysologus, or "golden speech," was ordained bishop of Ravenna in 433, a position he held until his death. He was evidently a splendid orator, and some two hundred of his discourses are still extant. His feast day is December 4.

PETER DAMIAN, ST. (1007?–1072). By choice as ascetic hermit, by appointment the cardinal-bishop of Ostia, Peter Damian rose from an unusually humble beginning to a place of great importance in the Church of his day. After being orphaned at a young age, he was saved from one brother, who put him to the most menial work, by another brother, Damian, whose name he later took in appreciation of that rescue. A zealous reformer, he bitterly attacked such sins as simony and lechery which were prevalent among the clergy of the time. He was first a teacher, but lived most of his life as a member of an austere monastic group, using it as a model for the hermitages which he founded. He is designated a Doctor of the Church; his writings are considerable, including letters, sermons, and lives of the saints. His feast day is February 23.

PETER THE HERMIT, BLESSED (c. 1050–1115). To the Frenchman, Peter the Hermit, must be given at least some credit for arousing thousands of the poor of Europe to take part in the First Crusade, although he was probably not as influential as was once thought. He was, evidently, a fiery preacher, for, inspired by his fanatic zeal, his group marched through the Rhineland on the first lap of the route to the Holy Land slaughtering the Jewish residents of the area and bringing chaos wherever they marched. Peter and his people reached Palestine in 1096, before the better led and better disciplined Crusaders-proper, but they accomplished nothing and were easily defeated by the Turks when they went into Asia Minor. After the conquest of Jerusalem by the Crusaders in 1099, Peter returned to Europe and died in an Augustinian monastery in Belgium.

PETER'S CHAINS, ST. August 1, also called the Feast of St. Peter Advincula, marks the dedication of a basilica of this name where a few links of the chains which bound St. Peter were preserved. August 1 is also called Lammas Day (Old English "loaf mass"), and was once celebrated as an early harvest thanksgiving.

PETER'S PENCE. Contributions made toward payment of the expenses of the Holy See. The name originated from the tax of a penny levied against every household during the Middle Ages.

PEW. Now, an undivided, fixed bench with a back, placed in a church for the seating of the congregation, a "pew" was originally an enclosure in the church that was set aside for a particular family. The word probably came from a Latin term meaning balcony.

PHARISEE. A member of the Jewish party that held itself entirely apart from the gentiles and adhered scrupulously to the literal interpretation of the Law, the ceremonies, and the old traditions. The party became quite powerful, representing the old and correct way, and, during Jesus' time, it grew more exclusive, proud, and self-righteous. Jesus inveighed against the Pharisees and their practices, according to Matthew 23:1-7 and 13-36.

PHILEMON, EPISTLE TO. A short letter of Paul's, included as a book of the New Testament and addressed to Philemon, his friend, whose slave had run away but returned bearing the letter. Paul requests that Philemon "receive him as myself."

PHILIP, ST. (first century). An apostle who is thought to have evangelized Asia Minor and died a martyr by crucifixion. His feast day is May 1, a day shared with St. James the Less.

PHILIP NERI, ST. (1515–1595). A native of Florence, Philip Neri went to Rome while still a young man and spent some fourteen years there studying theology, preaching, and working among the poor before entering the priesthood in 1551. His childhood had been happy, and his whole life apparently continued in that pattern. He was evidently a congenial and intelligent individual as well as a compassionate and devout priest. He founded a congregation of secular priests which grew and became known as the "Oratory." He was also influential in extending the use of the vernacular in church services. His feast day is May 26. See ORATORIO.

PHILIPPIANS, EPISTLE TO THE. A letter of St. Paul's included as a book in the New Testament, Philippians is addressed to the Christians of Philippi. It is highly personal and is filled with encouragements and exhortations.

PIE, THE. The general rubrics in the books of the so-called Sarum liturgy; the name is derived from the fact that they are printed in red and black and are thus particolored, or "pied."

PIETA (It.: pity; pyā-tä'). A statue or other image of the dead Jesus in the arms of his mother.

PIETIST. A member of the Fellowship of Piety, a Protestant sect of the seventeenth and eighteenth centuries. Beliefs had mystical overtones and members laid great emphasis on a devout daily life and strict morality.

PIETY (from Lat.: dutiful). Devoutness and dutifulness in religious matters; the related word "pious", however, has come to have a somewhat negative connotation in that it may carry overtones of excessive or pseudo-religiosity. To preserve its original meaning it often is used in combination, as "he was genuinely pious."

PILGRIMAGE (from Lat.: a stranger). A trip to a sacred place, whether made simply as an act of devotion or penance or to ask some favor or help.

PILGRIMAGE OF GRACE. The Catholic rising in northern England in 1536 to protest Henry VIII's abolition of papal supremacy and confiscation of Church land by the monarchy. Led by Robert Ashe, the large group was able to reopen monasteries in York, but upon being met at Doncaster by the King's representative with an offer of amnesty and a Parliament within a year, it dispersed. The leader went to London, where he was courteously received, and events seemed to be going well for them. Unfortunately, another man, Francis Bigod, tried to lead a similar movement the next year, and though Ashe had tried to stop him, he and other leaders of the first Pilgrimage were arrested, tried, and executed.

PILLAR SAINT. The generic name for any of a number of solitary individuals, who, from the fourth to the fourteenth century, expressed their devotion by living for lengthy periods of time on pillars or other elevations such as rocks. The pillar was usually equipped with a platform and a hermit's hut and might be only a few feet in height. Chief among the pillar saints, or stylites (from the Greek word for pillar), were the Simon Stylites, Older and Younger.

PIOUS. Possessing piety, which see.

PIX. A container to hold the Communion bread, or a small round box that holds the Host when it must be taken to the sick for a private Communion. In some early churches, the pix was shaped like a dove or a pelican. Also spelled "pyx."

PLAINCHANT, PLAIN SONG. Very early Christian church music developed during and after the time of Pope Gregory I in the seventh century, this entirely vocal music has one melodic line, no harmonies, and a rhythmical rather than a metrical composition. Notes are usually of the same length, but the chant itself may be fast or slow. The chromatic scale and progression are not parts of plainchant, which uses the major scale (from do to do) and the minor scale (from la to la). Often two choirs sing the melody alternately, its beauty depending on the purity and trueness of tone as well as the rhythmical variations. Gregorian chant is a type of plain song, which is the usual music of the liturgy in the Catholic Church. By extension of the term, "plain song" may also be used to describe the chants of the Orthodox Eastern Church, Ambrosian Chant (that developed by St. Ambrose), the chants of the Mozarabs, a Christian community that maintained some independence of worship during the time of the Moorish occupation of Spain, and the Gallicians, a French Catholic group.

PLENARY INDULGENCE. "An indulgence which remits the whole of the temporal punishment which has been incurred by a sinner

. . . the degree of its acceptance depends on the will of God . . . If gained for the living (i.e., oneself), there follows the complete remission of temporal punishment in this world and the next; but as we can never be certain of the perfection of our own dispositions, neither can we ever be absolutely certain of having profited to the full by a particular plenary indulgence. . ." (*Catholic Dictionary*, p. 385) The same uncertainty obtains in regard to plenary indulgences applied to a soul, or souls, in Purgatory, for acceptance depends on the will of God.

PLYMOUTH BRETHREN. A devout evangelical Protestant sect teaching extreme Calvinistic doctrines of justification and predestination, and rejecting a separate clergy and formal organization. They originated in Ireland, but take their name from Plymouth, England, where an association was formed in 1830. From there, the group spread to the Continent and then to the United States.

PNEUMATOLOGY (Gr.: spirit study). That part of Christian theology which deals with the Holy Spirit. In classical times, pneumatology was the study or discussion of the nature of the soul or of the self.

POLYCARP, ST. (d. c.156). One of the early bishops of Smyrna, St. Polycarp is said to have known those who had known Jesus, and especially to have been a disciple of St. John. He died a martyr, refusing to deny his Christian faith. According to the story, the flames of the execution pyre would not burn him and he had to be stabbed to death. His feast day is January 26.

POLYPHONIC. Used to describe music having a given or basic melody to which one or more melodies are added. Early church music, plainchant, was not of this nature.

PONTIFEX MAXIMUS (Lat.: Supreme Pontiff; pon'-tə-feks mak'-sə-məs). A title for the pope.

PONTIFF (Lat.: high priest). Any bishop is a pontiff, but when the term Supreme, or Sovereign, is added, the reference is to the pope, as it is when simply "the Pontiff" is referred to.

PONTIFICAL. Having to do with the pope or papal matters.

PONTIFICAL CHAPEL. Persons and representatives of groups who meet officially with the pope at solemn functions such as consistories.

PONTIFICAL FAMILY. Persons in the service of the pope and of the papal household, e.g., palatine cardinals, parish priest, sacristan of the household, and confessor.

PONTIFICAL MASS. A High Mass sung, or services celebrated, by a prelate such as a cardinal, bishop (from which the name derives) or an abbot.

PONTIFICATE. The office or the term of office of a bishop (pontiff) and particularly of the pope. To "Pontificate" means to celebrate Mass wearing the ceremonial vestments of a bishop.

POOR CLARES. The order of nuns founded by St. Clare under the direction of St. Francis of Assisi in 1212 and divided into two branches, one strictly enclosed (Colettines) and one more modified and working more in the world (Urbanists). The habit is brown, and the name is derived from the rule of the original group which did not allow the holding of any property, neither personal nor in common.

POPE (Lat.: Father). The title of the bishop of Rome as the Supreme Pontiff of the Catholic Church. It has designated the Supreme Pontiff exclusively in the West since the eleventh century, but forms of the title are used for the Orthodox patriarch of Alexandria and Greek-speaking priests. The pope is held to be the successor of St. Peter, who was given authority, according to Catholic faith, by Jesus. The pope is thus considered the supreme ruler of all Christians as the head of the Christian church, and further dogma asserts his infallibility when teaching *ex cathedra*. The full papal title is: Bishop of Rome, Vicar of Jesus Christ, Successor of the Prince of the Apostles, Supreme Pontiff of the Universal Church, Patriarch of the West, Primate of Italy, Archbishop and Metropolitan of the Roman Province, and Sovereign of the State of the City of the Vatican. There have been approximately 262 popes (early history is inexact) of which some 180 have been Italian. Seventy-six have been canonized, the last the Dutch Pope Adrian VI who died in 1523.

POPE JOAN. Joanna was the name of a female pope, according to a tale of the thirteenth century. The story, none of which is true, originated apparently with Jean de Mailly and was repeated by historians as late as the sixteenth century. Scholars have since rejected it as a complete fabrication, but it was long believed, especially by anti-Catholics. According to the account, Joanna, after gaining some renown as a scholar, disguised herself as a man and acted as pope for two years. Her secret was revealed only when she bore a child during a procession to the Lateran, after which she died. She was first said to have lived around 1100, and later, around the middle of the ninth century; both were periods which produced antipopes.

PORTABLE ALTAR. In the Catholic Church, a square or retangular block of natural stone which has been consecrated and has had relics sealed in it so that Mass may be said on it.

PORTER. A doorkeeper; the lowest of the minor orders in the ranks of the Catholic clergy, now, in practice, replaced in duties by a layman.

POSITIVE THEOLOGY. That theology concerned with historical fact, tradition, dogma, and doctrine in contrast to natural theology which is concerned with reason and experience.

POSSESSED. Being in the control of an inner demon or bad spirit, "demonic possession," manifests itself as control of limbs, speech, and behavior by some agent other than oneself. The Catholic and Anglican Churches recognize a need for exorcism of such demons; various Protestant denominations, perhaps more commonly those of a fundamentalist bent, also recognize the possibility of such possession and the need of a minister's aid in exorcising the evil spirit. Contrary to earlier belief, modern churches that accept the possibility do not believe that it indicates that the person possessed is particularly sin-ridden. Diabolical possession, does, however, seem to occur less frequently in predominately Christian, or modern, nations; further, it occurred, or seems to have occurred, far more frequently in pre-scientific or pre-psychological times.

POSTULANT. A person preparing to enter a religious order or community; during the period of postulancy, usually six months, the man or woman follows the routine of the monastery or convent and prepares for the novitiate, the next period which precedes the taking of final vows.

POVERELLO, IL (It.: the poor one; pō-va-rel'-lō, ēl). The Italian words for "The Little Poor One," a name often used to designate St. Francis of Assisi.

POVERTY, VOW OF. The vow taken, according to the prescription of the particular religious order, by every monk, friar, or nun, at the time of joining the order. Simple vows usually entail giving up the right to the use of personal property, although possession is retained and the property can be administered and its income disposed of at will. Solemn vows almost always entail disposing of all personal property; Jesuits, Friars Minor, and Capuchins are distinct in prohibiting any inheritance, while most orders provide that the disposition of any inheritance shall be at the discretion of the superior.

POWER OF THE KEYS. According to common usage, this term refers to the power of binding and loosing exercised by a priest in the sacrament of penance. It is derived from Matthew 16:19, "And I will give unto thee the keys of the kingdom of heaven; and whatsoever thou shalt bind on earth shall be bound in heaven; and whatsoever thou shalt loose on earth shall be loosed in heaven." It may also be used metaphorically to refer to the power of ecclesiastical authority.

POWERS. One of the nine choirs in the celestial hierarchy.

PRAYER. Speech or thought addressed in thanksgiving, petition, praise, etc. to God, Jesus, or, according to one's religious convictions, Mary or one of the saints. Prayer may be public or private, vocal or silent, spontaneous or formulated, and often good works are themselves considered a type of prayer. The original meaning of "pray" and "prayer" was a begging or an earnest entreaty or request; the Christian religion has enlarged this meaning, and often such prayers, if they alone are offered up, are considered sub-Christian. Nevertheless, the petitionary prayer, e.g., "God, help us. . .", "God, give us. . ." and "God, make us. . ." is probably still the most common.

PRAYER BOOK. A book containing prayers and devotions; the Catholic and Anglican Churches, especially, use prayer books.

PRAYER, BOOK OF COMMON. The book containing the services prayers, and texts of the hymns used in the Anglican Church. The Prayer Book of the Episcopal Church in America is only slightly different from that of the Anglican Church. The Book of Common Prayer is an amalgam, made during the time of the Reformation, of several smaller books: the Missal, containing the Mass; the Breviary, containing the hours or Daily Offices of worship in addition to the Mass; the Pontifical and Ordinal containing the Episcopal ministrations; and the Manual, containing the occasional offices. Further material was taken from books called Primers, containing instructions and devotions entirely for the laity. Of these, the Missal with the Mass, or liturgy, was the most ancient. The Book of Common Prayer has undergone some revision since the Reformation, and in some instances the Prayer Book of the Episcopal Church in American resembles more closely the Prayer Book of the Episcopal Church of Scotland, which is somewhat closer to the ancient forms, than it does the Book of Common Prayer.

PREACHER (from Lat., to proclaim or declare in public). A clergyman or minister in a Protestant denomination. The name was first attached to the individual who delivered the sermon, that is, who preached or proclaimed the Word of God before a congregation.

PREACHER, THE. The name given to the author of Ecclesiastes, a book of the Old Testament.

PREBEND. The portion of the income or revenues from a cathedral or collegiate church which is paid to the clergyman as his salary; also, the property or taxes from which such an income is derived.

PRECENTOR. In a contemporary sense, the cleric in charge of the arrangements for worship services, although the term once referred to the choir master in a cathedral, collegiate, or monastery church.

PRECEPT. A command or direction for moral conduct given to an individual by his superior. It is not a law and cannot be enforced any more than an example can be enforced (consider the phrase "by precept and example"), although it does, perhaps, carry more weight than the latter.

PRECIOUS BLOOD, THE. The blood of Jesus, symbolic of his sacrifice and redemption of man; also, a synonym for the Communion wine and, in the Catholic Church, for the bread as well, as the communicants (the celebrant excepted) receive the wine "under the species" of bread. A feast of the Most Precious Blood is observed on July 1.

PRECURSOR, THE. St. John the Baptist, considered as the one who came before, i.e., was the precursor of, and prepared the way for Jesus.

PREDELLA (It.: a stool). The third or highest step of a high altar; the platform on which a side altar stands; or, another term for the gradine, a shelf or shelves on the top and at the back of the altar on which a cross or candlesticks are often set.

PREDESTINATION. This familiar term cloaks a question far less simple than is usually thought. For Calvinists, the doctrine means that God foreordains eternal life for some and eternal damnation for others; for those who accept this "double predestination," the question still remains whether the foreordination occurred before the Creation or after the Fall. The former "hard line," or Supralapsarianism, holds that before the Creation God elected some for salvation regardless of their merit or lack of it; the "soft line" holds that God elected to save some after the Fall who would otherwise have been damned, and hence it is known as Infra, or post, lapsarianism. Within these two views there exists the split of opinion over double predestination itself; whether God elected only to salvation or to salvation and damnation. Just as some were selected for salvation, were others selected for damnation? This, of course, raises the further question: Does God withhold grace entirely from some, and if so, how does this action fit into the picture of a loving Father?

Predestination played a very small part in theology or Christian thought until the time of St. Augustine (c.400), but after his setting forth of the concept of double predestination it grew in significance. Never fully accepted by the Catholic Church, the idea was picked up and emphasized by Calvin and other Protestant reformers. Predestination still is most generally used to mean the election of some to grace and some to damnation, although more liberally it simply refers to the will of God in relation to mankind and his active participation in and determination of man's destiny, that is, "the act of foreordaining by which from eternity God decrees whatever he will do in time. . ." (*Catholic Dictionary*, p. 396)

PRE-EXISTENCE OF CHRIST. The term defining the coexistence of the Logos, or second person of the Trinity, with God the Father. It does not mean that the man Jesus so existed, but that the Son, the second person, did, and in due time was incarnated in the man Jesus.

PRE-EXISTENCE OF SOULS. The idea that each soul had an existence before it was embodied in a human being on earth. Where this life was lived or what its nature was is never precisely spelled out, but Christians who have found the idea attractive often envision the souls as existing in Heaven with God. Among those who have believed in the pre-existence of souls were Origen (c. 200) who was under the powerful influence of Greek thought, a small part of which included the acceptance of this idea. William Wordsworth, the Romantic poet of the late eighteenth century, also apparently accepted this thought, at least in part and for a while. Theologically, it is still considered heretical.

PREFACE. In the Mass, a prayer that introduces the canon and ends with the Sanctus. There are sixteen different prefaces appropriate for special occasions, as Christmas, Epiphany, and Lent.

PREFECT. An ecclesiastical dean or other authority having certain administrative responsibilities.

PRELATE. A general term used for a bishop, an abbot, or other ecclesiastical authorities.

PREPARATION AT MASS. Prayers said at the foot of the altar steps before the introit which begins the Mass.

PRESBYTER (Gr.: elder). This term, used originally by St. Paul to distinguish the priests of the New Law from those of the Old, called *hiereis,* means "a priest" and may refer to a member of the clergy in the Episcopal church. More usually, perhaps, it is used synonymously with "elder" in the Presbyterian church.

PRESBYTERIAN CHURCH. The Protestant church which is the inheritor of the doctrines of John Calvin is called "Presbyterian" because its government in spiritual affairs is handled by courts made up of "presbyters" or elders. The Presbyterian Church in the United States is made up of three divisions, the chief being the United Presbyterian Church, and has a total membership of about 4,500,000. The first Presbyterian Church in America was founded by an Irish missionary, Francis Makemie (1658?–1708), in Philadelphia in 1706, but the movement was strong in England by 1550, and especially under the direction of John Knox became of leading importance in Scotland. Governmentally, it stands about mid-way between Congregationalism, each of whose local churches is autonomous, and episcopally governed churches such as the Episcopal.

Basic doctrines of Presbyterianism include belief in predestination and salvation through God's grace alone, although it is doubtful if most modern Presbyterians accept the full implications of the former. The Bible is accepted as the rule of faith and the source of God's laws.

PRESBYTERY. In the Presbyterian church, this term refers to an ecclesiastical court made up of ministers and presbyters and its particular district, while in the Catholic it designates a priest's residence. It may also refer to the portion of a church that is reserved for the clergy.

PRESTER JOHN. A legendary figure of the Middle Ages, who, according to the popular stories of the time, was ruler and priest (Old French *prestre* means priest) of a Christian kingdom in Asia or Africa, perhaps Ethiopia. Other stories seem to identify this figure with a Christian prince, Owang Khan, of Karakorum, ruler of a settlement of Nestorian Christians.

PREVENIENT GRACE. The grace which arouses the will without its own volition to incline toward God; the inspiration, afterwards, may be freely accepted, by virtue of consequent or cooperating grace, or freely rejected.

PRICK SONG. The old English name for contrapuntal music, a name which means "pricked opposite." Melodies in such music were literally pricked, or dotted, on paper opposite each other.

PRIDE. The first and worst of the seven deadly sins, long considered the root of all the others. "Pride" in this sense refers to the self-elevation of man before God and a denial by man of his human limitations, not to the everyday feeling of satisfaction, or even vanity, in possessions or achievements.

PRIE-DIEU (Fr.: to pray God; prē'-dyōō). A small, low desk with a ledge, or a low chair with a high back, at which to kneel in prayer.

PRIEST. The minister of divine worship in the Catholic or Anglican clergy, although by extension the term may validly refer to a minister of any religion, or any clergyman in contrast to a layman. In the clerical hierarchy, priests rank just below bishops and may administer all the sacraments in the Catholic Church except that of holy orders.

PRIESTCRAFT. A derogatory name for the methods, policies, or artfulness of priests used to obtain desired ends.

PRIESTHOOD. The state of being a priest; the priestly office; or all priests considered as a unit, as "a member of the priesthood."

PRIESTHOOD OF ALL BELIEVERS. The Protestant, and essentially Lutheran, doctrine that all Christians are possessed of an inner liberty of conscience and personal access to Jesus that does not necessitate the mediation or ministration of an ordained priest. The ministry has been viewed by many as a practical working arrangement, although ministers are not considered to be a group especially favored in God's consideration. On the basis of this belief, some Protestant denominations such as Anabaptists did away entirely with the formal ministry and ceased to make any distinction between clergy and laity.

PRIMACY. The position of that bishop who has jurisdiction over the other bishops in any district or country, as, for example, a patriarchate. The primacy of the pope is supreme in the Catholic Church.

PRIMATE. In the Catholic Church, the highest-ranking bishop of a district or country, or an archbishop.

PRIME. The office that opens the new day in the Divine Office of the Catholic Church. Prayers and devotions are usually said at about 6 A.M., or at dawn.

PRINCE OF DARKNESS. The Devil.

PRINCE OF PEACE. Jesus.

PRINCE OF THE APOSTLES. St. Peter. In this title, "prince" is used as a translation of the Latin *"princeps,"* chief or leader.

PRINCE OF THE CHURCH. A cardinal in the Catholic Church.

PRINCIPALITIES. One of the choirs of angels in the celestial hierarchy.

PRIOR. The superior in a monastery or priory, or the superior just below the abbot in an abbey.

PRIORESS. The superior, or assistant to the abbess, in all convents of nuns having solemn vows, in contrast to other convents which are administered by a mother superior.

PRIORY. A monastery, or a convent, governed respectively by a prior or a prioress.

PRIVATE MASS. Usually, a Low Mass celebrated in addition to the Masses regularly celebrated to satisfy the needs of a congregation. A congregation may or may not be present.

PROCESSION. Often a part of worship services, processions are used frequently in Catholic and Anglican, less in Protestant churches. Their significance symbolically is man's approach, with reverence and dignity, to God's representative or into the place of divine worship. They may be preceded by the cross, or by the church flag, usually carried by a layman.

PROCESSION OF THE HOLY GHOST. The theological term defining the manner in which the Holy Spirit derives from the Father and the Son. It is held to be a "proceding from by spiration," the procession, rather than a "proceding from by generation," as the Son derives from the Father.

PROCURATOR. The permanent representative to Rome; a religious order; or a person acting lawfully for another. However, the term probably designates most commonly the individual in a monastery or convent who has charge of domestic affairs, i.e., food and clothing and similar concerns.

PROFANATION. As this term is frequently confused with "desecration" in popular speech, its use has become rather limited. It is, however, the correct way to describe the lawful process of turning over a church to a decent, though not a religious, use. Its origin is from the Latin sense of "profane," *pro,* or before, and *fanum,* a temple, and thus, before or in front of a temple and hence not sacred.

PROFANE. For derivation, see above. This term is properly used to describe anything unrelated to religion, although it has come to be thought of as showing irreverence or contempt for sacred matters.

PROFANITY. Although this term refers specifically to the condition of anything not related to religion, it is almost invariably used as a synonym for swearing that invokes irreverently the divine or religion-related things, e.g., "My God!" or "Damn it!" Protestant churches, and particuarly the more conservative, condemn such language, while the Catholic and Anglican are more lenient, holding that although profanities are unattractive, "if no definite blasphemous meaning or uncharitable intention is attached to them" the sin of using them is very minor. (*Catholic Dictionary,* p. 405).

PROFESSED. An adjective describing a member of a religious institute who has been admitted to simple or solemn vows, as "a professed nun."

PROFESSION, RELIGIOUS. The contract binding a man or woman to a religious order or community, or that life in a religious order or community itself. Vows of the professed religious, i.e., one who has entered the religious profession, may be simple or solemn and simple vows may be temporary or perpetual.

PROFESSION OF FAITH. A statement of the basic doctrines and dogmas of a Christian denomination.

PROMOTER OF THE FAITH, THE. The correct title for the official in the Congregation of Rites in the Catholic Church who is more often dubbed the "Devil's Advocate." The task of the Congregation is to investigate a man or woman's life prior to possible beatification and canonization, and it is the Promoter's job to examine in detail all claims for miracles and virtues, and to make certain that every question raised is satisfactorily answered.

PROOFS FOR THE EXISTENCE OF GOD. This extremely complex subject can be reduced, if not satisfactorily, at least usefully to the following: *a priori* arguments, such as the ontological argument, in which the conclusion follows from the definitions of the terms, and no appeal to experience is needed, and *a posteriori* arguments, those which start from experience and propose a solution which explains the experience. Of the latter, St. Thomas Aquinas' proofs are most famous. He argued, for example, that everything changes, particularly from a state of potentiality to a state of actuality. Yet everything must have an actuality before it, since no potentiality can begin its own existence suddenly. Eventually, this "pushing back" process must halt, and there must have been a "perfectly actualized being," or "first mover," and that must be, or must have been, God. Another of his arguments was based on the fact that nothing can be the cause of itself, and that the first cause was God. Those today who find proof of God's existence in the intricacy and marvelousness of the universe are, in effect, following such *a posteriori* arguments.

PROPER OF THE MASS. The parts of the liturgy of the Catholic Mass which vary according to the day or the feast in order to be most appropriate and, hence, "proper," e.g., the introit, collects, and epistle.

PROPHECY. The foretelling of events which are to occur in the future, or the events foretold.

PROPHET, THE UNKNOWN. Modern scholarship ascribes chapters 40–66 of the book of Isaiah in the Old Testament to some author other than that of the rest of the book, and he is called the Unknown Prophet.

PROPHETS, THE. In the Old Testament, and in the understanding of the Jewish people, prophets were first of all preachers and social reformers, and only secondarily foretellers of the future. The major prophets, so called because of the length, detail, and substance of their writings, were Isaiah, Jeremiah, Ezekiel, and Daniel. The minor prophets were Hosea, Joel, Amos, Obadiah, Jonas, Habakkuk, Zechariah, Micah, and Malachi.

PROPITIATION (Lat.: to appease). A prayer for mercy to sinners. "Propitiation" is often personified in Jesus, who is called "the propitiation for our sins."

PROSELYTE, PROSELYTIZE. One converted from one religion to another is a proselyte; hence, to attempt to convert is to proselytize.

PROTESTANT. A member of any Christian denomination which separated from the Catholic Church at the time of the Reformation, or of any sect which has become separate from those bodies or from the Catholic Church since that time. The name was originally applied to Lutherans who protested against certain decrees of the Catholic Church and especially against the corruption within the parent body. It is not applied to members of the Orthodox Eastern Church or its branches.

Protestantism in comparison with Catholicism emphasizes the individual's responsibility to God rather than to the church, makes a greater separation between secular and religious affairs, and stresses the individual's liberty to private judgment and interpretation of the Scriptures as against the authority of the church. The Bible as the sole rule of faith as against traditions and teachings of a church; the corruption of human nature; predestination, at least in some denominations; the acceptance of fewer sacraments, often only baptism and Communion; and de-emphasis of divine revelation characterize Protestantism to a greater or lesser extent. Lutheranism, Calvinism (Presbyterianism), and Methodism are important branches; Protestant by definition, Anglicanism is sometimes "protestant" mostly in its rejection of papal authority.

PROTOCANONICAL BOOKS. The books of the Old Testament which have been accepted as canonical by both Protestants and Catholics; they are those included in the Authorized Version. See APOCRYPHA.

PROTOEVANGELIUM OF JAMES. An early apocryphal gospel, attributed to James the Less, the brother of Jesus, and also called the Gospel of the Infancy, as it recounts something of the early life of Jesus. Actually, scholarship places its date as late as the second century, and rejects it as a source for authentic information.

PROVERBS. A "wisdom book" of the Old Testament consisting of maxims, proverbial sayings, and good advice, often attributed erroneously to Solomon. It dates from about 300 B.C. and contains a mixture of idealistic concepts and practical advice.

PROVIDENCE, DIVINE. The care and action of God, directing all things to their conclusions by sustained guidance of human destiny.

PROVOST. An authority; the first dignitary of a cathedral or collegiate chapter, i.e., one of the college or association clerics who carries out the liturgy in the cathedral or college.

PSALM (Gr.: song to be sung to a stringed instrument). A song or poem to be sung or said in praise or worship of God.

PSALMS, THE BOOK OF. This book of the Old Testament is a collection of 150 religious poems or hymns, notable for their sincerity, intensity, and beauty. They may be personal, as is Number 23, violent as is Number 137, or antiphonal as is Number 24. The variety of content and style is enormous. Although many have been attributed to David, the compilation itself dates from about 150 B.C., and it is probable that only a very few were actually composed by David as early as 1000 B.C.

PSALMODY. This ancient Jewish custom of singing psalms during a worship service was carried over into Christian practice, and still forms a fundamental part of many church services.

PSALTER. A book containing the psalms, or, in the Catholic Church, the part of the Breviary that has the psalms in it arranged for reading in each week's Divine Office.

PUBLICAN. A Jew who collected taxes for the Roman authorities. Because of the position, and also because many publicans used their office to extort money from their fellows, publicans were detested and ostracized by other Jews. Matthew, Jesus' disciple, is probably the most famous publican.

PULPIT (Lat.: a platform). A high reading desk behind which a minister stands, in many churches, to deliver the sermon. Frequently, in Protestant usage, "a pulpit" refers to the position of minister, as "he was assigned to the pulpit of the —— Church." In Catholic and Anglican churches, the pulpit is on the gospel, that is, the left-hand, side facing the altar, while it is often centered in Protestant churches.

PURGATORY. In the Catholic Church, the place or state in which saved souls, the souls of those who died in grace and friendship with God, and are destined for Heaven, are held after death in order to be purged of their minor sins and punished for the smaller sins for which they had not properly atoned in life. The belief in Purgatory is based on the further belief that only perfect souls, such as those of Jesus, can be granted the vision and presence of God immediately after death. Others must be purged, or cleansed, by both physical and spiritual punishment for a greater or lesser amount of time, but such punishment is not as horrible as that of Hell, nor is it eternal. The sins, afterall, have been forgiven, and it is only a matter of time until the soul will reach Heaven.

The concept of Purgatory was stated by St. Augustine and further developed by Gregory the Great (540–604). Since "indulgence" for the souls suffering in Purgatory could be purchased with prayers and Masses, and their time there reduced, it led to one of the abuses in the Catholic Church that was corrected during the sixteenth century Catholic Reform, that is, the indiscriminate selling of indulgences by priests in order to fill the coffers of the Church. Today, relatively little emphasis is given Purgatory and even less to the need for "buying" souls out of Purgatory.

According to the doctrines of the Catholic Church the belief in Purgatory must not be mis-read to lead to the erroneous conclusion that the Church does not hold the ultimate satisfaction and atonement offered by Jesus to be insufficient for salvation. Rather, according to Jacques Benigne Bossuet, a seventeenth century French writer and theologian, "having acquired an absolute dominion over us, by the price which He paid for our salvation, He grants to us pardon, upon such terms, such conditions, and with such exceptions as He thinks proper." For those who have sinned after baptism, this may include some physical pain and the deprivation, for a time, of the vision of God.

PURIFICATION, THE FEAST OF THE. Also called Candlemas, this feast celebrated on February 2 commemorates the ritual purification of Mary following the birth of Jesus as prescribed in Jewish law.

PURIFICATOR. The small cloth of linen used to dry the chalice and the celebrant's fingers after the Communion service.

PURITANISM. An extremely rigorous offishoot or development of religious faith and asceticism, most common among Protestants but also to be found among Catholics. In the common use of the term, "Puritan" refers to a member of a particular Protestant sect prevalent in the seventeenth century. From their customs, particularly, are derived modern concepts of puritanism, i.e., that it rejects dancing, drinking, gambling, noisy amusements, and almost all pleasures of the body, or, in fact, of the mind, except the pleasures of restrainéd and proper conduct. The "puritan" sees evil in all nudity, in speech that is to the point about physical matters, and in all enjoyment that is not of the spiritual. Historically, Puritanism arose at the time of the Reformation, which Puritans regarded as incomplete, but it has a close affinity with early Manichaeanism which regarded evil as an entity and the physical as synonymous with evil, and with the later Cathari and Albigensian heresies.

PURPLE. The liturgical color for the seasons of Septuagesima, Lent, and Advent; rogation and ember days (except at Pentecost); and most vigils, purple symbolizes penitence. Prelates of the Western church wear purple as the proper color of cassocks, birettas, etc., unless they are members of a religious order. As purple is associated with kingship, it may also, though unofficially, be used in relation with Jesus.

## Q

QUADRAGESIMA (Lat.; fortieth; kwäd'-rə-jes'-i-mə). The fortieth fasting day before Easter; the first Sunday in Lent is called Quadragesima Sunday. In early times the entire Lenten season might be called Quadragesima.

QUAKERS. The Society of Friends. This nickname was attached to members because of their purported trembling or quaking during meeting and at hearing the Word of the Lord. It became, later, the name by which the Society was popularly known.

QUENTIN, ST. (d. c.285). This saint, probably an actual historical figure, has collected many legends in the course of the centuries. The son of a Roman senator, he evangelized certain areas in France, where he was imprisoned, tortured, and killed for his faith. Legend has it that invoking St. Quentin is usually effective, especially when it is done on behalf of prisoners. Gregory of Tours recounts the story of a priest who had a man condemned to death for theft, repented of the severity of the punishment, and tried, unsuccessfully, to secure a reprieve. Invocation of St. Quentin was more successful, according to popular faith, for the rope broke while the man was being hanged, and he was, in consequence, set free. St. Quentin's feast day is October 31.

QUIETISM. An Oriental type of extreme mysticism whose essential teaching is "utter passivity." Ideally, according to Miguel de Molinos (1640–1696), its first proponent in the West, the soul gives up all activity—reasoning, worshiping, feeling, hoping for salvation, praying, everything. The purpose of this complete surrender was to "let God act," which was Molinos' motto. Such absence of activity could as easily lead to immorality as to morality, since the soul also gave up resisting temptation and paying heed to sin. Francois de Fenelon (1651–1715), theologian, archbishop, and author, defended Quietism, in a modified form, as a way toward the pure love of God; he was assisted by Madame Jeanne Marie Guyon, who was confined to a convent and later in the Bastille for the heresies contained in her Quietist writings. Eventually the entire movement was condemned by the Catholic Church as heretical.

QUINQUAGESIMA (Lat.: fiftieth; kwin'-kwə-jes'-i-mə). The fiftieth day before Easter; the last Sunday before the beginning of Lent is called Quinquagesima Sunday.

# R

RABBI (Heb.: master). Although in the broad sense of this title, a rabbi is the spiritual and legal authority of a Jewish community, more modern usage of the term limits it to the ordained spiritual head of a synagogue. The rabbi determines the ruling on laws, customs, and rituals; performs marriages; and in general ministers to the spiritual needs of his congregation.

RANSOM THEORY. An alternative term for atonement, which see.

RAPHAEL, ST. One of the three archangels mentioned in the Bible, the others being St. Michael and St. Gabriel. His feast day is October 24.

READER. A lector, one of the minor orders in the Catholic Church; the lector's duties have mostly been taken over by laymen.

REAL PRESENCE. The Catholic doctrine, defined especially by the Council of Trent, which asserts that the body and blood of Jesus as well as his soul and divinity, are really and substantially contained in the Eucharist, not only figuratively or symbolically.

REBAPTISM. Different Christian denominations have differing beliefs about rebaptism, i.e., baptizing for a second time. Those Protestant sects which maintain that baptism must be by immersion, or that infants cannot validly be baptized, usually require a previously baptized adult candidate for membership to be rebaptized according to the specifications of their particular faith. On the other hand, Catholic and Anglican doctrine holds that once a person has been baptized it is a sin to baptize him again; in the case of doubt about the validity of the previous baptism, he may, however, receive "conditional baptism" within the church. Most Protestant churches stand about midway in this

283

debate; if a person has been baptized in the Christian faith, it is so accepted, no matter what the form used, but if the candidate desires to be rebaptized, he can be.

RECEPTIONISM. The Protestant, and particularly Lutheran, doctrine that Jesus is present in the Communion bread and wine only when they are received by a worthy and devout Christian.

RECIDIVISM. Falling into the same sin over and over again, although one apparently is genuinely repentant and intends to reform. In the Catholic Church, recidivism is not reason for a priest to refuse absolution to a penitent, even though they both know that backsliding is most likely, unless it appears that the individual is not really repentant and doesn't honestly mean to mend his ways. Discipline, perhaps in the form of deferred absolution, may be administered, but it has always been true that absolution is not valid unless the penitent is sincere. It is likely though, that this recognition of man's weakness in spite of all his good intentions, and the Catholic handling of the situation, have led some Protestants to the erroneous belief that a Catholic is free to sin, be absolved, and sin freely again.

RECTOR. In the Catholic and Protestant Episcopal clergies, the rector is the head priest of a parish or the minister in charge of a parish. In the Church of England, however, he is the clergyman who holds the rights and tithes of a parish, and is distinct from the priest or vicar. The head of a church school or similar institution may also be called a rector.

RED. The liturgical color of vestments on the Feast of Martyrs, for Pentecost and its octave, and for various other festivals of the church, red symbolizes martyrdom for the Faith. It also is used to symbolize the Holy Spirit; it is the color proper to cardinals; and it has been considered the papal color since the sixth century. It may be called "sacred purple," but the color is usually a brilliant scarlet.

RED HAT. The red hat, or biretta, of the cardinal in the Catholic Church is so closely associated with the office that the term is often used to refer to the rank of cardinal or to a cardinal himself.

REDEEMER, THE. Jesus; in this title, special recognition is given his role as the savior of mankind.

REDEMPTION, THE. The buying back of man from his enslavement to the Devil, an act accomplished by Jesus through his suffering and death. It is generally held that man became so enslaved as a result of Adam's sin, which was a sin against God; no man could redeem man from such a sin, but God-in-man, that is, Jesus, was capable of atoning for man's sin and paying the price for all men. The "redemption" is the redeeming of man to the grace and friendship of God.

REFECTORY. A monastery or convent dining hall.

REFORMATION, THE CATHOLIC. See COUNTER REFORMATION.

REFORMATION, THE PROTESTANT. The sixteenth-century revolt against the Catholic Church which began with a desire to reform from within (as tried by John Huss, and, in fact, even by Martin Luther) and ended in the establishment of denominations either totally alienated from their Catholic origin, as the Lutherans and Presbyterians, or partially alienated, as the Church of England.

The essential cause of the drive for reform was the presence of enormous corruption within the Catholic Church. This was recognized by good churchmen, and attempts had been made since at least the fourteenth century to reform from within. However, the Church was weakened by internal rivalries, the Schism, and an hierarchical system that was almost impossible to break out of. It was, in short, incapable of reforming itself. The extent of corruption increased in the sixteenth century; simony, the sale of relics and indulgences, and the worldliness of some clergy with the lack of education of others, combined with two further factors to make reform inevitable. These other factors were the sweeping effect of the Renaissance that made life less spiritual and other-worldly, more secular and "this worldly," and the growth in the countries of Europe of powerful nationalistic fervor. These forces, together, brought about the collapse of what may be called the monolithic Christianity which had existed for at least a thousand years.

REFORMED. A term originally used in the sixteenth century to distinguish Calvinistic Protestants from Lutherans, it is now used frequently to refer to a branch of a church which, rightly or wrongly, believes itself to be practicing a purer form than its parent organization of the same basic belief and worship.

REFRESHMENT SUNDAY. Also called Mothering Sunday, this fourth Sunday in Lent commemorates Jesus' miracle of the five loaves, and that gospel story is read during the service. It also marks a rejoicing at the mid-point in Lent. See also LAETERE SUNDAY.

REGENERATION. That renewal of the self which occurs with the reception of grace, either through the sacraments or with the gift of the Holy Spirit.

REGINA COELI (Lat.: Queen of Heaven; rā-jē′-nə sē′-lē). A title of Mary, the mother of Jesus.

REGULAR CLERGY. In the Catholic Church, a general term for the men and women who are bound by vows and live a communal life in monasteries and convents, as distinguished from priests, the parochial or secular clergy, who take only the vow of chastity and have the charge of churches, or other duties, which they perform in the secular world.

RELIC. Anything intimately connected with a saint or member of the Holy Family, whether it be part of the body, clothing, or possessions. The Catholic Church authorizes the veneration, but not the worship, of relics, but insists that they be properly authenticated. Although no single specific relic is guaranteed as genuine, investigation is required into the evidence of its authenticity before public honor may be given it. Honor to a false relic, when given in good faith, is still held to be profitable, but relics known to be false must be withdrawn, and the making of "relics" has long been forbidden. It is further forbidden to buy or sell genuine relics. In practice, relics are not prayed to; rather, the veneration given them "passes over" to the individuals with whom they are associated. Catholics are not required to venerate relics, but they are forbidden to say that relics should not be venerated.

RELIGION. Any system of beliefs and practices that has to do with man's relationship to his god or gods.

RELIGION, NATURAL. The relations between man and God that are known apart from the truths of revelation, or revealed, religion. The existence of God is generally held to be the first fact of natural religion, as it is said to be apparent in creation.

RELIGIOUS. A term used to refer to a member, or the members, of a religious order or institute, as "He is a religious of the Dominican order." By the same token, a monastery or convent may be called a "religious house," and members may be said to follow the "religious life." In much more general terms, any individual may be described as "religious" if he is devout or pious, if he spends time in church work and worship, or if a considerable portion of his thought is of God and man's relation to the divine.

RELIQUARY. Any appropriate container into which a relic is sealed. It may be large or small and may vary from a simple box to an ornate, gem-encrusted casket.

REMINISCERE SUNDAY. The second Sunday in Lent. The name is derived from the Latin for "remember," and is taken from the first word of the day's introit in the Mass.

REMISSION OF SINS. The forgiveness of sins through baptism, penance and absolution, or, sometimes, sincere desire.

RENUNCIATION OF SIN. The renouncing or rejection of sin, the Devil, and the works of the Devil, made at the sacrament of baptism. The promise to reject sin is made either by the one being baptized, if an adult, or by godparents on behalf of an infant or child.

REPENTANCE. Repentance, or penitence, implies a rejection of and hatred for one's sin because it is an offense against God, and not just out of fear of punishment or getting caught. It differs thus from remorse, which is being deeply sorry for and ashamed of one's behavior, and from regret, which is a less deep sorrow that may result from a fear of consequences.

REQUIEM (Lat.: rest). In the Catholic Church, the first word of a portion of the introit in masses for the dead, "requiem" has come to be used synonymously with the Mass or service or music for the dead. The rest of the line in the introit is: *Requiem aeter-*

*nam dona eis, Domine, et lux perpetua luceat eis,* that is, "Eternal rest give to them, O Lord, and let everlasting light shine on them." It is taken from Esdras 2, not a book in the canon of Scripture, but found in the Apocrypha of the Authorized Version.

REQUIESCAT IN PACE (Lat.: May he rest in peace; rek-wē-es'-kät in pä'-sä). This brief prayer is used at the conclusion of the Catholic Church's Requiem Mass and is common in many prayers for the deceased. It is also well known in its abbreviated form, R.I.P., initials that were often engraved on tombstones in early American graveyards.

REREDOS (Anglo-Fr.: to rise at the back; rêr'-dōs). A carved or ornamented wooden or stone screen or painting at the back of the altar in a church. In the past, the reredos was often quite decorative, sometimes at the expense of the altar. Properly, it may be structurally a part of, or separate from, the altar, but it should not attract attention away from it.

RESERVATION OF THE BLESSED SACRAMENT. The keeping of the Communion bread for the Communion of the sick who could not attend worship service and receive it there. The term may also refer to the preservation of the Host in a ciborium and within a tabernacle on an altar of a Catholic church, where it serves as a point for private or public devotions.

RESPONSE. The answer given by a choir, the congregation, or other group to the words of a minister's formal greeting, bidding to worship, or prayer. The response may be either said or sung, but it is usually short, e.g.; *Minister*: The Lord be with thee. *Response*: And with thy spirit.

RESPONSIVE READING. The reading during worship service of a psalm or other devotional matter in which the minister and congregation read verses alternately until the selection is completed. It is similar to the Response, but the portion read by each, as well as the entire reading, is longer.

RESURRECTION OF THE BODY. The Christian belief that on the Day of Judgment every member of the human race, living or dead, saved or damned, will be "raised," that is, be alive again in the strictest physical sense. The particulars of the bodily resurrection have been much debated: Will the exact physical matter of the body come back to life? Will the body become alive again as it was at the moment of its death? or as it was in the fullness of its strength? Whatever the answers may be to specific questions, Christians in general agree that resurrection of the body is a divinely revealed truth.

RESURRECTION OF CHRIST. The return to physical life of Jesus on the third day after his crucifixion, death, and burial. According to 1 Corinthians 15:14, and much Christian teaching, the resurrection is the basic argument for Jesus' divinity, and the truth of Christian belief may depend upon the actuality of this one event. Discrepancies in the gospel resurrection stories have, as a consequence, been studied minutely. Responding to a modern inability of most men to accept the truth of miracles, and especially the miracle of the return to life, some theologians have reinterpreted the resurrection as a symbolic "rebirth" of man through faith or a triumph of the spirit over the grave.

RETREAT. A withdrawal from the ordinary pursuits of life to a place of relative quiet and solitude for the purpose of prayer, meditation, and spiritual regeneration. Retreats may be made individually or as part of a group. Certain churches, especially the Catholic, give retreats, or make retreats available, systematically to their members. Protestant churches offer retreats primarily for young people, and these not infrequently deteriorate into holidays with emphasis on "fellowship" at the expense of "spiritual refreshment," but the intention is usually devout.

RETRIBUTION. Although generally used in the meaning of God's punishment of a sinner through suffering or ill-fortune, "retribution" may also refer to God's reward of virtue as promised by Jesus.

REVELATION. The supernatural showing forth of a truth about man's relation to God, or the workings of the divine will. It is commonly taught that the first revelation was to the Jews, as expressed in the Old Testament, and that the second was to all mankind through Jesus and the Apostles. "Revealed religion" differs from "natural religion," although the term "revelation" is sometimes inaccurately used to refer to divine truths discovered through the use of the natural faculties, and it is then called "natural revelation." A third revelation, or type of revelation, is that given to a single person, as, for example, to Joan of Arc, but belief in such revelation is not a point of faith for either Catholics or Protestants. See also APOCALYPSE, for book of Revelation.

REVERENCE. The feeling for something sacred that is compounded of respect, love, and a certain amount of awe, almost equivalent to veneration. It is often shown by a bow, curtsey, or other gesture indicative of the highest respect, though not worship. The feeling of "reverence" is usually felt for a thing or an abstract idea, but one may "revere" a person.

REVEREND. That which is worthy of the highest respect; "Reverend" is often used as a title, or form of address, for a clergyman, but it is then most properly followed by the name.

REVISED VERSION OF THE BIBLE. An 1885 revision of the Authorized Version of 1611. Although more accurate, and also less archaic, it has never been very popular.

RHEIMS-DOUAY BIBLE. Also called the Douay Bible, this English translation based on the Vulgate was made at Rheims and Douay in France between 1582 and 1610. Dr. Gregory Martin and others who did the work followed the Latin Vulgate almost word for word, which made for a less graceful text than that of the Authorized Version, and also, in some cases, for very obscure reading. The Douay is still considered the Catholic Bible, just as the Authorized Version is the Protestant, but it has in fact been replaced by a thorough revision made by Richard Challoner in 1749–1752, and called Challoner's Bible.

RICHARD, ST. (d. 1253). This English saint was a scholar, a lawyer, a chancellor of the University of Oxford, and a legal advisor to St. Edmund, then archbishop of Canterbury. His life was marked by kindness to the poor and sick and by pointed criticism of clerical corruption. He preached the cause of the Seventh Crusade, and himself died just before he was to have embarked on it. His feast day is April 3.

RIDDEL (Fr.: curtain). An altar curtain.

RIGHT REVEREND. The title or proper form of address for a bishop or other ecclesiastical dignitary.

RIGHTEOUS (from the Old Eng. meaning "right-wise"). Virtuous and God-fearing; law-abiding and devout.

RIGHTEOUSNESS OF GOD. The justice of God, but extended to include an element of mercy and compassion for the weak not present in the strict concept of "justice." The righteousness of God was interpreted generally by medieval theologians to include retributive justice, both the punishing of the wicked and the rewarding of the good. This concept Martin Luther rejected as leading man to hate and fear of God rather than to love and trust, and he looked to St. Paul's statement that the Gospel of Jesus reveals God's righteousness to formulate his own definition which stressed God's goodness and grace to confer favor.

RING. A plain ring worn by many nuns signifies spiritual marriage with Jesus. Those rings worn by cardinals, bishops, and abbots are insignia of the office. That of the episcopate is a seal of faith and signifies the marriage of the bishop with his diocese. The "Ring of the Fisherman" (St. Peter) worn by the pope is a seal ring used for sealing papal briefs.

R.I.P. See REQUIESCAT IN PACE.

RIPIDION. A fairly good-sized flat metal disc mounted on a staff and designed with a cherub's head surrounded by six wings. It was, in the early church, an accessory used to fan away flies; it was replaced by the fan, or *flabella,* but is still used in some rites of the Eastern Church, though with more ritualistic than practical purpose.

RISEN CHRIST, THE. Jesus risen from the tomb. The Risen Christ symbolizes Christian victory over death, spiritual rebirth, and belief in personal salvation through Jesus.

RITE. A formal religious act including its accompanying prayers and words. "Rite," however, is not to be confused with "ceremony" or "ceremonial," the dressing up of the basic ritual action.

Such additions include the use of candles, genuflection, kneeling, and decorations of all sorts in the church. The word "rite," on the other hand, is used to identify a complete system of worship including ceremonies and songs, and it is correct to speak, for example, of the "Byzantine rite" or "Coptic rite" of the Orthodox Eastern Church.

RITES, THE CONGREGATION OF SACRED. The supervisory body within the Catholic Church established in 1588 to deal with questions about liturgical matters, beatification and canonization, and holy relics.

RITUAL. The rites of a church; in the past, the term was reserved mostly to refer to the worship services, and other formal services, of churches following ancient and set forms of worship. In this sense, the Catholic Church was said to be "ritualistic." However, modern practice has seen the growth of the use of this term in relation to the less stylized Protestant worship also.

A "Ritual" is also a book containing the prayers, ceremonies, etc., for a worship service.

ROCH, ST. (d. c.1327) One of the most popular of saints in France, St. Roch is invoked in many countries against contagious diseases. His short life, he lived only to about the age of thirty, was distinguished by kindness and the gift of healing. He paid particular attention to the plague-stricken, and is credited with having preserved those attending the Council of Constance from the plague altogether. On his way from his home in Montpellier to Rome, he stopped at hospitals to assist in the care of the ill and dying; it was during this or another journey that, as he lay dying of starvation and plague, he was befriended by a dog who stole enough food from his owner's table to save St. Roch's life. His picture is usually shown with this dog. Returned after some years and severe illness and privation to his home city, Montpellier, St. Roch was picked up as a suspected spy and died in a dungeon there, unrecognized but uncomplaining. Both Dominicans and Franciscans later claimed him. His feast day is August 16.

ROCHET. A knee-length, narrow-sleeved garment made of white linen and lace and usually worn under the mazetta by bishops, abbots, or other clergy.

ROCK. In Aramaic, *kepha;* in Greek, *petra;* the symbolic meaning of "Peter" as "the Rock," and "the Foundation" only becomes clear when both words are known. In Aramaic, Jesus' words, "Thou art Peter, and upon this rock will I build my church," comprise a pun on the name and the meaning, and might be paraphrased, "Thou art Peter, a rock, and upon this "rock" (i.e., foundation) will I build my church."

ROGATION DAYS (Lat.: entreaty). The Monday, Tuesday, and Wednesday before Ascension Day, during which the mercy and blessings of God are especially entreated.

ROMAN CATHOLIC. The Catholic Church centered in Rome, or a member of that church. It was founded, according to tradition, by St. Peter, and was the original, universal church from which other Christian churches have stemmed. It is also called the Western Church or the Roman Church.

ROMAN COLLAR. A stiff, short, white collar that stands upright and is fastened at the back of the neck, the Roman collar is part of ecclesiastical dress originally used only by priests of the Catholic and Anglican churches. The Roman collar has also been a symbol of Catholic priesthood.

ROMAN QUESTION, THE. The question of the position of the pope and Vatican City in relation to the civil government of Italy. Rome was seized by the Piedmontese in 1870, and the popes as a consequence confined themselves voluntarily to the Vatican in protest, as sovereigns having been deprived of their territory. The question was settled in 1929 by the Treaty of the Lateran.

ROMAN RITE. The Latin rite in its most authentic form and distinct from the Eastern rites and Western rites of Carmelites, Dominicans, etc. It is the most widely used liturgy.

ROMANS, EPISTLE TO THE. A book of the New Testament written by St. Paul at Corinth, Romans contains Paul's fullest development of his doctrine of salvation by faith; it is also his most profound work.

ROMISH. A derogatory term for the quality of being similar in rites or faith to the Catholic Church or beliefs. Also, "Romanish."

ROOD. The Old English term for the cross of Jesus, often spoken of as the Holy Rood. The more modern reference, in the Catholic Church, is to a large crucifix; the "rood-beam" is a large beam which stretches across the chancel arch and supports the crucifix; a "rood-loft" is a gallery above the "rood-screen" or choir-screen, a decorated wood or stone screen which is set across the chancel opening of a church to separate the sanctuary from the nave. Use of all of these was common in the Middle Ages and survives in some modern churches.

RORATE SUNDAY (Lat.: to drop; rō-rä'-tä). The fourth Sunday, and the last, in Advent. The name is derived from the first word, in Latin, of the introit.

ROSARY (Lat.: *rosarium,* a rose garden, and, by extension, a garland). A strand of small beads used for formal prayers and meditation by Catholics. The rosary most properly consists of fifteen sets of ten little beads and a large bead, to correspond with the fifteen mysteries which are meditated on while repeating the Lord's Prayer, and the Gloria Patri for each large bead and a Hail Mary for each small bead. However, the usual rosary consists of five sets, called decades, each containing ten small beads, one large bead, and a crucifix with two large and three small beads. The object of saying the rosary is concentration on intelligent meditation and prayer, and mechanical repetition of prayers is discouraged; the beads are reminders for keeping count. Tradition says that the rosary was revealed to St. Dominic (1170–1221), but there is no proof of this. Catholics celebrate the Feast of the Most Holy Rosary on October 7.

ROSE OF LIMA, ST. (1586–1617). Born in Lima, Peru, to a family which had seen better days in its native Spain, St. Rose was devout as a child, and, as an adult, was granted visions of Jesus, Mary, and her guardian angel. She was continually ill, a condition which she ignored in fasting and prayer, and even practised self-mortifications which induced more physical discomfort. She was humble and tried to avoid notice, but her reputation was great, so great, in fact, that inquisitors of the time subjected her to severe questioning and examination. She was, however, recognized as sincere and orthodox. Her feast day is August 30, and she enjoys considerable importance as the first American saint.

RUBRICS, THE (Lat.: *ruber,* red). Directions given in the liturgy for the carrying out of the services in the Catholic Church are printed in red for ease of reading and hence were given this name.

RULE, RELIGIOUS. The rules of daily communal life followed in monasteries and convents. There are four principal rules into which most congregations may be grouped, although reforms and adjustments are not rare. The basic ones are: Rule of St. Basil followed by all Eastern monks; Rule of St. Augustine, followed by Canons Regular, Dominicans, Austin Friars, etc.; Rule of St. Benedict, followed by Benedictines, Cistercians, and many others; and the Rule of St. Francis, followed by the Friars Minor, Poor Clares, Franciscans, etc. The Carthusians, Carmelites, and Jesuits have individual rules, as do many modern groups.

RULE OF FAITH. The teaching of a church, comprised of biblical truths, their interpretations, and, as in the Catholic Church, traditional Christian beliefs embodied in the writings of the early Fathers.

RUTH. A short narrative book of the Old Testament dating from about 350 B.C. It tells the story of Ruth, a Moabitess, and is a lesson demonstrating that racial, or tribal, intermarriage is not always wrong.

RUTHENIANS. Ukranians and other Slavonic peoples, some four million in all, who are Catholics of the Byzantine Rite, which is not the same as the Byzantine Rite of the Eastern Church. The group is in communion with the Catholic Church at Rome.

*S*

SABAOTH (Heb.: armies). Armies or hosts; in the phrase "Lord God of Sabaoth" the reference is to God as a leader of such multitudes. There is no connection between the words "sabaoth" and "Sabbath," although because of similar spellings the two are frequently confused.

SABBATARIANISM. The belief in following, on the Christian Sunday, the old Jewish customs regarding rest on the Sabbath. The Jews placed emphasis on desisting from all secular activity, but those such as Puritans who follow Sabbatarianism stress abstaining from secular pleasures and amusements. The term may be applied to Christians, for example, Seventh Day Adventists, who observe Saturday as the day of rest.

SABBATH (Heb.: rest). The seventh day of the week, when, according to Genesis, God rested from his efforts of creation. Jews traditionally observe it by resting from secular work, joining in divine worship, and enjoying some form of recreation. It was replaced for Christians by the first day of the week, although the old term "Sabbath" is often used to designate this "Lord's Day."

SACERDOTAL. Having belief in the divine authority of the priesthood; also, in an older usage, priestly or having to do with the priesthood.

SACKCLOTH. A rough cloth originally woven of goats' hair and worn as a symbol of penitence or mourning. "Sackcloth and ashes," a phrase found in the Bible, refers to the ancient custom of expressing penitence through the self-punishment of wearing this rough cloth next to the skin and sprinkling ashes on the head.

SACRAMENT (Lat.: a sacred pledge, from a word used to translate the Greek term for mystery). A religious rite instituted by Jesus, or the church, and generally accepted as "an outward and visible sign of an inward and spiritual grace." Catholics accept seven sacraments as having been ordained by Jesus; baptism, confirmation, the Eucharist, penance, extreme unction, holy orders, and matrimony. Protestants, excepting most or all Anglicans, recognize only baptism and the Eucharist (the Lord's Supper). God's saving grace is held to be especially active in the sacraments, although belief in the necessity of the sacraments for salvation is not universal. In general, it may be said that Protestants place less emphasis on the necessity of the sacraments than do Catholics, while Catholics do not make the claims for their remarkable efficacy in effecting salvation (for instance, that they "work" even when faith is lacking) of which they are often accused.

SACRAMENTAL ACT. Any deed which has about it something of a sacramental tone or nature; of a consecrated or sacred aspect.

SACRAMENTAL GRACE. The grace produced by each of the separate sacraments, as recognized by the Catholic Church, e.g., regeneration by baptism or increase of charity by the Eucharist. It is generally held to be habitual grace, though when the need of actual grace arises for the better fulfillment of the purpose of the sacrament, it partakes of the nature of actual grace, also.

SACRAMENT OF THE ALTAR. The Eucharist or Communion service.

SACRED HEART OF JESUS, THE. A feast day of this name is observed in the Catholic Church on the Friday after the octave of Corpus Christi. Worship of the sacred human heart of Jesus, considered as the symbol of his love for mankind and especially for ungrateful mankind, is always in conjunction with worship of the divine, and the heart itself is represented in association with the whole person. The heart is venerated as the place of origin of Jesus' love in much the same way as any human's heart is considered the place of origin of his human love.

SACRED ORDERS. In the Catholic Church, these are the orders of the priesthood, the diaconate (deacons), and the subdiaconate. See MINOR ORDERS.

SACRIFICE. To Christians, the one complete, perfect sacrifice was that one offered by Jesus in the crucifixion; every other true sacrifice is, also, a giving of oneself or of a part of one's self for another.

SACRIFICE OF THE MASS. The Catholic Mass is "a representation and a renewal of the offering made on Calvary" carried out in a bloodless manner. The sacrifice of Jesus was made at the Last Supper in this manner, prior to the sacrifice at Calvary, and it is this form which the Mass renews. "The sacrifice of the cross was the one universal and absolute sacrifice; from it consequently the Mass derives its efficacy, consisting in an application of its fruits. Thus the Mass gives supreme honour and glory to God and offers him thanks for his benefits, . . . and is effective in obtaining further graces and blessings, . . ." (*Catholic Dictionary,* p. 443)

SACRILEGE. Profane treatment of a sacred thing or place; or irreverent use, misuse, or abuse of a church, a sacramental object, or the person of a clergyman or member of a religious order.

SACRIST, SACRISTY. A sacrist is the person who has the daily responsibility of caring for a church, but especially for the sacristy, which is a small room near the sanctuary in which are kept various accessories of worship, books, vestments, and the like. The sacristy is not consecrated, but respectful behavior is required of those who enter it.

SAINT. Although this term is informally used to designate any person who leads a particularly self-sacrificing and devout life, it has a much more technical meaning. In the Catholic Church, one whose holiness in life is recognized officially by beatification and canonization after his death is called "saint." Further, the feast of All Saints, November 1, especially honors all the unknown and uncanonized saints, for it is acknowledged that not all true saints have actually been canonized. In the history of the Catholic Church, canonization has been bestowed on people from all orders of life, and it has been not infrequently bestowed on someone whose actions and behavior were disapproved of by many of his contemporaries. See CANONIZATION.

SALT. Ritualistically, salt which has been blessed is placed on the tongue of baptismal candidates in the Catholic Church as a symbol of wisdom and spiritual cleanliness. It is also used in the blessing of holy water and, among certain Eastern Catholics, some is mixed with the Eucharistic bread.

SALVATION. The state of being saved, that is, of having one's soul attain Heaven and the vision of God after the death of the body. Salvation depends upon God, but the way is usually held to be open to all through grace, cooperation, and free will. The varieties of beliefs among Christians on this subject are numerous, and the relative importance of "faith," "grace," and "cooperation" have long been debated. Contrary to one popular Protestant misunderstanding, Catholics do not believe that only Catholics can achieve salvation.

SALVATION ARMY, THE. Founded by William Booth in England between 1865 and 1880, the Salvation Army is a Protestant sect which accepts the Bible as its sole rule of faith; rejects Calvinistic predestination; and recognizes no ordained ministry. As the name indicates, the Salvation Army is militaristic in form of organization, identifying itself as an "army for Christ." It is a highly evangelistic group, working mostly in the slums of large cities where its efforts to feed, clothe, and give shelter to the desperately poor have usually been accompanied by efforts to bring them back to religion through hymn singing, praying, and sympathetic listening.

SAMUEL, BOOKS 1 and 2. Books of the Old Testament which recount stories of the reigns of Saul and David.

SANCTIFICATION. That state of the Christian who has been released from the power of sin and guilt through the action of the Holy Spirit. He is, then, more able to love God and his neighbor, to make moral decisions, and to succeed in his daily struggle toward Christian perfection. Also, the act of purifying or making holy.

SANCTIFYING GRACE. That grace which remits original sin and

which makes it possible for the soul to pursue the virtue which will make salvation eventually possible.

SANCTITY. Especial goodness, charity, and faith; saintliness; next to holiness.

SANCTITY, ODOR OF. See ODOR OF SANCTITY.

SANCTUARY. The part of a church around the altar, or, sometimes, all the parts within the altar rails. Occasionally in Protestant churches, all the main area of the church, including the portion usually called the nave, will be referred to by this name.

SANCTUS (Lat.: holy). The words "Holy, Holy, Holy [Sanctus, Sanctus, Sanctus] Lord God of Hosts. Heaven and earth are full of thy glory" used in the Mass and some Protestant church services. This Sanctus is derived from early worship practices of the synagogue.

SANCTUS BELL. A small bell rung at various places in the Mass, the first time just before the Sanctus, in order to call the attention of the congregation to a particularly significant portion of the worship.

SARUM USE. The form of the Catholic ritual codified in the late eleventh century by St. Osmund, for use in his church at Salisbury, England. "Sarum" is in fact an abbreviated form of the Latin *Sarisburia,* or Salisbury. It is highly ceremonious in form, resembling the Dominican rite, and survives in part in the marriage ceremony of present-day English Catholicism. After the Reformation, it was replaced in England, Scotland, and Ireland by the reformed Roman rite.

SATAN (Heb.: adversary). The Devil, also known as Lucifer, the Tempter, and Beelzebub.

SATISFACTION. Making or giving reparation to God for offenses committed against him; usually satisfaction takes the form of penance or punishment. The "satisfaction" made by Jesus through his death was made for man's sins, according to Christian theology.

SCAPULAR (Lat.: shoulder). Usually, two strips of cloth put together so that they can be placed over the head with one strip down the front and one down the back of the body. The scapular is about shoulder width and ankle length, and generally is the same color as the tunic with which it is worn by members of several religious orders. It symbolizes the yoke of Jesus.

SCHISM. A separation or rift into two, or sometimes more, divisions.

SCHISM OF THE EAST. The great split in the original Christian Church which led to the formation of two separate parts, the Catholic or Western Church and the Orthodox or Eastern Church. The schism took place over several centuries and was caused in part, if not in whole, by the rivalry between Constantinople (East) and Rome (West). Briefly, it occurred also because of disagreement over several theological points: the Iconoclastic debate prior to 800, the debate over the inclusion of "filioque" in the Creed, and the excommunication of Cerularius, patriarch of Constantinople, in 1054. A brief reunion was effected between 1274 and 1282, but the break between the two churches became final after 1472. Recent communication between the two apparently aims at a healing of the long-existent schism.

SCHISM OF THE WEST. See GREAT SCHISM, and cf. "Babylonian Captivity."

SCHOLASTICA, ST. (480?–533). The twin sister of St. Benedict, St. Scholastica spent her life as a nun in the shadow of her brother's famous monastery at Monte Cassino. Her feast day is February 10.

SCRIPTURES. The Bible; when the term is used in the New Testament, the Old Testament alone is, of course, being referred to.

SEAL OF AN ALTAR. In the Catholic Church, the relics and the sepulcher in which they are contained in an altar are known by this term.

SEAL OF CONFESSION. In the Catholic Church, the inviolable secrecy of the confessional; it is almost universally recognized by secular as well as by ecclesiastical law. A priest may not under any circumstances use in any way information he has received in the confessional to hurt or offend the penitent; if he does so, he automatically incurs excommunication.

SEBASTIAN, ST. (d. 288). As a soldier in the Roman army, St. Sebastian was able to bring about many conversions and frequently to secure the release of Christians who had been condemned to death for their faith. His role was, for a long time, not known to the Emperor Diocletian, who rewarded him for good and faithful service by making him captain of the Praetorian guard. Eventually, however, he was discovered, and in spite of his protests that he had always fulfilled his military duties scrupulously, he was condemned to death. He was shot with many arrows, but he recovered. Still, desiring to become a martyr, he threw himself in Diocletian's path and accused him of shedding innocent blood, and for this offense he was slain. His feast day is January 20.

SECOND COMING. The Parousia, or second coming of Jesus, was foretold by Jesus. It was to be the coming of Christ in his glory, the advent of the Kingdom of God, and the Last Judgment. Yet certain difficulties of understanding have arisen, partially because Jesus himself indicated both that the Parousia was to occur quite soon and that the time was unknown, and partially because the exact meaning of "the Kingdom of God" is not clear. Catholicism identifies the coming of Christ into his kingdom that was to occur "before this generation shall pass" (Matthew 24:34) as the founding of the Church at Pentecost, and states that the time of the second coming was repeatedly said to be unknown, as it is in Mark 13:32. Two directly opposed interpretations are possible: that the second coming, while imminent, is delayed, but can be expected to occur as foretold, and that the second coming is merely a symbolic way of expressing the fulfillment, or goal, of history, when a judgment must be passed on mankind, but need not be expected to happen literally as it was foretold.

SECT. A small group that has broken away from an established Protestant denomination because of specific views or beliefs which it does not share with the parent group. It often refers, also, to a small Protestant organization not obviously the offshoot of a parent group, but independently arising, perhaps as a result of a vague generalized dissatisfaction of certain people with any other sect or denomination. Sometimes "sect" is used synonymously with "denomination," and "Protestant sects" is often used to mean "Protestant denominations."

SECTARIAN. Having to do with religious sects or denominations, or referring to a person especially involved with some particular sect. Something that is "nonsectarian," perhaps the way in which the word is most commonly used, is not related to or limited to any particular church or faith.

SECULAR. Not of a churchly or religious nature, but having to do, rather, with the world and things of the world; concerned or related to temporal and material, rather than spiritual, affairs.

SECULAR CLERGY. Members of the clergy, such as priests and ministers, who do their work in churches and parishes; members of religious orders who live in monasteries and take holy orders are called the "regular clergy."

SECULARISM. The placing of emphasis on material things of the temporal world rather than on spiritual things of the metaphysical or religious world; also, the exclusion of faith or religion from any role in everyday affairs.

SEE (Lat.: a seat). The official area of a bishop's authority, deriving its name from the seat, or throne, placed in the main church of a diocese, which is then called the "cathedral church" (*cathedra*: throne or chair). The area of a bishop's diocese is also called the "see;" hence, the holy See, which includes the pope, the bishop of Rome, and his court.

SEMI-PELAGIANISM. That position midway between the viewpoint of St. Augustine, which was that God's grace is irresistible and that man can do nothing at all on his own to move toward faith without grace, and the viewpoint of his opponent, Pelagius, which was that man is free to resist the grace offered him and that faith is a free act of man's will. Semi-pelagianism, now, is the view that the will has the ability to cooperate with divine grace, although over the years, the orthodox Catholic position has itself been considerably modified.

SEMINARY. A school or college for the training of ministers and priests. The term has been used in the past to refer to a type of finishing school for young ladies.

SEPTUAGESIMA (Lat.: the seventieth; Sep'-tōō-ə-jes'-ē-mə). The third Sunday before Ash Wednesday. It is not seventy days or the seventh Sunday before Easter, as the name might suggest. Rather, it is named apparently only in relation to Quinquagesima Sunday, which is the last Sunday before the beginning of Lent and which falls close to Quinquagesima, the fiftieth day before Easter; Sexagesima Sunday is the Sunday before Quinquagesima Sunday, and Septuagesima Sunday is the Sunday before Sexagesima.

SEPTUAGINT (Lat.: seventy; Sep'-too-ə-jint'). A Greek translation of the Old Testament made between 250 and 100 B.C. by seventy-two scholars in as many days. It was done at the command of Ptolemy II of Egypt, and it stood as authoritative until the Reformation. The Vulgate of St. Jerome was based on the Septuagint, but Protestant reformers at the time of the Reformation rejected parts of it as uncanonical because they were not included in the later Jewish Masoretic text. These parts, or a portion of them, are included in the Apocrypha of the Authorized Version. The Septuagint is often abbreviated to LXX, the Roman numerals for "seventy," referring to the number of scholars who worked on the text.

SEPULCHER. A tomb or vault; specifically, in the Catholic Church, the place hollowed out in the altar stone to hold the required relics.

SERAPHIC. Angel-like; resembling the seraphim, the highest order of angels in the celestial hierarchy.

SERAPHIM. The highest order of angels in the celestial hierarchy.

SERMON (Lat.: speech). A speech given in order to instruct the listeners in religious and moral matters. Sermons usually, though not always, are given by a clergyman and are often based on biblical quotations.

SERMON ON THE MOUNT. Delivered by Jesus and recorded in Matthew, chapters 5–7, the Sermon on the Mount contains all the essentials of Christian moral teachings and beliefs.

SERVATUS, ST. (d. 384). A bishop in Belgium, St. Servatus was an orthodox Christian at a time when a majority of the converts in his area were Arian Christians, that is, while professing Christian faith, they denied the divinity of Jesus. St. Servatus supported St. Athanasius, also orthodox, who was at that time in exile; he died shortly after moving relics out of his church to save them from the approaching Huns. His feast day is May 13.

SERVER. One who assists a minister or priest in the sanctuary during worship service. In the Catholic Church, as well as in the Anglican, laymen and boys often act in this capacity, and are commonly known as acolytes.

SEVEN WORDS, THE. The words Jesus spoke from the cross, recorded in Luke 23:34, 43, and 46; John 19:26–27, 28, and 30; and Mark 15:34.

SEXAGESIMA (Lat.: sixtieth; sek'-sə-jes'-ē-mə). The second Sunday before Ash Wednesday. See SEPTUAGESIMA.

SEXT. The sixth hour of the Divine Office in the Catholic Church; it is most correctly said at noon, but is often included as a part in an earlier service.

SEXTON. A corrupted form of "sacrist," the person who has the care of church property and especially of the sacristy.

SHEOL (Heb.: to dig). In the Old Testament, Sheol is the underworld abode of all the dead, a place of shadows and gloom. It is often used synonymously with Hell, although that interpretation is not in keeping with its original meaning.

SHEPHERD OF HERMAS, THE. An anonymous Christian writer of the second century; he records visions and moral experiences which aim to bring the reader to repentance and faith. The writings were accepted as canonical at one time prior to St. Jerome's work.

SHRINE. The original use of this word was to refer to a box in which the bones or other relics of a martyr were kept; from this limited sense it was expanded to include the entire tomb of a saint or a venerated person, or to a place of worship or special devotion associated with something holy. Although almost always "shrine" implies a place of private or public worship closely associated in some way with a person, it is possible that a shrine may be simply an altar or a chapel dedicated to a saint or a holy thing, as roadside shrines may be.

SHROVETIDE. The three days before Ash Wednesday, "Shrove" is derived from the Old English word "shrive" or "to confess and receive absolution," and the period was one during which confessions were to be made and a last period of festivity was to be indulged in before the beginning of the penitential Lenten season. Shrove Tuesday, in England, has long been a day for eating quantities of pancakes, and other Shrovetide festivities include Carnival and Mardi Gras.

SIGN OF THE CROSS. The representation of the cross; the Catholic and Anglican custom of making the cruciform gesture on the body, with the thumb and finger tips of the right hand moving from the forehead to the chest and from the left shoulder to the right. Symbolically, making the sign of the cross testifies to one's belief in Christ crucified, and invokes his blessing. It is made at several points during the worship service, before or after prayers, at moments of spiritual or physical danger, and at numerous other times. Often the words "In the name of the Father, and of the Son, and of the Holy Ghost" are said when the sign is made. Eastern churches have various practices that differ, but they do use the sign; Protestants, with the exception of Anglicans, do not.

SIMON STYLITES, ST. (d. 459). Probably the most famous of the pillar saints. His feast day is January 5.

SIMON AND JUDE, STS. (first century). See JUDE.

SIMON OF CYRENE, ST. (first century). The man who was forced to carry Jesus' cross, "a passer-by who was coming in from the country . . . , one Simon of Cyrene" (Mark 15:21). His feast day is December 1.

SIMPLE VOWS. The vows which members of religious houses of the Catholic Church take may be divided into solemn and simple. Simple vows are public, i.e., received by the superior in the name of the Church; they render contrary acts unlawful but not invalid; and they permit those who take them to retain ownership of property. A religious society of those taking simple vows is called a congregation, in contrast to one for those taking solemn vows, which is called an order. Women who have taken simple vows are called "sisters"; those who have taken solemn vows are called "nuns." In practice, of course, this distinction is often not made. There are numerous congregations of women who have taken simple vows, such as the various Sisters of Mercy and Sisters of Charity; there are also several men's organizations, such as the Redemptorists and Passionists, whose members take simple vows.

SIN. Sin is defined as an act of the human will in opposition to God, or the Divine Will, as interpreted by the individual conscience; as the breaking of a moral or religious law; and as the self-aware and deliberate rebellion against a universal authority, usually identified as God. Catholic theology provides the more thorough categorizing of sin, although Protestant thought recognizes shades of distinction even if it does not place them in specific categories. Catholic theology identifies the following: Actual sin, an act of omission or commission against God's law; Formal sin, any deliberate breaking of what the conscience feels to be the divine law; Habitual sin, the state of a person who has sinned and not repented; and Material sin, the unintentional breaking of the divine law, that is, the committing of a transgression either without knowing that it is a transgression or without having given free consent to the act. Only the last is not regarded as a real sin.

Sin may also, in the terms of Catholicism, be mortal or venial, that is, very serious or less serious. Mortal sin is held to be a transgression of the moral law in a serious matter; it is deserving of eternal punishment and it deprives the soul of its supernatural life and sanctifying grace. Venial sin does not deprive the soul of sanctifying grace, and it may be remitted by prayer, penitence, and good works.

Many Protestants identify "sin" as breaking any of God's laws, especially those spelled out in the Ten Commandments, and in general it is these transgressions which Catholics identify as mortal sins.

SINDON (Gr.: linen cloth). The shroud in which Jesus' body was wrapped for burial. Liturgically, it may refer to any veils and cloths.

SINS, SEVEN DEADLY. The capital sins are pride, covetousness, lust, anger, gluttony, envy, and sloth. Each is the result, or the evidence, of inordinate attachment to something in the physical world. Of them all, pride is distinguished as the worst, as it is interpreted as a refusal of man to accept his human limitations and his consideration of himself as a god.

SISTINE CHAPEL. The main chapel in the Vatican Palace, deriving its name from Pope Sixtus, or Sistus, under whose direction the work was begun in 1473.

SLOTH. One of the Seven Deadly Sins, which may be summed up as "it's too much trouble to be good." Physical laziness is sinful when it hurts others, and leads, as it may, to other character deterioration.

SOCIAL GOSPEL. The name given to the generating idea of a Protestant movement in the late nineteenth and early twentieth centuries which stressed that man was a social being and that "sin" was the result of evil conditions of his social environment. It tended toward utopianism, its members holding that God was working toward an achievement of His kingdom in this world. Although it was shown to be theologically unsound by orthodox and even more liberal theologians, its emphasis on the need for social reforms in, especially, economic areas has lived on.

SOCIETY OF JESUS. See JESUITS.

SODALITY (Lat.: a companion). A group of church members associated together to do works of piety and charity. Sodalities are most often thought of as associations of church women, especially in the Catholic Church, and are often named in honor of the Virgin Mary.

SOLEMN MASS. High Mass.

SOLEMN VOWS. Vows taken by members of religious orders of the Catholic Church. In contrast to simple vows, solemn vows make acts that are contrary to them not only illicit but invalid; members who take solemn vows renounce all property ownership. Compare with SIMPLE VOWS.

SOLIPCISM. The view which places the self and its perceptions at the center of reality; it states that, in fact, this self is the only thing which truly exists and all other "realities" depend upon it.

SOLITARY. One who lives in solitude in a remote place, or the condition of living in such a way. A "solitary" devotes his life to worship and prayer; a modification of this type of life, which is almost impossible today, may be found in the modern world in a regulated form in some religious communities.

SONG OF SIMEON, THE. See NUNC DIMITTIS.

SONG OF THE THREE CHILDREN. See BENEDICITE.

SON OF GOD, THE. The second person of the Trinity; Jesus, the incarnation of the second person, the only begotten son of God. The Son of God is held to be co-equal and co-eternal with God, and begotten "from all eternity," not at the time of the Incarnation itself.

SON OF MAN, THE. The Messiah, according to Daniel 7:13. A title by which Jesus referred to himself, according to translation and theological interpretation of the biblical text.

SORROWFUL MYSTERIES, THE FIVE. In the Catholic rosary, these are identified as: the agony in Gethsemane, the scourging, the placing of the crown of thorns, the carrying of the cross to Calvary, and the crucifixion.

SORROWS OF MARY, THE SEVEN. These are often identified as: the prophecy of Simeon (Luke 2:35); the flight into Egypt; the three-day disappearance of the boy Jesus, after which he was found in the temple; the walk to Calvary; the crucifixion; the removal of Jesus' body from the cross; and the burial.

SOTERIOLOGY (Gr.: the study of the savior, or redemptive concept). The study of the work of Jesus as redeemer and savior, and the doctrines of salvation.

SOUL. The concept of the soul as the seat of reason and will in the human being, indeed, as the essential "being" or person, is primarily Platonic. There is no very clear identification of "soul" to be found in the Bible, and it really only became necessary to identify it specifically when Hebraic Christianity encountered Hellenic philosophy. Platonism stressed the existence of an immortal soul which was, in a sense, held captive in a "bad" body.

Christianity, on the other hand, held the body to be good and badness only a perversion of the will. These two concepts had to be reconciled. The work of synthesis was accomplished over the centuries, some of the finest being that of Thomas Aquinas (thirteenth century), who "rejected the Platonic idea of the soul using the body the way a pilot uses a ship and regarded soul and body as but two distinguishable factors in one substance or person . . . the soul can survive the body, although this is not its natural state . . . [and] will be rejoined to the body after the resurrection." (*Catholic Dictionary*, p. 227) In general, Protestants agree, holding that the soul of man is his invisible, immortal part, his "true self," his share, as it were, in the divine. See SPIRIT.

SOUTANE (Lat.: under, beneath; sōō-tän'). The cassock, a part of a priest's vestments.

SPEAKING IN TONGUES. Glossolalia, the ability to speak in a language or languages other than the one normally used, a gift miraculously received.

SPIRATION. The technical theological term used to define that process whereby the Holy Spirit originates from the Father and, in Catholic doctrine, also from the Son. Both the Son and the Holy Spirit are said to "proceed from the Father," but the Son is "begotten," or actively generated, while the Holy Spirit more literally proceeds, through "passive spiration."

SPIRIDION, ST. (270–344). A bishop in Cyprus, St. Spiridion is credited with at least two miracles, which, while interesting, may well be apocryphal. One attributed to him was the silencing of a deacon who was reading the gospels in such a way as to attract attention to his own fine speech rather than to the words; the deacon became a stammerer. St. Spiridion suffered under the persecutions of the Emperor Galerius before the Edict of Milan (311) gave toleration to Christians. His feast day is December 14.

SPIRIT. A term often used synonymously with "soul," "spirit" yet requires at some points to be considered as defining an entity apart from the soul. "Spirit" is, most accurately, the animating presence; for example, it is the Spirit of God which is held to function in the world and to animate man so that he, too, has a spirit, which may then mean the same as "soul" or, in the least physical sense, "heart." However, Hebrews 4:12 opposes soul and spirit in the passage "For the word of God is quick, and powerful, . . . even to the dividing asunder of soul and spirit." And again, it was the "spirit" which Jesus committed to God's hands as he hung on the cross whereas the portion of Jesus which "descended into Hell" has often been identified as his soul. In such cases it becomes almost essential to distinguish between the thinking principle, human will and reason, perhaps the soul of man, and the animating principle, or spirit.

SPIRIT, HOLY. The Holy Ghost, the third person of the Trinity.

SPIRITUAL. Having to do with things of the spirit, or of a spiritual nature, rather than with things of the physical, or of a material nature; remote or removed from secular concerns; religious, holy, or devout. Also, a type of religious song originating, usually, with Negro congregations, and characterized by rhythm and emotionalism.

SPONSOR. The person, or persons, who bring another to be baptized and who assume some responsibility, mostly spiritual but to a degree worldly, for that person's care and upbringing. The sponsor is often called a godparent.

SPY WEDNESDAY. The Wednesday in Holy Week, so-called, perhaps, as an allusion to Judas Iscariot described as a traitor or spy in the biblical passage read at the service for the day.

STABAT MATER (Lat.: The Mother was standing; stä'-bat mä'-tĕr). A hymn about the sorrows of Mary at the crucifixion; the first Latin words are *Stabat Mater dolorosa,* "The sorrowful Mother was standing. . ." The name also refers to a musical setting for the words.

STALL. A pew, or a fixed bench with a back, in the nave of a church for members of the congregation, or more usually, in the choir for its members.

STAR OF BETHLEHEM. The star which appeared to the Magi to stand in the sky over Bethlehem when Jesus was born. The identity of the Star has always been a matter for speculation, whether it was truly miraculous or a natural event which appeared to be a sign; whether it was a single star or a conjunction of several stars or planets that looked like one; and whether it appeared to be in the East or was seen at its rising.

STAR, THE. The Star of Bethlehem.

STATE OF GRACE. The state of being forgiven for one's sins; the condition of being saved. In Catholic theology, the state of the soul that is free of original sin and actual mortal sin, held to obtain directly after a true and valid confession, penance, and absolution. In some Protestant theology, the known condition of the elect.

STATIONS OF THE CROSS, THE. There are fourteen stations of the cross which mark the path of Jesus to the Tomb. The devotions which are termed the Stations or the Way of the Cross consist of entirely personal meditations and prayers made before each station. There are fourteen stations which may be marked with simple crosses or elaborate statuary or paintings. Whichever is the case, the Stations are usually placed on the walls of Catholic churches. The custom of making the Stations of the Cross originated in the fifteenth century with the Friars Minor. The same name is also sometimes applied to the Via Dolorosa in Jerusalem, the route tradition says Jesus followed as he walked to Calvary. The fourteen Stations are: (1) the condemnation of Jesus; (2) Jesus receives the cross and sets out toward Calvary; (3) He falls the first time; (4) He sees his mother; (5) Simon of Cyrene carries the cross; (6) the woman called Veronica wipes his face; (7) He falls the second time; (8) He speaks to the women of Jerusalem; (9) He falls the third time; (10) He is stripped of his clothing; (11) He is crucified; (12) He dies; (13) His body is taken down from the cross; (14) it is laid in the tomb.

STEPHEN, ST. (first century). The first martyr, St. Stephen's devotion to Jesus and his death by stoning are recounted in The Acts of the Apostles, chapters 6–8. His feast day is December 26.

STIGMATA (Gr.: marks). Marks which appear to resemble the crucifixion wounds on the hands, feet, and brow of Jesus, and which are believed by the devout to appear supernaturally on any or all of these parts of some especially devout Christians. The

Catholic Church recognizes their supernatural nature and holds that they may be wounds or scars; that they are actually painful; that they may be visible or invisible; and that they may be of a temporary or permanent nature. The best substantiated cases are those of St. Francis of Assisi, the Impression of the Stigmata being commemorated on September 17, and those of St. Catherine of Siena, commemorated April 3.

STIPES (Lat.: a post; stī'-pēz). The part of the altar on which the *mensa,* or table-like top, rests. It may be solid, a single central pillar, or a cluster of columns.

STOLE (Gr.: robe). A vestment which is distinctive of the deacon by whom it is worn over the left shoulder and joined under the right arm, but which is also worn by other members of the clergy as well. It is a silk strip about four inches wide and eight feet long; its color is in keeping with the other vestments. The origin of its use is not known, but it symbolizes immortality and the hierarchical order.

STOUP (Old Eng.: a container for liquid). A font for holy water.

STRIKE THE BREAST. An ancient sign of anguish and repentence. It is used liturgically by the celebrant in the Mass at such places as the repetition of *mea culpa,* "my guilt," and at the Agnus Dei.

STRIP THE ALTAR. The removal of all linens and cloths from altars in the Catholic and Anglican churches after services on Maundy Thursday, leaving them bare except for cross and candles. The stripping of Jesus' garments is symbolized, and the leaving of the door open on that day further symbolizes the temporary suspension of services.

STYLITE, A (Gr.: pillar). One who lives on top of a pillar, rock, or other such high point as a form of penance and solitude. See PILLAR SAINT.

SUB-APOSTOLIC. The times between the deaths of the apostles and the deaths of those who could have known them personally. Roughly, it is figured to be between A.D. 75 and 150, although a more realistic figure might limit the extension of the period to 125.

SUBDEACON. The lowest of the major or holy orders. The subdiaconate involves such duties as assisting with the ceremonies at Mass, the singing of the epistle, and bringing of Communion vessels to the altar. Obligations include that of celibacy and the recitation of the Divine Office each day. The vestments particular to the order are the maniple and tunicle, and the order is bestowed by delivery of a chalice, paten, and a book of the epistles.

SUBORDINATIONISM. The view that the second person of the Trinity, the Son, is subordinate to, rather than equal with, the Father; also, that the third person, the Holy Spirit, is subordinate to the Father, or the Son, or both. Catholic and most Protestant theology rejects subordinationism as heretical.

SUBSTANCE. A technical and complex theological term whose meaning is still much debated. Classically, however, it may usually be understood to refer to the defining characteristic of anything, or the enduring reality that underlies the "accidents" of appearance and change.

SUBSTANTIAL GRACE. The Holy Spirit dwelling within the souls of the just is called by this term; an alternative expression is "uncreated grace." (See Romans 5:5)

SUFFICIENT GRACE. Opposed to efficacious grace, sufficient grace is the grace which does not bring about the effect it should have, not because it was not "sufficient," but because of lack of cooperation on the part of the receiver.

SUFFRAGAN BISHOP. In the Anglican Church, someone appointed to assist a bishop, who, because of age or illness or excessive duties, is no longer capable of performing all the work of the diocese alone. In the Catholic Church, the bishop of a diocese who is subject to an archbishop, or metropolitan, or, possibly, directly subject to the Holy See.

SUMMA (Lat.: a whole). When capitalized, "Summa" refers to the *Summa Theologica* of Thomas Aquinas, one of the greatest theological works, if not the greatest, in the Western world. A "summa" may, however, be any definitive theological text, and the name was rather widely used in the Middle Ages.

SUNDAY. The observance of the first day of the week, Sunday, as the Lord's Day replaced observance of the Jewish Sabbath, the seventh day, as the New Law of Jesus replaced the Old Law of the prophets. It commemorates the resurrection and is the day on which most churches hold the principle worship service of the week.

SUNG MASS. In the Catholic Church, that worship service which is midway between High and Low Mass, and is the Mass usually celebrated. There is no deacon or subdeacon to assist the celebrant, and incense is not used without the special permission of a bishop. It is called "Sung Mass" because the celebrant must sing rather than say such portions as the collects and preface.

SUPERIOR. The person in authority in some ecclesiastical unit, as "Mother Superior" is the title of the nun in authority in certain convents.

SURPLICE. The long, loose white garment with wide sleeves worn over the cassock by priests and by laymen acting as acolytes. A short form which comes just below the hips and which has short sleeves is usually called a *cotta*.

SUSANNA, ST. (d. c.390). The life of St. Susanna is told only in legends, which are obviously full of misdatings and inaccuracies. Veneration has long been given her, and she has been a very popular saint, because of the tremendous struggle she made to preserve her innocence in the face of imperial persecution and corruption. She died a martyr, and her feast day is August 11.

SWITHIN, ST. (d. 862). A bishop of Winchester, St. Swithin is today best remembered for a superstition about the weather on his feast day, July 15, the day on which his relics were moved from an old grave to a new shrine in Winchester Cathedral in 1093. The little predictive verse reads:

> St. Swithin's Day if it doth rain
> For forty days it will remain.
> St. Swithin's Day if it be fair
> For forty days 'twill rain nae mair.

SYLVESTER, ST. (d. 335). St. Sylvester was pope during one of the most important periods in all Christian history, but nothing whatsoever is known of his life. His papacy included the years immediately following the issuance of the Edict of Milan (311) which gave toleration to Christians and ended the persecutions and it spanned the time of the conversion of the Emperor Constantine. Perhaps most important of all, St. Sylvester also headed the Church during the conflict with the heretic Arius, which led, partially, to the convening of the Council of Nicaea in 325 and the establishment of the tenets of the Athanasian creed as orthodox belief. It was at this time that the divinity of Jesus was proclaimed as dogma. St. Sylvester's feast day is December 31.

SYMBOL (Gr.: password). A "symbol," in the most usual sense, is, of course, a thing which stands in the place of and which represents another. The picture of a fish or of an anchor were early Christian symbols; they stood for "Christ" or a cross. Other symbols have been the cross itself, as a symbol of Christian faith, the dove as a symbol of the Holy Spirit, and the triangle as a symbol for the Trinity. The four evangelists have their own symbols which in turn represent the characteristics of their respective gospels: Matthew, a winged man, the historical importance of Jesus' life; Mark, a winged lion, the kingly dignity of Jesus; Luke, a winged ox, Jesus' sacrificial character; John, an eagle, Jesus' divinity.

A creed or a confession of a church may also be called a "symbol," and, in fact, the Nicene Creed is sometimes called the Major Symbol and the Apostles' Creed the Minor Symbol. This usage grew from the necessity within the early church to be sure that a messenger sent between congregations was the true messenger; he was required to match a fragment of a dish or bone with another piece that had been sent on ahead, and this was called the *symbolon,* or password. Later, verbal passwords or symbols were used, and knowledge of the creed or Christian beliefs came to be accepted as proof of membership in the Christian group.

SYNCRETISM. The effort to combine the teachings and beliefs of two or more divergent faiths to form a new and more attractive religion.

SYNOD (Gr.: a meeting sin'əd). A meeting of church authorities; an ecclesiastical assembly.

SYNOPTIC GOSPELS (Gr.: a general view). The Gospels according to Matthew, Mark, and Luke are called the Synoptic Gospels because they have a great deal of material in common, a style that is at least vaguely similar, and a tendency to treat the life of Jesus biographically. John, on the other hand, has a style that is totally different; it includes material not found in any of the Synoptic Gospels; and, most important, it treats Jesus' life less biographically and far more subjectively, searching for the theological meanings to be found there rather than recording the facts alone.

SYNOPTIC PROBLEM. That problem in biblical criticism which concerns the first three, or Synoptic, Gospels. Mark is generally, although not universally, accepted now as having been written first, partly because of the style and partly because most of the material from Mark is repeated in Matthew and Luke. Another source for the "sayings of Jesus" is hypothesized to account for that type of material found in Matthew and Luke: it is called Q, and the theory of the two sources for Matthew and Luke, that is, Mark and Q, is called the Two Source Hypothesis. Some scholars, unsatisfied with this answer to the puzzle of certain material included in the two gospels, insist that there must have been another source besides Mark and Q. This entire question is known as the Synoptic Problem.

# T

TABERNACLE. Occasionally used synonymously with "church," "tabernacle" may also refer to the container for the Eucharist on the altar in the Catholic Church. By extension, it is a place for keeping any sacred thing.

TEACHING ORDER. A religious order in the Catholic Church, especially founded for the purposes of establishing schools and teaching young people. The Brothers of the Christian Schools for men and the Ursulines for women are among the best known; nearly all religious institutes now have some teaching members or branches.

TE DEUM (Lat.: We praise thee, O God; tā-dā'-ōom). An old hymn of thanksgiving and praise, or a musical setting for the words of the hymn. It is still called the Ambrosian Hymn, although now St. Niketas (d. c.414) rather than St. Ambrose is thought to have composed it.

TEMPLARS, KNIGHTS. One of the two wealthy and powerful military orders within the Catholic Church, the other being the Knights Hospitallers, the Knights Templars or Poor Knights of the Temple was founded by crusaders in 1118 to defend Christian Jerusalem against the infidels. It became extremely strong and extended its possessions and influences to Italy, France, Spain, Germany, and England. The Rule of St. Benedict was adopted, but did not prevail, and abuses and luxury, indulgence and vice, grew with the Order's fortune. In 1312, Pope Clement V tried the Order for heresy and immorality, decreed its suppression, and transferred most of its possessions to the Knights Hospitallers. Although there were many things wrong within the Order, the true facts in the case are little known, and there is at least some suspicion that the jealousy and greed of Philip IV of France, who was responsible for many repressive measures, were partly the incentives to action. The Order was well entrenched in England, where many place names still include "Temple," a reference to this Order. The Templars derived that name from the fact that their early headquarters were near Solomon's Temple in Jerusalem.

TENEBRAE (Lat.: shadows, darkness; ten'-ə-brī). The special mourning service of the Catholic Church when Matins and Lauds for Maundy Thursday, Good Friday, and Holy Saturday are said or sung on the preceding evenings. From the extinguishing of the candles, which signifies the crucifixion and death of Jesus, the name "Tenebrae" is derived.

TERCE (Lat.: third). The hour of the Divine Office which is said at about 9 A.M., the third hour of the day. This hour particularly commemorates the Pentecostal event and the descent of the Holy Spirit to the apostles.

TERESA OF AVILA, ST. (1515–1582). St. Teresa of Avila is one of the best known and most venerated of saints. Her life has been found meaningful by many because she recognized quite clearly and for many years the pleasures of a secular existence. She was quite devout as a child, but during her adolescence she was apparently as flirtatious and frivolous as most girls her age. At about the age of eighteen, however, she again came under religious influences and entered a Carmelite convent in her home town. At that time, nuns of the Order enjoyed the freedom of entertaining guests both in the convent rooms and in their own cells, and St. Teresa participated in this daily life for twenty years. However, as time drew on, she found the secular world less and less rewarding, and decided at last that she could be content only in devoting her entire life and energy to God. Shortly after this, she began her long and difficult efforts at reforming the Carmelite Order. She established convents throughout Spain that were distinguished by their poverty, their austerity, and their devotional sincerity; in this task she had the support of St. John of the Cross, but the job was not easy. Eventually, however, her reforms were extended to all Carmelite houses. She suffered much, but her rewards were in her success and her ecstatic visions and supernatural experiences.

Her death occurred in a convent of Alba, quite peacefully and blessedly. Her feast day is October 15.

TERTIARY. Any member of a third order in the Catholic Church. A secular tertiary is a member, a man or a woman, of a third order who lives in the world, while a regular tertiary is a member of a religious community.

TESTAMENT. A testimony, a bearing of witness, or a covenant. The Bible is composed of the Old Testament, an historical and philosophical account of Jewish history in thirty-nine books composed between about 1000 B.C. and 150 B.C. and the New Testament which is made up of twenty-seven books, four biographical and philosophical gospels, a Church history (Acts of the Apostles), twenty-one epistles, and an apocalypse. It recounts the beginning and early growth of Christianity and is called the "New" Testament because in many ways the new faith was held to supersede the old.

TETRAGRAMMATON (Gr.: four letters). The usual verbal construction referred to by this name is JHVH, the ancient Hebraic "name" for God. The full word was so holy it could not be written out. In translation to other languages, however, it became necessary to create a pronounceable word, and probably the vowels from Elohim or Adonai, two alternate names for God, were inserted between the four consonants to form versions of Jehovah and Jahweh.

THAUMATURG(US) (Gr.: a wonder-worker; thô′-mə-tūrj). A worker of miracles. Among saints especially deserving of this designation have been Sts. Cosmas and Damian (c.297), St. Stephen (c.816), and St. Antony of Padua (c.1231).

THEANDRIC ACTS. Those acts of Jesus which were a union of the purely human and the purely divine. In classical theology, Jesus was considered the blending in perfect harmony of the human and divine natures and wills, but certain actions were determined as proper to each. Theandric acts, on the other hand, represented a unity of both.

THEANTHROPIC (Gr.: "God" plus "man"). Having a nature both human and divine, as did Jesus according to orthodox theological doctrine.

THEATINES. A Catholic religious order founded by Cajetan in 1524 and named after its co-founder, a bishop of Chieti, or "Theate," to fight heresy and personal evil living. The group was relatively successful, but declined during the nineteenth century.

THECLA, ST. (first century). St. Thecla was probably the most highly venerated female saint in the first centuries of the Christian era and her name is still invoked in Catholic prayers for the dying. She was converted by St. Paul and underwent much persecution to remain loyal to her faith and her vows of virginity, but she died peacefully. She was praised by St. Ambrose and St. John Chrysostom, among others, but beyond these few facts nothing is known about her life. Her feast day is September 23.

THEISM. The system of belief which includes belief in a perfect being that is the creator and ruler of the universe.

THEODICY (Gr.: from "deity" and "justice"). The study of the problem presented by the existence of evil in a world ruled by God, and the attempt to justify and support God's goodness in the face of the evil. The attributes of God are called into question by the presence of evil. "It [the problem] may be expressed in a famous dilemma: either God is able to prevent evil and will not, or he is willing to prevent it and cannot. If the former, he is not merciful; if the latter, he is not omnipotent." (*Theological Terms*, p. 236) The traditional Christian solution has been to leave the question unanswered, but to assert that all things work eventually for good under God's rule, no matter how evil they may seem. The number of "solutions" to this problem is too great to be included here; it is still a very real one to theologians, for many of whom no really satisfactory answer has yet been put forward.

THEOLOGY. The study of the divine Being, or God, and His relations to man and the universe, including the study of religious doctrine and dogma.

THEOPHANY (Gr.: from "god" and "bright"). The appearance of God in a visible or otherwise tangible form. In general, Christian belief is that God may not be seen or perceived in any of the three persons of the Trinity. The "appearances" in the Old Testament, such as to Moses, are held to have been of an angel representing God. The Incarnation is understood in another sense entirely.

THESSALONIANS, FIRST AND SECOND EPISTLES TO THE. Two of St. Paul's letters, written during his second missionary journey especially to encourage the Christians of the young congregation, and to answer questions regarding the second coming.

THIRD ORDER. The branch of a religious order of the Catholic Church which, when secular, is composed of men or women who live in the world and pursue a normal secular life though bound by modified forms of the laws of their order, or, when regular, is made up of members who leave the world to live under simple vows in a religious community of their order. It is called the "third order" to distinguish it from the first order, composed of the monks of a religious order, and the second order, the women's branch of the religious order. Members of a third order are called tertiaries; the purpose of such orders, which originated in the thirteenth century, is, primarily, to carry the religious spirit into the world, and even the regular tertiaries, those who live in community, are engaged in such works as teaching and nursing in the world.

THIRTY-NINE ARTICLES. The statement of beliefs of the Anglican and Episcopal Churches. It dates from 1562, when Queen Elizabeth I called a "meeting of Convocation" to draw up such a statement, and from 1571, when it was made the official dogma for the Church of England. The Thirty-nine Articles specifically state that "The Bishop of Rome [i.e., the Pope] hath no jurisdiction in this Realm of England," and further, that "the Church . . . ought not to decree anything against the same [Holy Writ], so besides the same ought it not to enforce anything to be believed for necessity of Salvation." The Articles recognize also that men in religious assemblies "may err, and sometimes have erred, even in things pertaining unto God." In the Articles which deal with God, the Trinity, Jesus, sin, salvation, Scripture, justification by faith, and the Sacraments, the agreement with other Protestant churches in Europe is very close. The Thirty-nine Articles still form the basic rule of the Anglican Church. (*Protestantism,* p. 87).

THOMAS A KEMPIS, BLESSED. (1379–1471). A monk in the Nether-
lands, Thomas a Kempis, or Thomas Hemerken, is usually
credited with authorship of the *Imitation of Christ*. However,
some scholars give credit, instead, to Gerard Groot, founder of
the Brothers of the Common Life, a religious community which
later joined with the Augustinian canons, and to which Thomas a
Kempis belonged. His feast day is August 25.

THOMAS AQUINAS, ST. (1225–1274). Called the Angelic Doctor,
Thomas Aquinas achieved in his *Summa Theologica* a blending of
Aristotelian and Christian philosophies and beliefs which still
stands as the high point of scholasticism and one of the greatest
philosophical studies ever produced. "Thomism" is the name by
which his philosophy is known, and the Catholic Church in 1879
declared it to be official; although Catholics are not required to
accept Thomistic doctrines, Thomism is respected by all Catholics.
Essentially, St. Thomas Aquinas held that truth is indivisible and
that science and theology cannot contradict each other. Evil, he
felt, was only the absence of good. Everything, he stated, was
arranged in ascending order to God, in whom alone the distinction between form and matter, existence and essence, does not
exist. His rational and logical treatment of theology still stands
as an unrivalled achievement. It is interesting that in his own
time he was not particularly appreciated. He belonged to an important Italian family that did not want him to follow the religious
vocation, and, in fact, went to considerable lengths to prevent it.
However, he prevailed, joined the Dominicans, and studied under
Albertus Magnus in France. Because he was quite heavy and slow
moving, he was nicknamed the Dumb Ox, and he and his teachings were frequently misunderstood and even frowned upon. Today, there is a Neo-Thomism which attempts to apply Thomistic
concepts to political, social, and economic problems, and it exists
not only among Catholics, but among those outside the Church
as well, an indication of the far-reaching influence of this Doctor of the Church. The feast day of St. Thomas Aquinas is
March 7.

THOMAS, GOSPEL OF. An apocryphal gospel which attempts to fill
in the gaps in knowledge about Jesus' boyhood, giving an account
of the miraculous powers and actions of the child which is both

coarse and tasteless. "The Infancy Gospel," an Arabic book popular among Nestorians, was based on this "gospel," which apparently originated with the gnostics and is now included in the Pseudepigrapha.

THOMAS MORE, ST. (1478–1535). Perhaps best known for his book *Utopia,* St. Thomas More, or Sir Thomas More, was among those Catholics who became martyrs for their faith following the passing of the Act of Supremacy in England in 1534. He had opposed King Henry VIII's divorce from Catherine of Aragon, and retired from his official post as lord chancellor in 1532. He was finally beheaded on a charge of treason, having refused to acknowledge Henry as a spiritual leader. This great humanist, a friend of Erasmus and a man noted for his wit and good humor even to the very chopping block, was canonized in 1935, and his feast day is July 9.

THOMAS, ST. (first century). This apostle is probably best known as "doubting Thomas," a reference to his refusal to believe that Jesus was risen until he had himself felt the wounds in his body. Thomas is not mentioned specifically except in the Gospel according to St. John; it is to Thomas that that author gives the question which inspired Jesus to respond, "I am the way, the truth, and the life: no man cometh unto the Father, but by me." There is an apocryphal Acts of St. Thomas which describes a portion of his journey to India, on which, according to tradition, he evangelized the Parthians, Medes, and Persians. His feast day is December 21.

THREE. The number of the Trinity; hence, three rings, circles, crosses, or marks of any sort are always a possible symbol for the Trinity.

THREE CHILDREN, THE. In Babylonian, the names of these three, whose story is recounted in the Book of Daniel in the Old Testament, are Shadrach, Meshach, and Abednego. Condemned to the fiery furnace, they were saved by their faith from the flames, and the song that they are said to have sung, or recited, has been given a place in the worship services of Catholic and Anglican churches, where it is known as the Benedicite. Actually, the Song was probably a later addition to Daniel, and it is found in the Apocrypha of the Authorized Version.

THREE HOURS, THE. The "Three Hours" are between noon and 3 P.M. on Good Friday, the time when Jesus hung on the cross. They are observed by special devotions, often meditation on the seven words or phrases spoken by Jesus during this period. The custom of the devotions of the Three Hours is said to have originated with the Jesuits in 1687.

THREE KINGS, THE. The Magi or Wise Men. See MAGI.

THREE MARYS, THE. The three biblical Marys are identified as Mary Magdalen, Mary Salome (Mark 15:40 and 16:1, though there is at least doubt that "Salome" was preceded by "Mary"), and Mary the wife of Cleophas and sister of the Virgin Mary. Legend has it that these three preached in southern France, and three ancient tombs in the Camargue were once identified as theirs.

THRONE. An honorary name for the chair used by a cardinal, abbot, etc., when he is not at the altar during a service he is conducting. Usually it is a permanent armed chair with a canopy. "Throne" is also the name used for a small canopied platform which holds the monstrance at certain times during the Mass.

THRONE OF GOD. A usage at one time more prevalent than it is now, when, taken literally, the throne was envisioned as an elaborate but realistic ruler's throne which one's soul approached after death to be judged by God the King. Now, the expression is more likely to be used in the figurative sense to denote the majesty and authority of God.

THRONES. One of the choirs, or levels, of angels in the celestial hierarchy.

THURIBLE (Lat.: from "frankincense"). A container for the incense used in worship services. It is a metal dish suspended by three chains, with a fourth chain holding the lid, and filled with charcoal and incense.

THURIFER. The acolyte who has charge of the thurible.

TIMOTHY, FIRST AND SECOND EPISTLES TO. Pastoral letters from St. Paul to Timothy at Ephesus. They deal with church discipline, organization, and doctrine.

TIMOTHY, ST. (first century). A disciple and companion of St. Paul, Timothy accompanied his master on many of his missionary journeys and undertook some, such as to Macedonia and Corinth, on his own. The Epistles to Timothy are letters addressed by St. Paul, in captivity in Rome, to Timothy in Ephesus, and II Timothy is distinguished by St. Paul's moving words of farewell. Timothy lived for some thirty years after St. Paul's death, and during that time served as bishop of the church in Ephesus. According to tradition, he was stoned to death by members of his group while he was trying to keep them from attending a pagan festival. His feast day is January 24.

TITHE (Old Eng.: a tenth). A tenth of one's income, supposed to go to one's church as an offering. Tithing was an ancient custom which survived into the twentieth century but which is now almost extinct.

TITUS, EPISTLE TO. A Pastoral Epistle directed by St. Paul to his envoy, Titus, on the island of Crete. It emphasizes salvation by faith, but good works are not neglected. St. Titus remained as missionary to Crete, where he died in 96. His feast day is January 4.

TOBIT. A book included in the Apocrypha of the Authorized Version dealing with Tobit's story and illustrating, especially, the goodness of God.

TONGUES, GIFT OF. See GLOSSOLALIA.

TONSURE. The shaving of the hair on the head of a cleric of the Catholic Church symbolizes Jesus' crown of thorns. The shaved portion may be as small as a half dollar on the crown of the head, usual among the secular clergy, or as extensive as the entire crown with the exception of a circular fringe called a corona. The most extensive is that of the Dominicans, which is called the great tonsure.

TRADUCIANISM. Opposed to Creationism, Traducianism is the doctrine that the soul is given to the child by the parents either as a material or a spiritual generation. Most Christians believe in Creationism, that the soul is created directly by God.

TRANSCENDENCE. This term is used in the theological context with much the same meaning as in the material context, and it thus may be fairly broadly interpreted. In general, it means a "being above or beyond," or a "surpassing." It may also, more specifically, refer to an attribute of God, as he transcends or stands above the world. Philosophies of a transcendent God stress his remoteness, his separation and removal from the world, and thus reduce to some extent the element of concern God is held to feel for each human being. In such a sense, transcendence is contrasted to immanence, which emphasizes God's involvement with and activity in the day-to-day life of people.

TRANSFIGURATION, THE. The revelation of the divinity and spiritual brightness of Jesus which occurred on Mt. Tabor in Galilee in the presence of the apostles Peter, James, and John. The story is recounted in Luke 9:28-36 which describes how "the fashion of his countenance was altered, and his raiment was white and glistering." Moses and Elias appeared with him, and God spoke from a cloud saying, "This is my beloved Son: hear him." The feast of the Transfiguration is celebrated on August 6.

TRANSLATION. The term used to refer to the removal of a saint's relics from one tomb to another, or from one burial site to a more suitable one, often a shrine.

TRANSUBSTANTIATION. This Catholic doctrine states that the substance of the Eucharistic bread and wine is changed into the body and blood of Jesus at the Communion service. It may be better understood if one knows that "substance" is, in the philosophical sense, "The inner substantial reality" which underlies appearance and is "not perceptible to the senses but can only be grasped by the intellect. It is this inner reality that is transformed, not the accidents that are perceptible to the eye. [e.g., taste, color, smell]" (*Theological Terms,* p. 244) It is contrasted to Luther's "consubstantiation."

TRAPPISTS. The term by which Cistercians of the More Strict Observance have commonly, though incorrectly, been known since about 1892 when the group absorbed Cistercians who followed the reformed constitution of La Trappe abbey. Until that time, Cistercians following the La Trappe constitution, reformed in

1664, were the only ones known as Trappists. The choir monks' habit is white, the lay brothers' is brown; perpetual silence is observed; meat, eggs, and fish are not eaten; and there is manual work, usually farming, for choir monks as well as for lay brothers.

TREASURY OF MERITS. The Treasury from which the Catholic Church grants indulgences, made up, first, of the superabundance of merits and satisfactions of Jesus, and, second, the superabundance of those of the saints. This doctrine, that such a Treasury does exist and is usable, has been subjected to many attacks, not least of all by Martin Luther.

TREE OF KNOWLEDGE. The tree planted in the Garden of Eden, the fruit of which contained the knowledge of Good and Evil. It was from this tree that man ate in disobedience of God's order and thus incurred the Fall from grace and expulsion from the Garden, the story told in Genesis.

TREE OF LIFE. The twin of the Tree of Knowledge, its fruit gave immortality, and it was from this tree that man did not eat. Because he might have done so, he was expelled from the Garden of Eden after breaking God's commandments in eating from the Tree of Knowledge.

TRINITARIAN. One who believes in the doctrine of the Trinity; also, anything having to do with that doctrine. In the Catholic Church, a member of the religious order of the Holy Trinity, founded in 1198, and now engaged mostly in teaching and nursing, may be called a Trinitarian. Nuns of the name now have no connection with the original Order of the Holy Trinity, but were founded in the seventeenth century to do teaching and nursing.

TRINITY. God the Father, God the Son, and God the Holy Spirit are the "three persons in one substance" of the Christian God, or Trinity. The persons are considered to be co-equal and co-eternal; each is fully divine and each is closely unified with the other, although each has an individual character or individual characteristics. The doctrine was not emphasized until the fourth century, when it became necessary to clarify beliefs because of the rise of certain heretical groups, especially Arians, who denied the divinity of Jesus. Orthodox belief is spelled out in the Athanasian creed, but the Trinity is directly named in Matthew 28:19.

TRINITY SUNDAY. The first Sunday after Pentecost, observed since about the fourteenth century as the special feast day of the Trinity.

TRITHEISM. A form of Trinitarianism which claims the existence of three separate consciousnesses in the Trinity which share the nature of deity; it does not accept the unity of that deity, however, and in not doing so closely approaches polytheism.

TROPE. A phrase or short passage that was inserted into the liturgy of the medieval church worship service. It was often a fragment of dialogue that emphasized or brought alive a particularly significant liturgical point. As such, tropes are identified as the portion of the service from which drama was revitalized. The first tropes were inserted into the resurrection and Christmas stories.

TRUTH, REVEALED. A truth given man by God through revelation, as in the Bible. Catholicism recognizes formally and virtually revealed truth. Formally revealed truth may be either explicit, as those truths stated in the Apostles' Creed, or implicit, as those of the Immaculate Conception. Virtually revealed truths are those such as the impeccability of Jesus.

TUNIC, TUNICLE. The basic garment of the habit of most religious orders, an ankle-length, loose-fitting gown with narrow sleeves. Another "tunic" is the vestment identified especially with the subdeacon, and is often almost identical with the dalmatic of the deacon. It is referred to as "the garment of gladness and the vesture of joy."

TWELFTH DAY. The twelfth day after Christmas, January 6, also known as Epiphany. It was once celebrated as Christmas, and is also called Old Christmas. Twelfth Night is the evening of January 5, the eve of Twelfth Day. This time still marks the end of the Christmas season for many people.

TWELVE APOSTLES. See APOSTLE.

TYPE. The term may refer, as it does in Platonic philosophy, to an exemplary idea or highest realization of a concept or species, or it may be used to designate a person or event that functions as a forerunner of the later, fully actualized person or event. In the latter sense, Melchisedek is a "type" of the Christ, for he was an early priest-king; the sacrificial lamb is a "type" of the sacrificed Jesus; and Jonah's three days in the whale's belly and eventual release form a "type" of Jesus' burial and resurrection. Contrasts are drawn, too, as a "negative type." Thus the "tree" by which man fell (the Tree of Knowledge) is a negative type of the "tree" by which man was saved, that on which Jesus was crucified.

UNBAPTIZED. Although baptism is generally held to be necessary for salvation, the Catholic Church recognizes that the desire for baptism fulfills the requirement, and that a perfect act of contrition or act of charity indicates such a desire.

UNCTION. The anointing with oil for religious purposes. See EXTREME UNCTION.

UNFROCK. To depose, or remove, a member of the clergy from his office.

UNITARIAN UNIVERSALIST ASSOCIATION. Although not a church by name, the Unitarian Universalist Association, formed by a merger in 1961 of Unitarian and Universalists, functions as one. Unitarians reject most or all orthodox theological doctrine, but, specifically, belief in the Trinity and in the divinity of Jesus. They deny the infallibility of the Bible and affirm, instead, the strength of man's reason, the importance of natural virtue, and the conception of God in one person.

Although there are strong doctrinal resemblances with Arianism, the Unitarian movement actually began in the Reformation; it became organized in England in 1774 and in America in 1785. In 1819, W. E. Channing delivered an ordination sermon which defined the doctrines, but no creed has ever been formalized, and neither ministers nor members are required to make a particular profession of faith. The American Unitarian Association was formed in 1825; present United States membership in the Unitarian Universalist Association is about 170,000.

UNIVERSALISM. The belief that eventually all souls will be saved; it is also called Redemptionism. Theologians such as Clement and Origen, both writing around A.D. 200, emphasized the power

331

of God's love and would not believe that such love could be manifested as total wrath against any human soul. Origen was condemned by the Church as a heretic.

UNIVERSALIST CHURCH. Merged with the Unitarian Association in 1961, the Universalist Church was founded in the United States in the eighteenth century and held its first convention in 1790. It changed from being Calvinistic to Unitarian in nature, accepted the principle of universalism, and asserted the fatherhood of God and the spiritual leadership of Jesus. Combined membership with the Unitarians is about 170,000 in the United States.

URBANIST POPES. Urban VI (1378), Boniface IX (1389), Innocent VII (1404), and Gregory XII (1406), who reigned at Rome during the Schism of the West.

URSULA, ST. (third or fourth century). The old legend of St. Ursula and the Eleven Thousand Virgins recounts how a girl named Ursula, accompanied by eleven thousand young women, fled from England to the continent to avoid the attentions of invading Saxons, only to be slaughtered by the Huns who had invaded Europe. The more likely story is thought to be that eleven girls were killed, perhaps by the Huns, near present-day Cologne, and that their story was subsequently embroidered and added to over the centuries until it reached its present form. The feast of St. Ursula and the Eleven Thousand Virgins is October 21.

URSULINES. Any of several Catholic congregations of sisters whose work is the education of girls. The main group is called the Company of St. Ursula and was organized in 1535 by St. Angela Merici; it was the first women's teaching order. Congregations are unenclosed or semi-enclosed, and a black habit is worn.

VALENTINE, ST. (d. c.270). There are two martyrs who bear the name of Valentine, but since their stories are remarkably similar, it is a question whether they did not, actually, have a single origin. Both Valentines were clergymen, though one was a priest in Rome and one was reputedly a bishop in Umbria; both performed miraculous cures of children, whose families were thereafter converted to the Christian faith; and both were beheaded. It is perhaps difficult to see the connection with these martyrs and the traditions of St. Valentine's day, but in the Middle Ages, February 14 was not only celebrated in memory of the Sts. Valentine but was also believed to be the day in spring when birds mated. Thus two traditions united "St. Valentine" with "love." The feast day of both saints is February 14.

VATICAN, THE. The papal palace and other buildings in Vatican City; the government and/or power and influence of the Catholic Church headed by the pope; and, sometimes, the Catholic Church itself. The name is derived from the fact that the palace is built on Vatican Hill.

VATICAN COUNCIL, FIRST. This council of cardinals and others met from December 8, 1869, until October 20, 1870, and defined such matters as the infallibility and primacy of the pope. It was the twentieth ecumenical council of the Catholic Church. "Vatican Two" of the first half of the 1960's was actually the Second Vatican Council.

VEIL. A covering for the head and shoulders, usually black for professed nuns and white for novices, is part of the habit of all enclosed nuns and most others, although various active orders have dispensed with it either entirely or in part. It is derived from the veil worn in early times by married women and is the symbol that the nun is a bride of the Church.

VENI CREATUR SPIRITUS (Lat.: Come, creating Spirit; vā'-nē krā'-ä-tur spir-ē'-tōōs). A ninth-century hymn invoking the Holy Spirit, it is still sung at Mass on many occasions, as well as during the Divine Office for Pentecost.

VERONICA, ST. (first century). According to tradition, Veronica or Berenice was the name of the woman who wiped Jesus' face with a scarf as he walked toward Calvary. Hence, the scarf or veil is called a "veronica." St. Veronica's feast day is February 4.

VERSICLE. Literally, a little verse; usually, a short sentence said or sung by a minister or priest during a worship service and responded to by the congregation.

VESPERS (Lat.: eventide). The evening hour of the Divine Office in the Catholic Church, to be said about 6 P.M. or between 3 P.M. and 6 P.M. It is the evening assembly in a religious community, or the evening service in a church, and in the latter sense, the term is used by Protestants as much as by Catholics.

VESSELS, SACRED. In the Catholic worship service, the chalice, paten, ciborium, pyx, monstrance, etc., which may not be handled by any layman except the sacristan.

VESTMENTS. The special clothing worn by members of the clergy. The general vestments always worn at Mass in the Catholic Church by priest, deacon, and subdeacon are the amice, alb, girdle, and maniple; the priest adds the stole and chasuble, the deacon the stole and dalmatic, and the subdeacon the tunic. Other vestments are the surplice, cope, and pallium. Clergymen of many Protestant churches wear a greatly modified form of these vestments.

VIATICUM (Lat.: provision for a journey; vē-at'-ē-kōōm). Communion bread and wine given to the dying or to those in danger of death, as a soldier before a battle. The accompanying words are "Receive, brother, the viaticum of our Lord Jesus Christ, that he may preserve thee from the malignant enemy and bring thee to everlasting life. Amen." It is said before extreme unction when that sacrament is administered.

VICAR. In the Episcopal Church, a vicar is a minister in charge of a parish chapel, as deputy for another minister. In the Anglican Church, he is a priest who receives only a salary, other incomes going to a layman or a religious corporation, or, often, a priest who is not a rector. In the Catholic Church, a vicar is one who acts as a deputy for another, as a priest or other clergyman acts for a bishop, and as the pope acts for Christ, as evidenced in the title Vicar of Christ. A "vicarage" is a vicar's residence, or, sometimes, his income.

VIGIL. The day before a religious holiday, to be used in preparation for, and, in earlier days, in fasting before the festival itself. Among those having vigils are Easter, Christmas, and Pentecost. The Easter vigil, a fairly recent renewal of the ancient custom, and midnight services on Christmas Eve, are survivals of the old vigil observances.

VIGIL LIGHT. A light perpetually burning before a shrine, statue, or the like.

VINCENT, ST. (d. 304). A victim of the persecutions of the Emperor Diocletian, St. Vincent was the deacon who spoke and preached for the very old and tongue-tied Valerius, bishop of Saragossa. St. Vincent, speaking for himself and Valerius, refused to apostasize, and was tortured to death for his faith. His feast day is January 22.

VINCENT DE PAUL, ST. (1580–1660). Remembered for his work among the poor and the homeless, work, in fact, which is continued to this day in his name, St. Vincent de Paul's life divides into three uniquely separate portions, only the last of which is related to his work among the destitute. He was a child in a fairly good-sized and well-off peasant family; intelligent and ambitious, Vincent was sent to the University of Toulouse for theological studies which would enable him to rise in the world by a route often chosen by those who desired to improve their position but lacked funds to do so. At first he was unsuccessful. However, trying to return by sea from Marseilles where he had gone to collect a debt, he was captured by Corsairs and taken to Tunis. He escaped somehow, and carried a secret message from the court in Rome, which he had been given at one point in his escape, to the French king. That king, Henry IV, immediately became his protector, and at that time, about 1610, begins the second phase of the life of this man. For the next seven years St. Vincent lived the life of a favorite, receiving good positions and benefits from the king and court. Indeed, he seemed to have achieved all he had hoped for. However, in 1617, he abandoned all his honors and favors and began the third phase of his life, that for which he is so well known. He founded the Lazarists or Priests of the Mission, to evangelize the poor of the countryside, and he founded the congregation of the Sisters of Charity to work with the city's poor and homeless. A great deal of his work was done with foundlings and abandoned babies. He continued in this work, with only a few brief interruptions, until his death. His feast day is July 19.

VIOLET. The liturgical color usually called purple.

VIRGIN BIRTH. The doctrine that Jesus was conceived by the Holy Spirit and that Mary thus both conceived and bore him while yet a virgin. Catholic doctrine refers to Mary as "ever virgin," holding that the biblical "brothers" of Jesus were not true brothers but only relatives or otherwise closely associated with him.

VIRTUE. Catholic theology identifies a "virtue" as a disposition toward right conduct and such an inclination is called a "habit." The natural virtues, those which improve human nature, are prudence, justice, fortitude, and temperance, and the theological virtues, those which have to do with man's destiny and salvation, are faith, hope, and charity. Protestants generally reject the formal doctrine of virtues while recognizing the "virtues" of prudence, justice, and the like.

VISITATION, THE. A feast day celebrated on July 2 commemorating the visit of Mary, Jesus' mother, just after the Annunciation, to her cousin Elizabeth, who was to bear John. The story is recounted in Luke 1:39ff.

VISITATION, ORDER AND SISTERS OF THE. The Order of the Visitation of the Blessed Virgin Mary was founded in 1610 by St. Francis de Sales and St. Jane Frances de Chantal to provide for widows and women in poor health. The Order is enclosed and contemplative; the Sisters of the Visitation is a teaching congregation founded some fifty years after the Order. It is unenclosed. The habit of both Order and Congregation is black.

VISITATION OF THE SICK. One of the duties of clergymen, or specifically designated laymen, is to call upon the members of the church who are, through illness, confined to their homes. Usually the visit is accompanied by prayer, and some reading from the Bible, as well as with more general conversation.

VITUS, ST. (fourth century). More commonly known as Guy, St. Vitus was a martyr of the fourth century, and for reasons unknown today was invoked against epilepsy, called the "falling sickness," and related seizures which came to be known as St. Vitus' dance. His feast day is June 15.

VOCATION. A person's work is usually called by this term; although the word should designate the particular work toward which he feels attracted, or called, and which he does in response to such an attraction or call. In a more religious context, having a "vocation" is having the fitness, will, and sense of duty to enter the religious life.

VOTIVE OFFERING (Lat.: a wish or vow). Something offered God or a saint as a sign of gratitude, or in fulfillment of a promise or a vow. Sometimes a votive offering is made in the form of a candle lighted before a shrine or an image, which is then called a votive candle. A votive Mass, on the other hand, is a special service held at the discretion of the priest for a specific reason.

VOWS OF RELIGION. These three vows, taken by one who enters a religious order of the Catholic Church, are of poverty, chastity, and obedience. They are taken to secure assistance in resisting the enemies of spiritual life which they combat: envy, fleshly desires, and pride.

VULGATE, THE. This Latin Bible is still a basic Catholic text and is still considered authoritative. It is the work of St. Jerome, done in the fourth century, by the order of Pope Damasus. St. Jerome set Hebrew and Greek versions into Latin, the popular or "vulgar" tongue of the day, and thus made the Bible far more accessible than it had previously been. Books of Wisdom, Ecclesiasticus, Baruch, and two of the Maccabees, included in the Vulgate and the Apocrypha of the Authorized Version, were not worked on by Jerome; however, the whole New Testament was revised from the old *Itala Vetus*, the Book of Psalms was given a new revision, and the other books of the Old Testament were translated directly from the Hebrew, Aramaic, or Greek. St. Jerome's decisions about what books to include in the Vulgate amounted to setting the canon, and, indeed, the books included in the Vulgate are known as the Western Canon. Essentially, the choice was based, so far as the Old Testament was concerned, on what was included in the Septuagint, and it was to this that Protestants took exception at the time of the Reformation. St. Jerome is honored as one of the Doctors of the Church, and his feast day is celebrated on September 30. He ranks, perhaps, with St. Paul, St. Augustine, and St. Thomas Aquinas in importance in shaping the Christian church.

WAFER BREAD. Bread for the Communion service often made in the form of small, flat, crisp disks.

WAKE (Old Eng.: watch). Passing the night before a burial in the house where the deceased lay was originally an entirely religious custom, practiced mostly in Ireland. Praying and comforting of the bereaved relatives distinguished the early wakes.

WATER. The symbolism of water is multiple. It represents cleansing, and hence purity and purification. When mixed with the Communion wine, it symbolizes especially the union of the human and the divine in Jesus as well as the water which issued from Jesus' pierced side. Water is used liturgically in baptism, consecration, and, in the Catholic Church, in the form of holy water.

WAX. By ancient tradition, church candles are made entirely, or mainly, of beeswax, which symbolizes, in its purity and naturalness, the purity of Jesus' body.

WAY OF THE CROSS. See STATIONS OF THE CROSS.

WENCESLAUS, ST. (903–935). The "good King Wenceslaus" of the English Christmas carol was actually Duke Wenceslaus of Bohemia, a tenth-century ruler of that section of Czechoslovakia. He was raised as a Christian by his grandmother, or, as some accounts say, by his mother, St. Ludmilla. As a ruler, he practiced the teachings of his faith, giving to the poor, protecting the weak and the helpless, and generally bettering the lot of the downtrodden. It is this aspect of his reign which is told about in the well-known song. St. Wenceslaus is considered a Christian martyr because he was assassinated by a jealous and far less kindly brother, or by a band of conspirators under his brother's direction, who took exception to his Christian piety and practice. He was killed on his way to Mass, September 28, 935, and was later canonized and made patron saint of Bohemia. His feast day is September 28.

WESTERN CANON. The books of the Bible accepted as inspired and official by the Church at the time in the fourth century when St. Jerome edited and translated the Bible into Latin. This book, called the Vulgate, was adopted by the Council of Trent in 1546 as the official Bible of the Catholic Church, and from it, from 1582 to 1610, was made the official English translation, the Douay, or Rheims-Douay, Bible. Thus the Western Canon and the Douay Bible are the same. The King James, or Authorized Version, differs from Western Canon in that it omits those books of the Old Testament which appeared in the Septuagint, a third-century B.C. Greek translation of the Old Testament, but not in the tenth-to-fifteenth century A.D. Masoretic text. At the time of the Reformation, English Protestants decided that such non-Masoretic books should be used only for instruction and should not be considered inspired, for the Masora represented the best efforts of Hebrew scholars to establish the authentic Old Testament text. All, or parts, of fourteen such books are included in an appendix, or the Apocrypha, to the Authorized Version. The A.V. did, however, preserve the arrangement of the books in the Old Testament, so that, with the exception of the books which were omitted, it contains the same material in the same order as the Western Canon.

WESTERN CHURCH. An alternative name for the Catholic, or Roman, Church whose head is the bishop of Rome, i.e., the pope. As a name, it makes the distinction between this church and the Eastern Orthodox Church, or Eastern Church.

WHITBY, SYNOD OF. The assembly held in 663 at Whitby, in Yorkshire, England, when the Catholic Church with headquarters at Canterbury secured the agreement of the northern, or Celtic, branch of the Catholic Church to conform to Roman ritual and practice. It also led to a settlement of the long-standing Easter Controversy and was especially significant in that it brought English Catholicism into the main stream of the Church's development.

St. Wilfrid led the group from the south; St. Chad and King Oswy led the group from the north; and St. Colman, bishop of Lindisfarne, led the group that opposed the decisions and later retreated with some of his loyal monks to Ireland.

WHITE. Symbolically, white represents joy, and, of course, purity. In the Catholic Church it is used on many occasions, for example, on all of the feasts of Jesus except that of the cross and the passion.

WHITE FRIARS. The Carmelites; the name is derived from the fact that they wear white cloaks.

WHITE LADIES. A group of teaching nuns founded in 1796 and formally called the Daughters of the Presentation. Also, an old name for Cistercian nuns.

WHITE MONKS. The Cistercians, so-called from the color of their tunics and cowls.

WHITSUNDAY. White Sunday, the older English name for Pentecost, so-called because Pentecost was originally a time for baptism, and white was worn by the candidates for that sacrament.

WHITSUNTIDE. The week following Pentecost, or Whitsunday, but especially the first three days of the week.

WILL, FREE. See FREEDOM OF THE WILL.

WILLIAM, ST. (1085–1142). An active founder of monasteries and abbeys following the rule of St. Benedict, St. William worked in Italy, the land of his birth and peaceful death. His feast day is June 25.

WINE. With bread, wine forms the Eucharistic sacrifice, its primary liturgical use. It is specified that it should be pure grape juice naturally fermented, but it may be either red or white.

WISDOM. Used with a variety of meanings, "wisdom" is sometimes interchangeable with "the Word," as in I Corinthians 1:24, when Jesus is called "the wisdom of God." More often, it refers to a gift of the Holy Spirit which enables a man to judge according to divine standards, or it may refer to a superior intellect which enables a man to examine the nature of things effectively.

WISDOM OF JESUS, SON OF SIRACH. Ecclesiasticus, a book of the Old Testament in the Western Canon, is included in the Apocrypha of the Authorized Version. Because the excellence of wisdom is stressed, this book is considered to be in the same class as such writings as Job, Proverbs, Ecclesiastes, and the Wisdom of Solomon. Also emphasized are praise of God for nature and praise of many of the great men of Israel.

WISDOM OF SOLOMON. Included in the Western Canon and in the Apocrypha of the Authorized Version, this book exhorts the reader to wisdom and justice and examines Israelite history from those two points of reference.

WISE MEN, THE. See MAGI.

WITNESS, TO BEAR. To testify by words and deeds, or through the goodness of one's life and works, to a personal acceptance of the Christian faith.

WORD, THE. A metaphysical and complex concept of the unity of God, Jesus, and the Holy Spirit, expressed in John 1:1-14, "In the beginning was the Word, and the Word was with God, and the Word was God . . . and the Word was made flesh and dwelt among us." Thus, Jesus may be spoken of as the Word, as is frequently done, but the Word may also be interpreted to mean God, the holy Spirit, or the Trinity. It is sometimes used in the Greek form, LOGOS.

In practice, also, the term is often used as an abbreviation for "The Word of God," that is, the Bible, or devout discussion of the biblical message. When it is said that a minister preaches "the Word," the expression implies that the clergyman teaches a fundamentalist, generally literal, reading or interpretation of the Bible.

WORKS. See JUSTIFICATION BY FAITH.

WORLD COUNCIL OF CHURCHES. The organization that numbers in its membership some 170 Protestant and Orthodox churches which share concern in secular and religious affairs. The body has no administrative or legislative power over its member churches, but it does provide a forum for discussion by representatives of the various churches of things of common interest. The organization was first assembled in Amsterdam in 1948, but presently its activities are carried on from headquarters in New York.

WORSHIP. The adoration and reverence paid to God and Jesus. Christian worship is not only private, in spirit and in truth, but also communal. However, without the inner spirit, external worship is valueless, according to most teachings. The technical term by which Catholicism refers to the worship due God is *latria,* which is contrasted to the veneration due saints, *dulia,* and the special veneration due Mary, *hyperdulia.*

WYCLIF, JOHN (c. 1328–1384). A vigorous English reformer, John Wyclif defied the established Church by condemning the doctrine of transubstantiation; asserting that Jesus was man's only overlord and that the Scriptures, not the Church, were the supreme authority; and declaring that the clergy should not own property. He was instrumental in bringing about the first translation of the Bible into English, and two translations bear his name although one of his followers, Nicholas of Hereford, probably did much of the work. The Wyclif Bible is almost a word-for-word translation of the Vulgate; it was completed in 1382, but even before the end of the century a more satisfactory and up-to-date text had appeared. However, the fact remains that the ground had been broken by Wyclif. Although he was condemned as a heretic, John Wyclif was never imprisoned or otherwise disturbed in his work. His followers were termed "poor priests" and Lollards, and the movement survived, although grown fanatic and secret, for some time, having considerable influence, for example, on John Huss. Among its achievements was the making of manuscript copies of the Wyclif Bible, of which an almost unbelievable 170 copies still survive to this day.

*Y*

YAHWEH. See JAHVEH.

YEAR, CHRISTIAN. The Christian calendar begins with the first Sunday of Advent, that which is nearest the feast day of St. Andrew, November 30. It proceeds to Christmas, followed by the Feast of the Circumcision (January 1), Epiphany (January 6), and the Purification (February 2). The Easter cycle then opens with Septuagesima, Lent, Holy Week, Easter, Ascension Day, and Pentecost. The time after Pentecost begins on Trinity Sunday and extends to Advent, including many important saints' days. The Christian year, obviously, traces Jesus' life and the life of the Church; during the early years of the Church, and perhaps especially during medieval times, it was well known to every Christian.

# Z

ZACHARY AND ELIZABETH, STS. (first century). The parents of John the Baptist; their story is recounted in Luke 1:5-64. Their feast day is November 5.

ZECHARIAH (Heb.: remembered by God). A prophetic book of the Old Testament, urging the rebuilding of the temple and prophecying the coming of Jesus.

ZEPHANIAH. A short, prophetic book of the Old Testament, reproving the Jews and exhorting them to repent.

ZITA, ST. (1218-1278). The "little maid of Lucca" presented during her life the ideal personification of Christian self-sacrifice. She worked from the age of eighteen until her death as a maid in the service of the wealthy Fatinelli family; although she was, thus, rather poor herself, she gave all that she could to those who were even less fortunate than herself. Her feast day is April 27.

ZWINGLI, ULRICH (1484-1531). A Swiss religious reformer, Zwingli began as a priest but ended by becoming a Protestant and rejecting Catholic ritual, the use of statues, clerical celibacy, the monastic life, and the papacy. He went farther than Luther in rejecting transubstantiation as a Eucharistic doctrine, maintaining that it was a commemorative feast and nothing more. Zwingli was a soldier, too, and was killed in a battle between Protestant and Catholic cantons of Switzerland. He had hoped for a political reform that would establish Protestantism in Europe, and though he was far from attaining this goal, Calvinism was at least partly built on the foundation he laid.

345

# BIBLIOGRAPHY

Attwater, Donald, ed. *A Catholic Dictionary*. New York: The Macmillan Company, 1961.

Bouquet, A. C. *Comparative Religion*. Baltimore: Penguin Books, 1964.

Bultmann, Rudolf (R. H. Fuller, trans.). *Primitive Christianity*. New York: Meridian Books, 1957.

Cross, F. L., ed. *The Oxford Dictionary of the Christian Church*. London: Oxford University Press, 1963.

Dunstan, J. Leslie. *Protestantism*. New York: George Braziller, 1961.

Englebert, Omer (Christopher and Anne Fremantle, trans.) *The Lives of the Saints*. New York: Collier Books, 1964.

Enslin, Morton Scott. *Christian Beginnings,* Parts I and II. New York: Harper and Brothers, 1956.

———. *The Literature of the Christian Movement,* Part III of *Christian Beginnings*. New York: Harper and Row, 1956.

Fremantle, Anne. *The Age of Belief*. New York: The New American Library of World Literature, Inc., 1955.

———. *A Treasury of Early Christianity*. New York: The New American Library of World Literature, Inc., 1960.

Harvey, Van A. *A Handbook of Theological Terms*. New York: The Macmillan Company, 1964.

*The Holy Bible: Authorized King James Version.*

Tenney, Merrill C., ed. *Handy Dictionary of the Bible*. Grand Rapids, Michigan: Zondervan Publishing House, 1965.

Trawick, Buckner B. *The Bible as Literature*. New York: Barnes and Noble, Inc., 1963.

———. *World Literature,* Vol. 1. New York: Barnes and Noble, Inc., 1966.

Watts, Alan W. *Myth and Ritual in Christianity*. New York: Grove Press, Inc., 1960.